CONTENTS

OVERCOMING INFORMATION POVERTY

Chandos

Information Professional Series

Series Editor: Ruth Rikowski
(email: Rikowskigr@aol.com)

Chandos' new series of books is aimed at the busy information professional. They have been specially commissioned to provide the reader with an authoritative view of current thinking. They are designed to provide easy-to-read and (most importantly) practical coverage of topics that are of interest to librarians and other information professionals. If you would like a full listing of current and forthcoming titles, please visit www.chandospublishing.com.

New authors: We are always pleased to receive ideas for new titles; if you would like to write a book for Chandos, please contact Dr Glyn Jones on g.jones.2@elsevier. com or telephone +44 (0) 1865 843000.

OVERCOMING INFORMATION POVERTY

Investigating the Role of Public Libraries in The Twenty-First Century

ANTHONY McKEOWN

AMSTERDAM · BOSTON · HEIDELBERG · LONDON
NEW YORK · OXFORD · PARIS · SAN DIEGO
SAN FRANCISCO · SINGAPORE · SYDNEY · TOKYO
Chandos Publishing is an imprint of Elsevier

ELSEVIER

CP

CHANDOS
PUBLISHING

Chandos Publishing is an imprint of Elsevier
50 Hampshire Street, 5th Floor, Cambridge, MA 02139, United States
The Boulevard, Langford Lane, Kidlington, OX5 1GB, United Kingdom

Library of Congress Cataloging-in-Publication Data
A catalog record for this book is available from the Library of Congress

British Library Cataloguing-in-Publication Data
A catalogue record for this book is available from the British Library

ISBN: 978-0-08-101110-2 (print)
ISBN: 978-0-08-101231-4 (online)

For information on all Chandos Publishing publications
visit our website at https://www.elsevier.com/

**Working together
to grow libraries in
developing countries**

www.elsevier.com • www.bookaid.org

Publisher: Glyn Jones
Acquisition Editor: Glyn Jones
Editorial Project Manager: Harriet Clayton
Production Project Manager: Debasish Ghosh
Designer: Maria Ines Cruz

Typeset by TNQ Books and Journals

LIST OF FIGURES

LIST OF TABLES

PREFACE

Overcoming Information Poverty is an adaptation of a recently completed PhD thesis at Ulster University. Writing this book was the appropriate way to disseminate the knowledge gained during my academic studies at Ulster University from 2008 to 2014. I gained first-hand experience of the changing public library service, how information poverty theories can be applied in practice and how public libraries play a vital role in assisting those without the financial means or the skills to access information. The research upon which this book is based was a case study that used Libraries NI, the public library service of Northern Ireland, to investigate how information poverty can be addressed at societal, community and individual levels. This research is, to my knowledge, the first external, large-scale study to investigate Libraries NI since it was set up in 2009.

Overcoming Information Poverty establishes a theoretical framework that demonstrates how information poverty can be conceptualised and targeted at three levels: macro (strategic), meso (community) and micro (individual). The book is innovative, valuable and significant in that it is the first time a unique macro-, meso- and micro-based model of information poverty indicators has been developed and applied to illustrate the impact of public libraries at strategic, community and personal levels. This study applied mixed methods using quantitative and qualitative data obtained from semi-structured interviews with library staff and external stakeholders, a survey of branch library managers and focus groups with library users and nonusers. Secondary data from the Northern Ireland Census (2011) and a content analysis of documents strengthened the primary data from the interviews, survey responses and focus groups. In addition, the information poverty literature – for example, a 1975 study by Childers and Post of localised information environments, Chatman's small-world theories, and more recent writings from Britz (2007) and Thompson (2006) – have shaped my thinking and are integrated within this book.

Overcoming Information Poverty is very topical; public libraries now have a significant role in facilitating and supporting access to online government, social, commercial, financial and educational services. It focuses on the role public libraries play in tackling social and digital exclusion and in developing the knowledge base of society. In doing this, the book gets to the heart of the role and purpose of public libraries in the 21st century and develops a vision for the future. *Overcoming Information Poverty* concludes with recommendations that public libraries in other countries and contexts can use to improve their capacity to address information poverty. So, while this book specifically investigates public libraries in Northern Ireland, it has wider implications, and the three-level framework of information poverty indicators can be applied within other countries and contexts.

Overcoming Information Poverty has unique educational value and should appeal to academics, information professionals from various sectors, public library leaders and managers, students, educational specialists and government policymakers who are interested in tackling poverty and social and digital exclusion. Moreover, I hope that this text may lead to further research, debate and policy development regarding information poverty and public libraries, as well as areas farther afield.

ACKNOWLEDGEMENTS

Firstly, I would like to thank the course tutors of the Postgraduate Certificate/ Diploma/MSc in Library and Information Management at the Ulster University who were influential when I embarked on this academic journey. Secondly, I extend my sincere gratitude to Dr Jessica Bates, Professor Linda Clarke and Dr Victor McNair for their invaluable feedback and guidance during my doctoral studies. Thirdly, thanks to Libraries NI for allowing me to take a three-year career break and to everyone who participated in my PhD research.

Finally, a special thanks to my parents for encouraging me to write this book and for their belief in me.

ABBREVIATIONS

A2B	Access to Benefits
ALBs	Arm's Length Bodies
BLM	Branch Library Manager
CHS	Continuous Household Survey
CILIP	Chartered Institute of Library and Information Professionals
CyMAL	Museums, Libraries and Archives Wales
DARD	Department of Agriculture and Rural Development
DCAL	Department of Culture, Arts and Leisure
DCMS	Department of Culture, Media and Sport
DEL	Department of Employment and Learning
DETI	Department of Enterprise, Trade and Industry
DFP	Department of Finance and Personnel
DIU	Digital Inclusion Unit
ELFNI	Electronic Libraries for Northern Ireland
EU	European Union
GB	Great Britain
GCE A-Level	General Certificate of Education Advanced Level
GCSE	General Certificate of Secondary Education
IALS	International Adult Literacy Survey
ICT	Information and Communication Technology
IFLA	International Federation of Library Associations and Institutions
IPI	Information Poverty Indicator
ISAS	International Survey of Adult Skills
IT	Information Technology
LIS	Library and Information Science
LISA	Library and Information Science Abstracts
LISC (NI)	Library and Information Services Council (Northern Ireland)
LMS	Library Management System
LNI	Libraries NI
MLA	Member of the Legislative Assembly (Northern Ireland Government)
MOT	Ministry of Transport
NEET	Not in Employment, Education or Training
NFIL	National Forum on Information Literacy
NGN	Next Generation Networks
NIMDM	Northern Ireland Multiple Deprivation Measures
NISRA	Northern Ireland Statistics and Research Agency
NS-SEC	National Statistics Socio-economic Classification
OECD	Organisation for Economic Cooperation and Development
OFCOM	Office of Communications

OFMDFM	Office of the First Minister and the Deputy First Minister
ONS	Office for National Statistics
PATs	Public Access Terminals
PCs	Personal Computers
PCs	Public Computers
PwC	Pricewaterhouse Coopers
Q	Quintiles
PfG	Programme for Government
PN	People's Network
PULLS	Public Libraries in the Learning Society
RNIB	Royal National Institute of Blind People
ROI	Republic of Ireland
RPA	Review of Public Administration
TSE	Targeting Social Exclusion
TSN	Targeting Social Needs
TV	Television
U3A	University of the Third Age
UK	United Kingdom
UN	United Nations
UNESCO	United Nations Educational, Scientific and Cultural Organisation
USA	United States of America
VIP	Visually Impaired People
WTP	Working Together Project
YPBAS	Young Persons' Behaviour and Attitude Survey

CHAPTER 1

Introduction

1.1 INTRODUCTION

In a changing social and technological environment, the content of this book advances our understanding of the instrumental role libraries can play in overcoming information poverty. The book conceptualises information poverty using a macro-, meso- and micro-level framework. This framework is applied to demonstrate how public libraries address it at macro (strategic), meso (community) and micro (individual) levels. In doing so, *the book* provides an understanding of the wider economic, social and political contexts within which public library services operate and the information services they provide. This introductory chapter outlines the primary motivation for creating this book and considers why its content is important at this time. There is a brief discussion of what information poverty is, how this book creates a new perspective on information poverty and the role of public libraries in addressing it. In addition, the chapter discusses how the three-stage methodological framework was operationalised: the research design and the data collection methods. The chapter concludes by providing an outline of the subsequent chapters.

1.2 BACKGROUND AND RATIONALE

The book is timely given the emphasis by government to tackle poverty and digital and social exclusion. A challenge for government, educational specialists and public libraries in modern society is improving access to information for those without the literacy, information and digital literacy skills or the socioeconomic means to acquire information, with a goal to create a more socially and digitally inclusive society. When considering the challenges facing and the changing role of public libraries, this book articulates and promotes the purpose, role and ethos of public libraries and provides a vision of how library services can remain relevant and influential in order to meet the needs of 21st-century users. This book demonstrates the value of public libraries in this age of austerity and provides evidence of their continued relevancy in society, communities and

Overcoming Information Poverty
ISBN 978-0-08-101110-2
Published by Elsevier Ltd.
All rights reserved.

people's individual lives. This book is therefore particularly pertinent now, when public library services face cutbacks and increasingly need to be accountable to justify future investment. In light of current debates in the United Kingdom on public libraries and the recent Sieghart Independent Library Report, this book offers fresh insights and recommendations for public libraries based on a comprehensive analysis of the findings of recent United Kingdom–based research on information poverty and public libraries.

Specifically, this book uses the findings of an original PhD study conducted by the author[1] at the Ulster University that investigated how the public library services of Northern Ireland (Libraries NI), address information poverty at the macro level (with information infrastructure, policies and strategies); at the meso level (with targeted community interventions); and at the micro level (by improving literacy and information and digital literacy skills). Library services in Northern Ireland – as elsewhere in the United Kingdom and farther afield – are likely to be threatened increasingly by budget cuts, which mean less money to spend on stock, the library premises or library staff. In these circumstances the need for libraries to demonstrate their impact on tackling government priorities for poverty, social and digital inclusion is imperative. While the book looks at Libraries NI, it has wider implications; the three-level framework of information poverty indicators can be used within other contexts and at an international level. Thus, in essence, the local context is purely a means of showing how the three-level framework could be applied to libraries in a way that readers can interpret, adapt and apply the framework within their own library context/sector. I consider how the findings can be used to contribute to strategic policy and makes recommendations about how policy to alleviate information poverty might be improved. The empirical data from interviews with both strategic and community-level library staff and external stakeholders, a survey of branch library managers (BLMs) and focus groups with library users and nonusers are used throughout the book to illuminate (1) views and perspectives of what information poverty is, (2) how it can be addressed by public libraries and (3) how public libraries can improve their approaches to addressing it.

The next section reviews what information poverty is. Following this are discussions of how this book further develops the concept and how this conceptualisation can be applied to public libraries.

---

[1] See: McKeown, A. (2015) How can information poverty indicators be used to demostrate the impact of Libraries NI'S information services, Available in print at the Ulster University library, Jordanstown or accessible online from: http://ethos.bl.uk/OrderDetails.do?uin=uk.bl.ethos.648024?

1.3 INFORMATION POVERTY

For people to change their circumstances or improve their lives – whether socially, culturally or economically – they need access to information. The elusiveness and complexity of information poverty has led researchers to consider it from different perspectives. Information poverty describes a situation where individuals are unable to access information as a result of inter-related social, cultural, educational and economic factors that prevent information access. It is often defined in terms of a lack of both literacy and the information literacy skills needed to participate in society. Information poverty can be characterised by a lack of information and a lack of skills to access information, as well as a result of the cultural norms and information behaviours that exist within communities. Furthermore, it is a 'global phenomenon that can vary from context to context' and is 'not purely an economic phenomenon' because it 'can be linked to the cultural and social spheres of society' (Britz, 2007: 75). Moreover, information poverty is a multidimensional concept with various interpretations and applications, several different causes and many different impacts. The factors creating information poverty and the ways in which public libraries can alleviate information poverty are discussed throughout this book.

Information poverty suggests a scarcity of information that is vital to citizens' ability to engage effectively in society and make informed life choices. The concept of information poverty, in which individuals suffer from a lack of needed information, is an issue of growing importance in contemporary society, with its enhanced focus on information and communication technology (ICT) for personal and social development. In contemporary society the need to be online and to access digital information means that ICT is now viewed as an essential tool to reduce poverty and for economic and social development. Having access to ICTs and the Internet, as well as the ability to use these, are now vital assets to escape poverty and hence be included in society. Furthermore, individuals who experience information poverty are less able to access the information they need to improve their social, economic and cultural positions; as a consequence they are often at risk of exclusion from participation in wider society.

Public libraries have traditionally addressed information inequalities 'especially for people from the lower socio-economic groups' who may not have the financial means to afford it (Ptolomey, 2011: 98). Public libraries now play a fundamental role in providing access to ICTs/the Internet for those who cannot afford the technologies or need support to access online information. In facilitating access to digital information public libraries can develop and empower individuals who lack the financial resources to pay for home Internet access. As well as providing access to ICTs and the Internet, public libraries have a leading role to play in developing citizens' information and digital literacy skills and in supporting the United Kingdom government's Digital by Default agenda. The role of public libraries in creating a more culturally, digitally and socially inclusive society by facilitating access to information and providing a space for social participation is discussed throughout this book. Bates (2008: 96) observes that 'there is the danger that increasingly, non-use of the Internet can perpetuate a cycle of poverty and exclusion'. Being without access to ICTs and the Internet can therefore restrict personal development, social participation and access to a range of government services. So, information poverty can exclude individuals without information or the skills to access information and can prevent people from achieving their full potential and participating as full and equal members of society.

The 'information society', which emphasises the importance of information in contemporary society, has an enhanced focus on access ICTs. Haider and Bawden (2007: 546) aver that the lack of 'affordable' access to ICTs and the Internet leads to a 'state of deprivation' and exclusion described as 'information poverty'. Information poverty is discussed variously in the literature with terms like the 'information society', the 'digital divide' and 'information inequality'. Yu (2006) states that two overlapping research communities have emerged: first, information poverty, information inequality, information gap and information divide research, and second, digital divide and universal access research. Both research communities focus on social inequity in information distribution; however, their research methods and policy recommendations are different (Yu, 2006: 230). Yu (2006: 230) argues for an 'exchange of ideas between the two communities'. The terms 'information inequality, information gap, information divide, information disparity, information inequity, information rich vs. information poor or information haves vs. information have–nots, [and] knowledge gap' are used to 'describe the state of social division between those who are favourably' placed in information resource distribution and those who are not' (Yu, 2006: 230). While the information divide can often be seen as that which exists between developed and developing countries, there is often a similar dichotomy within societies between:

…those with easy access to an abundance of information and those who do not know how and where to find it and even, perhaps, do not understand the value of information and how it can help them in their day-to-day lives
Goulding, 2001: 109

Information poverty is 'often mentioned together with equally con-
tested concepts' such as the digital divide and the information society
(Haider and Bawden, 2006: 372). With the growth of ICTs in the 1990s, the
Internet was 'widely recognised as the most significant divider between the
information rich and information poor', and consequently the 'digital
divide' became 'the major embodiment of information inequality' (Yu,
2006: 203). The digital divide concept emerged, often referring to (in economic terms) those who can and cannot afford technologies. In the digital
divide discourse the 'information have-nots' are 'frequently conceptualised
as the economic poor' (Hersberger, 2003). Digital divide research considered the infrastructural approaches to access to ICT/the Internet and 'was
thought to be binary: one was either an ICT *have* or a *have not*' (Thompson,
2006: 20). While the 'digital divide literature often blurred with information
poverty literature', they are not the same: the digital divide is only one part
of the information poverty problem (Thompson, 2011: 137). Putkey (2009)
concurs, stating that the digital divide is 'one component of the larger problem of Information Poverty'.

Moreover, this approach excludes other cultural, educational and personal
factors that impede information access. Viewing information poverty in binary
terms makes measurement even more problematic. Digital divide studies con-
centrate on lack of information access, whereas others for example (Gebremichael and Jackson, 2003 and Britz, 2004). present a 'more complex account,
saying that they lack in information access, skills and use' (Yu, 2010: 907). The
complexities and problems associated with the digital divide research are noted
by Van Dijk and Hacker (2003), Boekhorst (2003) and De Beer (2007). De Beer
(2007: 196) posits that the digital divide is 'a highly questionable term', arguing
that it is more of a 'human divide' because the digital divide oversimplifies the
real issues and neglects the 'humanness of the divide', the capacities, intellect and
skills or willingness to use technology, which in turn makes it difficult to find
solutions (De Beer, 2007: 199–200).

Instead of looking at a digital divide, Potter (2006) offers an alternative
perspective to describe those who are excluded from the network society,
and advocates a 'zones of silence' framework that emphasises that, first, 'there
are not simply two types of people - information "haves"/"have-nots"',
second, differences exist within a zone of silence, not only in access to ICTs
but also 'in opinions, everyday life, experiences, and modes of communication'; and third, there 'is also more than one type of information'. Zones of
silence, Potter argues, exist within countries, communities and households,
where lack of access to ICT results in exclusion and where 'people's voices

are, effectively, outside of their immediate community, unconnected and unheard'. Potter (2006) suggests that the '"information poor" may lack what the digital divide defines as "information", but this does not mean that the knowledge they have is less useful or less valuable'. Potter (2006) acknowledges the local information and knowledge contexts. For instance, socially deprived communities may be information rich in some generalised local, community knowledge. Public libraries can play a vital role in breaking down these zones of silence and facilitating access to ICTs and the Internet, which can subsequently provide those at risk of social exclusion with a connection to the wider society.

The growing demand to be able to communicate in contemporary society, to access government information through electronic, social networks and virtual communities on the Internet and to share information (videos, photos) has led some scholars to suggest there is a move from an information society to a 'communication society' (Hamelink, 2003; Komito, 2008). Some studies refer not only to 'information' poverty but to 'information and communication' poverty, which Barja and Gigler (2007: 16) describe as 'a lack of the basic capabilities needed to participate in the information society.' Similar to digital divide research, information and communication poverty studies consider ownership of ICTs, Internet, radio, television, cable television, fixed telephones, mobile phones and smartphones, focussing on 'the importance of information and communication assets and how they are used' (May, 2012: 36). Information and communication poverty is similar to terms such as 'digital poverty', which May describes as incorporating:

1. a demand dimension (the ICT service cannot be afforded);
2. a capability dimension (the skills to use the service are unavailable); and
3. a supply dimension (the infrastructure to deliver the service is not in place) (May, 2012: 36).

May (2012) points out that digital poverty is sometimes referred to as 'digital literacy' and is a concept that 'moves away the dichotomous notion of a "digital divide" in which some have ICT skills and access, while others are deprived of them'. He argues that 'digital poverty can be seen as a continuum, perhaps with a critical threshold akin to a poverty line'. In this book the term 'information poverty' is preferred for various reasons:

1. It is the more established term within the literature.
2. The focus is on information in any form (print or digital), or the information communicated within groups, and is not confined to looking at poverty from a communication technologies perspective.

3. It addresses the social, cultural and personal barriers to information access rather than focussing on assets.

4. It incorporates literacy and digital and information literacy skills.

5. It is more applicable to the information provided by and the services of public libraries.

The prime concern of this section has been to emphasise the different approaches in the literature and interpretations of information poverty and to argue that a more integrative approach to understanding information poverty is needed. This presents a challenge for public libraries when seeking to address information poverty as they must consider range of factors which prevent information access such as economic, educational, personal and cultural.

Having briefly discussed what information poverty is and how it can exclude citizens from participating fully in society, I propose the following definition of information poverty:

Information poverty is one component of the wider problem of poverty and is the result of inter-related socioeconomic, educational and infrastructural factors. Information poverty can be examined at macro (societal), meso (community) and micro (personal) levels. At the macro level, information poverty is an ethical issue and should be addressed by government and education specialists to reduce the digital, educational and social inequalities in contemporary society. At the meso level, information poverty illustrates the constraining attitudes and behaviours towards information that prevent information access in localised environments. At the micro level, information poverty is the lack of literacy, information literacy and ICT skills needed to participate effectively in modern society, which can exacerbate social exclusion.

This definition reinforces the multilayered factors that contribute to information poverty and reflects the macro, meso and micro approach that is used throughout this book to explain information poverty and how it may be addressed at different levels. The opposite of information poverty is information richness. I define an ideal information-rich society or community as one which:

- has access to information
- has a strong information infrastructure embedded within its public library service
- is both information and digitally literate
- understands the value of ICT and the need for ICT skills
- shares information among the community
- has socially included and empowered citizens
- recognises the importance of information, learning and libraries.

Public libraries have a significant role to play in developing information-rich societies and developing knowledge societies. Alleviating information poverty is therefore fundamental to creating a knowledgeable and skilled society. The role that public libraries can play in developing knowledge and providing the opportunity for information access to enable digital and social inclusion is at the heart of this book.

1.4 A NEW PERSPECTIVE ON INFORMATION POVERTY AND PUBLIC LIBRARIES

This book adds to current understanding of what information poverty is and applies the theoretical lens of information poverty to demonstrate how public libraries address it through strategic policies, community engagement and developing citizens' literacy, information literacy and digital literacy skills. Information poverty theories and their application to public libraries warrant detailed investigation; as Pollock (2002) suggests, 'Information poverty and the information poor are inadequately researched within information science'. In addition, Thompson (2006: 12–13) claims that information poverty theories can improve libraries by strengthening 'information policy, provid[ing] a basis for improved information diffusion and/or service'.

Thompson (2011: 138–139) suggests that to create a better understanding of information poverty, we should look at both the structural/economic lens and the behavioural/cultural lens. Traditionally, poverty theories fall into one of the following categories (Rodgers, 2006: 63):

- cultural/behavioural, which implies that the 'only real cause of poverty is the behaviour, values, and culture of the poor'; or
- structural/economic, which argues that the main 'precipitating cause of poverty is a lack of equal opportunities'.

Thompson (2006) concluded that a holistic method embracing the infrastructural, sociocultural and personal dimensions of information poverty is needed. While Thompson's work is theoretical, presenting and discussing the information poverty theories, this book advances understanding of not only interpreting the theories but also in investigating these as they occur at a practical, real-life level. Thus this book builds on Thompson's earlier study by defining information poverty at macro (strategic), meso (community) and micro (individual) levels, and using this three-level definition as a framework for conceptualising information poverty, developing a set of indicators to measure it and applying these practically to demonstrate the impact of public library strategies and interventions to address it. While the practical application of the framework of information poverty used here – that is, within the Northern Ireland context – is original, earlier studies were influential in determining this terminology, as discussed in the following section.

1.5 THE MACRO, MESO AND MICRO FRAMEWORK

This book has been influenced by and builds on earlier three-level frameworks of information access, such as that described by Thompson (2006), and adapts Yu's the macro, middle (meso) and micro terminology defined by Yu (2006). Previous theorists have developed three-level approaches to interpreting information poverty and information access (Childers and Post, 1975; Yu, 2006; Thompson, 2006; Britz, 2007; Burnett et al., 2008; Thompson and Afzal, 2011). A tripartite approach is used by Yu (2006: 235), who observes that information inequality and poverty can be perceived at three levels:

1. *Macro*: a broad spectrum of economic, ethical and political concerns that can determine information poverty on a global and societal level
2. *Middle (meso)*: the social norms and information behaviour that result in information poverty in small communities/small worlds
3. *Micro*: an individual's cognitive and information literacy capabilities to process information

Each level is defined and explained in subsequent sections, but first it is important to state why the three levels are presented together. Those who are most 'information-impoverished' are disadvantaged in all three levels in their attempts to access information: first, by political and economic factors (macro level); second, by cultural and social factors (meso level); and third, by personal factors (micro level). Yu (2006) asserts that the macro, meso and micro approaches complement each other, and factors in each are interdependent; thus information poverty ensues where information access is impeded in all three levels. This interdependency is discussed in the following sections.

Thompson (2006: 69) notes three layers of information access: the information infrastructure (technology), the social sphere (broad) and the small world (local) must be considered in any discussion of information access and information poverty. Similarly, Burnett et al. (2008) discuss information access in terms of physical, social and intellectual lenses. This terminology is later adapted by Thompson and Afzal (2011). The three lenses of information access must be viewed holistically as 'three parts of a single theoretical model' in order to 'develop useful ways of addressing information access barriers' (Thompson and Afzal, 2011: 29). Thompson and Afzal (2011: 24) also suggest 'there is no existing theory or model that takes the varied approaches used thus far into account'. They comment that a holistic approach that includes all three lenses – physical, sociocultural and intellectual – 'is largely absent from the information studies literature' (Thompson and Afzal, 2011: 22), and that

that 'Information service providers can benefit greatly when using the tripartite model' when 'designing information spaces, services, programs, and products' (Thompson and Afzal, 2011: 35).

This book aims to show that the macro, meso and micro lenses related to information poverty are a useful way of examining public library services. While this framework builds on earlier models, it takes a more complete view of information poverty than the physical, sociocultural and intellectual factors of information access. A holistic framework has been created to measure how public libraries can address it at macro (societal), meso (community) and micro (personal) levels. Also, it is the first time that a three-level framework of information poverty indicators has been developed and applied to illustrate the role of public libraries. When looking at public library services, specific descriptions can be provided for each of the three levels of the framework:

- *Macro level*: developing strategies which facilitate access to information in order to alleviate poverty and create a more culturally, digitally and socially inclusive society
- *Meso level*: engaging the community and targeting information services that are tailored to the needs of various groups
- *Micro level*: developing individual literacy and digital and information literacy capabilities

At the macro level, public library priorities and strategies are often aligned to government agendas, for example, facilitating access to information, alleviating poverty a more culturally, digitally and socially inclusive society. Conceptualising information poverty at the macro level enables us to understand the broader ethical issues and the responsibilities of governments in addressing it, as well as the role for public libraries. The macro level approach also emphasises the importance of the information infrastructure of countries and the potential that the public library service has to reduce information poverty.

For a complete understanding of information access, we also need to understand it from a meso-level perspective – from within communities. It is important to consider the sociocultural factors that have an impact on information access and on an individual's attitudes towards information, information providers and learning. By conceptualising information poverty at the sociocultural level, public library staff can enhance their awareness of the information behaviours of specific groups and improve how they deliver information services to their communities. To encourage library usage, public library staff need to be able to understand the information needs and attitudes towards information, learning and information providers within disadvantaged communities. By developing a sociocultural perspective on information poverty, and applying small-world concepts, library staff can identify marginalised groups and target services to them.

To complete the conceptualisation of information poverty, the intellectual, educational, attitudinal and behavioural (micro-level factors) that impede information access also need to be considered. Conceptualising information poverty at the micro level enables library and information professionals to understand these factors and to develop strategies such as literacy initiatives or ICT skills training to address them.

Having briefly discussed what information poverty is and the development of the three-level framework, the following section outlines the local context from which the book originated.

1.6 RESEARCH DESIGN AND METHODOLOGY: LIBRARIES NI AS THE CASE STUDY

Public libraries in Northern Ireland face similar challenges to public library services in other parts of the United Kingdom and the Republic of Ireland in terms of declining usage, accountability and justifying future roles. In the United Kingdom library services in the four nations (England, Scotland, Wales and Northern Ireland) are operated and managed differently. In England public libraries are funded and run through local authorities and are currently supported by the Arts Council (Hull, 2011: 5). In Scotland the Scottish Library and Information Council is an independent body that advises the Scottish Government on library and information services. Similar to England and Scotland, public library services in Wales are coordinated by local authorities and are financially supported by CyMAL: Museums, Libraries and Archives Wales. In the Republic of Ireland local libraries are also coordinated by a local authority, with 32 separate library services, and are funded by the Department for Environment, Community and Local Government (Hull, 2011: 5).

However, there is a 'unique' situation in Northern Ireland, which has one relatively large library authority for the whole of the country, as opposed to public libraries in the Republic of Ireland, Scotland, England and Wales, which are funded and run by local authorities (Hull, 2011: 5). Public library services in Northern Ireland, Libraries NI, are remitted by the Department of Culture, Arts and Leisure (DCAL). Tackling poverty and social exclusion are prominent concerns for Libraries NI because they are DCAL's main priorities. Libraries NI was specifically selected as the case study through which to investigate information poverty because this organisation has appropriate structures and effects with which to conduct a three-level investigation of information poverty. Libraries NI is a relatively large organisation – the largest public library authority in the United Kingdom – employing 800 staff and serving almost 800,000 registered users. It provided me with multiple layers from which to explore information poverty. Libraries NI is also an appropriate case study because its organisational framework is typical of a public library organisation, which engages and affects at the macro, meso and micro levels of society. Pickard (2013: 108) argues that case studies 'are intended to allow for transferability of findings based on contextual applicability'. This implies that by using Libraries NI to investigate information poverty, the findings could lead to transferable and replicable research in other public library authorities. Denscombe (2007: 37) states that case studies allow the researcher to use multiple sources, types of data and research methods. Various methods were used to elucidate specific points of reference: for example, interviews with policymakers were useful for the macro-level phase; interviews and a survey with policy implementers were appropriate for the meso-level phase and finally, focus groups with library users and nonusers were effective at the micro level. Thus the case study afforded a more in-depth focus and allowed for multiple data collection methods and sources, and various stakeholders, to create a holistic picture of how information poverty can be understood and addressed.

Table 1.1 Methodological framework

Research design	
Macro level: Stage 1	Semistructured interviews with senior library staff ($n = 15$ interviewees) and external stakeholders from the Department of Culture, Arts and Leisure ($n = 2$ interviewees)
Meso level: Stage2	Electronic survey to 37 branch library managers in the 28 libraries that are located in the 10% most deprived areas, according to the Northern Ireland multiple deprivation measures
	Semistructured interviews with library staff, with a specific remit to target socially disadvantaged areas ($n = 3$ interviewees)
Micro level: Stage 3	Focus groups: one with library users ($n = 8$ participants) and one with nonlibrary users ($n = 8$ participants)
	Semistructured interviews with Department of Employment and Learning staff ($n = 2$)

The methodological framework reflected the three-level model of information poverty (see Table 1.1). Stage one involved semistructured interviews with external stakeholders and Libraries NI staff at the strategic (macro) level; these people had responsibility for the design of library policies and strategic direction. These data informed stage 2 of the study, which used data from policy implementers at the meso level – those who initiate library strategies within communities. Stage 2 consisted of a survey of BLMs and interviews with specialist library staff working in deprived areas. At the micro level, stage 3 involved two focus groups, one with library users and one with nonlibrary users. In essence, mixed methods enabled me to provide multilevel perspectives on information poverty: what it is, how it manifests itself and how it can be addressed. Evidence was gathered from multiple perspectives using both qualitative and quantitative data collection techniques. At each stage, the direction and shape evolved, based on data gathered, reflecting the interconnectedness of this framework.

1.6.1 Stage 1 Data Collection Methods: Macro Level

At stage 1, semistructured interviews were conducted to gain a deeper insight into thinking at a strategic level within Libraries NI, and at the government level with DCAL. Semistructured interviews enabled the interviewees to clarify policies and themes, and to elaborate on personal perspectives towards information poverty. Quotations from interviews with DCAL and Libraries NI staff are anonymous. To ensure anonymity and confidentiality, when verbatim extracts are used, Libraries NI interviewees are referred to as LNI1 to LNI15, and interviewees from DCAL as DCAL1 and DCAL2. Not including individual's names or titles gives me as the author greater objectivity and allows me to take a more critical stance, especially since I am an employee of the organisation that was being investigated. It is important to point out that I was not involved in designing or implementing the strategies or policies that this study refers to since my substantive post within Libraries NI is as a library assistant, and I did not have any previous personal and professional contact with most of the study participants. This enabled me to take a detached and objective stance on the subject matter (see Appendix 1: Macro and Meso Level Interviewees).

1.6.2 Stage 2: Meso-Level Questionnaire and Interviews

The data collected from the macro-level interviews shaped the second phase, in particular the discussion about the recent community engagement strategy developed by Libraries NI called targeting social exclusion (TSE). Stage 2 investigated the following themes: barriers to accessing libraries experienced by people in socially disadvantaged areas, the information behaviours of people in disadvantaged areas, targeting hard-to-reach groups and improving community outreach and services to attract new library users. To do this, data were collected via an electronic survey designed using Survey Monkey and sent to BLMs working in the 28 libraries in the 10% most deprived areas in Northern Ireland. While the survey has a local context in that it was sent to public library managers in Northern Ireland, its terminology could be adjusted and then the survey replicated in other public library settings.

The survey focused on library managers' awareness of the concept of information poverty, activities/services to address information poverty and the challenges of targeting hard-to-reach groups and developing community partnerships. In addition, semistructured interviews with specialist library staff in community engagement roles strengthened the survey data. The meso-level interviewees discussed the factors creating information poverty, why people in socially disadvantaged areas may not be using libraries and their knowledge of the information environments of those living in socially deprived areas. In this way the interviews supplemented the BLM survey data, gathered more in-depth information and contextualised the survey findings. Denscombe (2007: 111) observes that while questionnaires 'would not have provided the kind of depth of information' that semistructured interviews do,

> ...by combining the methods, the researcher is in a position to avoid potential criticism linked to either the relatively small sample size associated with the interview method or the relative superficiality of data collected via questionnaires.
>
> **Denscombe, 2007: 111**

The process of augmenting quantitative data from the survey's closed questions and the qualitative data from both the survey's open questions and the interviews provided a more comprehensive account of how library services are addressing information poverty. By combining both a survey and interviews at Stage 2, I gained a deeper insight into how public libraries can address information poverty in socioeconomically deprived areas. Sung et al. (2012: 2) observes that there is a 'lack of research literature on conceptualisation of the practical aspects of the Community Engagement process in the context of public libraries'. Thus, the survey findings contribute to existing knowledge of how public libraries target social disadvantage through community engagement. Verbatim abstracts from survey respondents are referred to only as BLM1 to BLM25. When quotations by the specialist community engagement staff are used, they are referred to TSE1 to TSE3. The names of community organisations or specific areas within Northern Ireland are omitted so that survey respondents, interviewees or specific areas cannot be identified (see Appendix 2: The Survey Questions).

1.6.3 Stage 3: Focus Groups (Micro Level)

Analysis of the macro- and meso-level data informed the choice of partici-pants at the micro level. For example, macro-level interviewees emphasised the importance of strategic partnerships with government departments to address information poverty. One such library partnership was with the Department of Employment and Learning (DEL) and involved Job Clubs in libraries. The unemployed also were identified in the meso-level inter-views and in the BLM survey as a demographic that could be at risk of information poverty. Evaluating information poverty using the Job Club partnership was an effective way of ascertaining the effectiveness of library partnerships. Furthermore, a common thread from the macro-level and the meso-level data was that libraries needed to do more to target groups that were not using libraries. There was also a need to obtain perspectives of libraries from nonusers.

Therefore I decided to focus on information poverty at the micro-level stage from two perspectives: unemployed library users and unemployed nonlibrary users. Krueger and Casey (2009: 2) assert that focus groups are a way of gathering information 'to better understand how people feel or think about an issue, product or service' and enable researchers to 'gather opinions'. Focus groups were important here for two reasons: First, they provided evidence of the impact library programmes are having on indi-viduals to reduce information poverty and allowed me to gather evidence of the peoples' 'perceptions' of library services (the Job Club). Second, focus groups enabled me to examine attitudes towards library access from among nonlibrary users, and to compare both groups.

The first focus group, a Job Club with young people aged 18–24 years, who were not in education, employment or training, was held at a commu-nity centre in a socially deprived area with no connection to their local library. This provided the opportunity to investigate libraries from the per-spective of a demographic group identified in the BLM survey as one that libraries could target more effectively. The second focus group, with library Job Club participants, provided the opportunity to investigate the partnership between Libraries NI and DEL. This enabled the author to investigate the impact of the library Job Club, and thus, be able to compare the advantages and disadvantages of the community centre Job Club with the library Job

Club. Pickard (2013: 244–245) explains that focus groups can be used as an 'evaluation device' at the end of data collection 'to confirm emerging findings'. At this final stage, focus groups were appropriate to investigate the efficacy of information poverty indicators. The questions asked during both focus groups were developed to ascertain what support the participants needed to obtain employment. In both focus groups the following topics guided the discussion:

- skills (ICT, literacy proficiency)
- Internet and ICT access
- information seeking (sources of help)
- support needed to apply for jobs, fill applications, write curricula vitae
- support received from friends, family, community organisations, library
- awareness, perception and usage of the library

Anonymity of focus group participants was needed because of the sensitivity of the topic, specifically when talking about skills and perceptions of being unemployed. As with participants in the macro and meso stages of data collection, focus group participants were coded, for example, unemployed male 1 (UM1) (see Chapter 9, Tables 9.1 and 9.2).

The process of data collection, using a top-down approach, meant that each stage informed the next. The mixed-methods approach showed that a combination of quantitative and qualitative data, as well as documentary analysis, could be used to provide a fuller picture of information poverty at strategic, community and personal levels. This three-stage methodological approach could be transported to investigate information poverty in other settings.

Having outlined the methodological approach, the following section concludes the chapter by presenting a brief synopsis of the remaining chapters.

1.7 STRUCTURE OF THE BOOK

As this introductory chapter details, the primary motivation for writing this book is to define, conceptualise and explore what information poverty is and how it can be addressed by public libraries. The book comprises nine subsequent chapters. Chapter 2 sets out the context from which the book emerged. The historical role of public libraries in alleviating educational and social disadvantage is discussed. It considers government policies to tackle social need and to facilitate information access in the United Kingdom, and outlines the role of the public library in providing access to information. It positions library services in Northern Ireland within the broader framework of library and information services in the United Kingdom and farther afield. Libraries NI is profiled, looking at their vision, mission and strategic priorities, as well as the challenges facing library services in Northern Ireland.

Chapter 3 examines what information poverty is. The chapter considers what information and poverty are separately and how the two terms are united in the concept of information poverty. The origins of this concept and the term 'information poor' are discussed and information poverty within the Library and Information Science discourse is presented. It provides an in-depth analysis of information poverty and social exclusion using the data gathered from both my research and the published literature. It examines the main factors that lead to information poverty and how these can be addressed by library services. Following this, Chapter 4 uses the data collected from interviews and surveys to paint a picture of the factors that create informa-tion poverty. The relevant literature is used to support my own research findings. In addition, this chapter considers the importance of measuring a library's impact. It discusses the creation of information poverty indicators and how these could be used to evaluate the impact of library services. I also discuss how the indicators could be adapted and applied within other library contexts as a way of evaluating the impact of their services.

The first findings chapter, Chapter 5, presents a description of what information is at the macro level and how it can be addressed by public libraries using strategies to tackle poverty and low educational attainment, and to facilitate social and digital inclusion. Statistics for home Internet access in the United Kingdom are presented. It considers the United Kingdom government's Digital by Default agenda and the role that public libraries play in this. It also examines the staff skills needed to support social and digital exclusion. Chapter 6 then considers how public libraries contribute to wider European agendas to support learning and facilitate access to information to promote social and digital inclusion. The chapter outlines how government agendas for lifelong learning are reflected in public library strategies and services. The role of libraries in developing literacy and improving ICT and information literacy skills is discussed.

Following the macro-level findings, Chapters 7 and 8 present the meso-level findings. Chapter 7 considers how information poverty theories at the sociocultural level can be used to illuminate how public libraries can have an impact on disadvantaged communities through outreach, engagement and encouraging learning and social participation. Following this, Chapter 8 explores how information poverty can be addressed within communities. It focuses on how the strategic approaches of Libraries NI are being implemented into policies and programmes within local communities. This chapter presents some of the findings of both the survey of BLMs working in the 10% most socially deprived areas in Northern Ireland and the semistructured interviews with specialist library staff who are tackling information poverty and social exclusion.

Chapter 9 focuses on the micro-level investigation into information poverty. It reports on two focus groups conducted: the first with library users participating in a Job Club in partnership with DEL, and the second with nonlibrary users in a Job Club in a community centre in a socially deprived area. In doing this, the chapter examines information poverty indicators and scrutinises the impact of Libraries NI's strategic policies on individuals.

Finally, in Chapter 10 I reflect on the themes raised in the book and the future challenges facing public libraries when addressing information poverty. In addition, the chapter summarises the key findings and proposes recommendations for policy and practice.

1.8 SUMMARY

Overall, this chapter highlighted the rationale for the book and discussed the macro-, meso- and micro-level framework and how it will be operationalised. The next chapter positions Libraries NI within the context of broader European, United Kingdom and Northern Ireland local government priorities to target information poverty and social and digital exclusion. It places in context both the book and the study upon which the findings are based. It considers the historical role of libraries in alleviating educational and social disadvantage, then narrows the focus to examine the challenges facing public library services in Northern Ireland.

CHAPTER 2

Setting the Context

2.1 INTRODUCTION

Chapter 1 discussed the rationale for the book and why it is important at this time. It briefly considered what information poverty is and outlined the methods that were used in the investigation. This chapter now narrows the focus to consider the broader social and political contexts in which public libraries exist and the role they play in providing access to information. It reviews the historical role of public libraries in addressing educational and social disadvantage. In addition, the macro-level interviews with library strategists and policymakers in Northern Ireland are used to support previous thinking on the historical role of libraries. Following this, the chapter considers how tackling poverty and social exclusion is now a priority for the government in Northern Ireland and for library services of Northern Ireland (Libraries NI). Library usage in Northern Ireland and the challenges of improving usage, in particular within socially deprived areas, is discussed.

2.2 HISTORICAL CONTEXT: PUBLIC LIBRARIES AND SOCIAL INCLUSION

Public libraries in the United Kingdom were initially set up 160 years ago to address social injustice and the educational and social disadvantages within society, although the term 'public libraries' 'can be traced back long before the 1850 Act of Parliament' (McMenemy, 2009: 19–20). He notes that the Act did not 'create a brand new network from scratch', but rather 'led to the formalisation of a pre-existing network of ad hoc libraries' (McMenemy, 2009: 34). Muddiman et al. (2000: 1) note that 'the public library has a long history of provision for "disadvantaged" or "excluded" individuals, social groups and social classes'. They argue that in the 19th century, public libraries 'were established partly as agents of social change - to educate the deserving poor - and partly as organs of social control - to manage the reading habits of the masses' (Muddiman et al., 2000: 12). McMenemy (2009: 5) concurs, stating that 'one of the key motivations' for introducing public libraries 'in the mid-19th century was for the working classes to use their leisure time in culturally beneficial ways'. Muddiman

Overcoming Information Poverty
ISBN 978-0-08-101110-2

et al. (2000: 12) explain that public libraries were set up in the 19th century by 'philanthropists and progressives', such as Andrew Carnegie, who had an interest in improving the education of the working classes. McMenemy (2009: 24) asserts that libraries 'can still be seen as social education vehicles for their communities', and that while they were 'not designed to offer formal education akin to schools or colleges, they have always formed a self-improvement function'. The historical and contemporary role and purpose was acknowledged by McKee (2006), who stated that public libraries,

...haven't changed in the last 150 years, [they] will never change. It's about giving people access to knowledge so that individuals, families, communities can reach their potential whether that's intellectual, creative, imaginative, personal potential.
McKee quoted in Goulding, 2006: 340

Hence, public libraries have 'always played an important role as an educational vehicle for the wider community', providing 'access' to 'self-educate' (McMenemy, 2009: 96–97). While the role of public libraries is evolving, their historical foundations and purpose for alleviating educational and social disadvantage is arguably still important today.

Muddiman et al. (2000: 12) cite Charles Dickens's speech at the opening of Manchester's first public library in 1852, in which Dickens claimed that the books would provide a 'source of pleasure and improvement in the cottages, the garrets and the ghettoes of the poorest of our people'. Muddiman et al. explain that, as public libraries 'developed in the late 19th century', they 'opened up a world of books and opportunity for some in the "labouring classes"'. However, they acknowledge that while there was a philanthropic interest in establishing public libraries, there was a 'contradiction of purpose' that 'has never been resolved' (Muddiman et al., 2000: 12). They assert that the '"inclusive" heritage of the Victorian public library is a superficial one': 'most Victorian libraries and their committees focused on the "deserving" poor and drew the line at criminals, vagrants and those condemned to the poorhouse' (Muddiman et al., 2000: 12). Pateman and Vincent (2010: 129) comment that while public libraries were originally established 'to meet the needs of "the deserving poor"', they did so 'to different degrees and at different times in history'. They further claim that libraries 'have never succeeded' in meeting 'the needs of the "undeserving poor" – in modern language, the homeless, the unemployed, Travellers, asylum-seekers, refugees, migrant workers, ethnic minorities, and so on' (Pateman and Vincent, 2010: 129). Pateman and Williment (2013: 123) explain that there are two schools of thought: one that argues that public libraries were 'introduced as an agent of social change, to enable the "deserving poor" to obtain work and other opportunities through access to free books and informal learning', and another that suggests public libraries 'were, and still are, to some extent...agents of social control by providing what the Victorians called "healthy" literature which would keep workers out of the pubs where they were exposed to "seditious" literature'.

While public libraries were originally set up for the educational and cultural improvement of the working classes, Muddiman et al. (2000: 12) note that as they 'developed towards the turn of the century, middle class librarians began to devise a broad range of services which appealed increasingly to middle class readers'. They further claim that, 'despite their origins as working class institutions, public libraries were never heavily used by the majority of working class people' and were subsequently 'taken over' by 'the middle class' (Muddiman et al., 2000: 13). They state that the 'philanthropy of the Victorian Public Library, and its concern for the "labouring classes" is part of the heritage of the institution, and by the mid-20th century public libraries claimed to provide free access to books and information "for all"' (Muddiman et al., 2000: 1). By the 1950s, library services to socially excluded people included mobile libraries, prisons and hospital library services (Pateman and Vincent, 2010: 22). In 1964 the Public Libraries Act was passed; it 'initiated a period of comprehensive community service, and an image of "universality" for public libraries which avoided the stigmatisation of the disadvantaged and in turn, led to a middle-class "strangle-hold" on public libraries' (Birdi et al., 2008: 580–581). Birdi et al. claim that in the 1970s there were attempts 'to "re-claim" the working classes, and the concept of community librarianship began to be re-invented by socially radical and committed librarians'. By the 1980s 'community librarians had developed specialised services' for 'perceived disadvantaged groups and potential users, such as housebound services, and tailored services for ethnic minority groups' (Birdi et al., 2008: 580–581). As Muddiman et al. (2000: 13) point out, 'the 1970 and 1980s saw the emergence of a new way of working-community librarianship which attempted to redress the mainstream and middle-class bias of the service'. While attempts were being made 'by some public libraries to reach out into their communities and to begin to serve previously unmet needs', there was 'a lack of prioritising' and 'staff attitudes to this kind of work', which meant that 'many of these strong links were never followed through and sustained' (Muddiman et al., 2000: 14).

While the motivations for creating the original public libraries have been debated, Hendry (2000: 334) acknowledges that in the 19th century libraries 'helped to revolutionise educational opportunities in the towns and cities of the first Industrial Revolution' and 'were often described as "the poor man's university"'.The traditional role of the library as the 'working man's university' has evolved into one where 'the introduction of [information and communication] technologies means that 'learning 'opportunities can be delivered in new ways' (O'Loan and McMenemy, 2005: 4). They explain that,

> ...the philosophy that underpins social inclusion – the right for every citizen to be included in society – is one that is familiar to a public library service which has always emphasised the importance of equity for all.
> **O'Loan and McMenemy, 2005: 10**

They further acknowledge that,

> ...the public library has the capacity and the general ethos with which to encourage social inclusion, yet more effort must be made to target the groups most unlikely to use its resources.
> **O'Loan and McMenemy, 2005: 10**

Goulding (2006: 264) states that some 'commentators and practitioners' view the current involvement of public libraries 'in learning as returning to the roots of the public library movement, with the potential to enhance the standing, relevance and credibility' of libraries 'within the community'.

Policymakers and strategists in Northern Ireland were asked during interviews how they perceived the current purpose of Libraries NI in relation to the historical role of libraries. There was consensus among the Department of Culture, Arts and Leisure (DCAL) and Libraries NI that the original role and ethos of libraries was still important today. Furthermore, the historical role libraries played in tackling social and educational disadvantage and increasing the skills of the workforce was still relevant today. For instance, one interviewee commented that the justification for building a library in Belfast in the late 19th century was to develop workforce skills and 'support worker's education' (DCAL1). DCAL1 further asserted that DCAL is revisiting the original justification for public libraries to improve the lives of those with a 'lack of education', focussing on 'areas of high social need' and tackling generational and 'cyclical issues' of low levels of ambition and educational underachievement within socially deprived areas.The other interviewee from DCAL agreed that DCAL's priorities to alleviate poverty and tackle social exclusion demonstrated that they were returning to the original argument for setting up public libraries which was to develop the 'reading and writing skills' of the most educationally and disadvantaged in society (DCAL2). Likewise, another participant claimed that since libraries historically provided people with an 'opportunity to educate themselves', improve 'their employment opportunities' and develop themselves 'as individuals', what public libraries were doing now to address information poverty 'has a lot of history' (LNI6). These views are similar to those expressed by participants in recent research conducted by Ipsos MORI (2013) which confirmed that 'when stakeholders' focused on the:

> ...fundamental purpose of libraries they found themselves returning to enduring concepts – almost identical to the arguments made when the very first rate-funded public libraries were established over a century ago ...providing knowledge and education as opportunities for social mobility.
>
> **Ipsos MORI, 2013: 17**

This Ipsos MORI report also cited the Dickens quote from 1852, mentioned earlier, which linked the purpose and value of public libraries today to their historical value in supporting a 'skilled workforce' and 'a knowledge economy' (Ipsos MORI, 2013: 21).

The views expressed previously were supported by the macro-level interview data. The interviewees typically observed that public libraries were the stepping stone to informal learning and personal growth: everyone's university. The role of public libraries in supporting society and acting as the 'street corner university', the 'people's university' or the 'university of life' was cited by five interviewees from Libraries NI. Another interviewee explained that 'libraries have always worked with people who have been excluded' (LNI4). This person acknowledged the history of public libraries providing access for people who could not afford education and books. As with other research across the United Kingdom, there was agreement that libraries were set up by Andrew Carnegie in the Victorian era to address educational and social disadvantage, and that the original argument for public libraries was as powerful today.

While information poverty is often a product of educational and social disadvantage, it is also a key factor in creating, exacerbating and maintaining disadvantage. One interviewee noted the role libraries play in 'helping the underprivileged' (LNI5). Another remarked that addressing educational and social disadvantage was 'in the psyche of most people' who work in public libraries (LNI2). Evidently, public libraries have traditionally had a responsibility and a role in mediating the information disadvantages of the underprivileged, an idea that permeates this book in three ways: first, in the conceptualisation of information poverty and the role of public libraries in addressing disadvantage; second, in the findings chapters, which examine how information poverty is addressed at strategic and community levels;

and third, in the book's recommendations, which can improve the capacity for public libraries to address information poverty.

2.3 POVERTY IN NORTHERN IRELAND

Enabling the economy to grow, regenerating deprived areas and tackling disadvantage and inequality within society are key priorities of the Northern Ireland Programme for Government, 2011–15. The most recent total population figure for Northern Ireland, as of 30 June 2013, is estimated to be 1.830 million people (Northern Ireland Statistics and Research Agency, 2014).[1] Poverty figures for Northern Ireland reveal that it is arguably more disadvantaged than other regions in the United Kingdom. For example, the number of unemployed people has increased since 2008, with Northern Ireland experiencing the highest level of persistent unemployment among countries in the United Kingdom.[2] As of August 2015, the employment rate in Northern Ireland 'for those aged 16–64 was estimated at 67.9%' (just over two-thirds), which remained 'below the UK average (73.6%)' and was 'the lowest rate among the twelve UK regions'. The Northern Ireland 'economic inactivity rate for those aged 16–64 stood at 27.6%', which is 'significantly higher than the UK average rate (22.1%) and is the highest of the 12 UK regions' (Department of Enterprise, Trade and Industry, 2015)). Additionally, the latest Northern Ireland seasonally adjusted unemployment rate of 6.0% 'is above the overall UK average rate' of 5.4%, and is 'the joint fifth highest rate among the twelve UK regions' (ibid). In addition, the 'youth unemployment rate (percentage of economically active 18-24 year olds who are unemployed) was 18.7%' which was 'higher than the UK average rate (13.8%)'.

A report by the Joseph Rowntree Foundation (2014: 4) states that 'unemployment increased by more in NI than in GB between 2007/08 and 2012/13 to reach 5.8%; a level now only slightly lower than GB'. The report also reveals that the 'Northern Ireland labour market stands out from Great Britain'; for example, in 'NI 36% of those unemployed have been unemployed for over two years, compared with 18% in GB', and 'the employment

[1] See Northern Ireland Statistics and Research Agency, 2014. Population and Migration Estimate Northern Ireland, 2013 – Statistical Report. Available from: http://www.nisra.gov.uk/archive/demography/population/midyear/MYE13_Report.pdf.

[2] See Northern Ireland Assembly, 2012. Poverty and Social Deprivation Mapping Executive and Departmental Strategies, Policies and Programmes in Northern Ireland. Paper 145/12, NIAR 464-12. Available from: http://www.niassembly.gov.uk/Documents/RaISe/Publications/2012/social_dev/14512.pdf.

rate of disabled people in Northern Ireland is 35%, compared with 50% in England and around 45% in Scotland and Wales', which reveals a 'much higher level of economic inactivity among disabled people in Northern Ireland' (Joseph Rowntree Foundation, 2014: 4). The report also indicated that the following occurred in Northern Ireland in the 5 years between 2006/2007 and 2011/2012:

- 'The poverty rate among adults aged 16 to 29 rose by 8% points to reach 26%'.
- 'Among those aged 30 to 59 poverty... also increased but... solely... among those in working families'.
- Household incomes, poverty rates and the labour market all worsened.
- The average (median) income fell by almost 10% compared with 7% for the United Kingdom as a whole. The decrease at the bottom of the income distribution was also much greater.
- 'The proportion of unemployed working-age people... almost doubled... to reach 5.8'.

As of July 2015, the employment rate in Northern Ireland was estimated at 67.9% (just over two-thirds) (Office for National Statistics, 2015). Areas where information poverty is most likely to be concentrated are those with the highest levels of unemployment, economic inactivity and poor educational attainment. Furthermore, deprived areas with limited home information and communication technologies and Internet access are key locales to target when addressing information poverty.

The next section describes the role of DCAL, which oversees and sets strategy for library services in Northern Ireland, to give the reader a sense of the context for the study upon which the book is based. Following this, the priorities and strategic plans of Libraries NI, and the challenges facing library services in Northern Ireland, are discussed.

2.4 THE DEPARTMENT FOR CULTURE, ARTS AND LEISURE AND LIBRARIES NI

In the Northern Ireland executive, DCAL is one of the departments that have a responsibility to deliver the Programme for Government's (2011–15) agenda to address poverty and social deprivation. Public libraries in Northern Ireland are sponsored by DCAL, which sets 'strategic direction and policy' for libraries (Osborn, 2008:12). In 2005 DCAL commenced a review of public libraries and in 2006 published *Delivering Tomorrow's Libraries*, which became the policy framework for public libraries in

Northern Ireland. *Delivering Tomorrow's Libraries* is DCAL's overall policy document for libraries; however, it does not contain any specific policies to address information poverty. The Review of Public Administration by the Northern Ireland Executive, which sought to review the delivery of public services and the ideas expressed in *Delivering Tomorrow's Libraries*, led to the establishment of a single library authority in 2009; it was hoped that this would improve public library services across Northern Ireland. Libraries NI is a nondepartmental public body that brought together public library services that were previously provided by five education and library boards. In the transitional period since 2009, library leaders and managers in Northern Ireland have faced the challenges of reframing a new organisation, putting procedures and processes in place and restructuring and managing organisational change. With the new organisation and structures now in place, there is an opportunity to develop a more community-focused organisation, and to develop strategies to encourage library usage and contribute to wider government priorities to tackle poverty and social and digital exclusion.

Having one library authority can be beneficial in a number of ways. First, it can raise the profile of libraries, allowing them to have greater influence at the national level and providing a better opportunity to deliver government initiatives. Second, it facilitates collaboration and the development of strategic partnerships with other government departments that are addressing similar areas such as poverty and digital and social exclusion. Third, it is more cost-effective and can facilitate more consistency across the service in relation to service standards and staff development. Fourth, marketing and branding can be improved, thereby improving the corporate image. Fifth, the stock budget can be used more efficiently, improving stock selection and distribution. Finally, as one library service serving the entire country, Libraries NI has the potential to have an impact at the strategic and government levels, as well as an impact on communities, as opposed to being delivered through local authorities.

Libraries NI has a responsibility to deliver the Northern Ireland Programme for Government and to contribute to DCAL's strategic plans. Public library policy is driven by government policy, and the main priority – and most important objective – of DCAL and its Arm's Length Bodies (ALBs) is to 'promote equality and tackle poverty and social exclusion' (Libraries NI, 2014: 13). Libraries NI's vision and mission statements, as outlined in the Libraries NI Business Plan, 2014/2015 (Libraries NI, 2014: 3), are the same as those contained in *Delivering Tomorrow's Libraries* (DCAL, 2006):

Vision: A flexible and responsive public library service that provides a dynamic focal point in the community and assists people to fulfil their potential.

Mission: To enrich and enhance the lives of individuals and communities through providing and promoting a range of high-quality library and information services.

The statements emphasise that the organisation seeks to be flexible and responsive and the potential value of public libraries in order to improve lives and libraries' importance to communities. The vision and mission statements could be modified to include an emphasis on a library service, which addresses disadvantage and digital and social exclusion. For instance, Pateman and Williment (2013: 164) argue that 'if social exclusion is not central to the public library strategy, vision and mission statements, then it will not be possible to successfully identify, prioritise and meet community needs'. Libraries NI's vision and mission statements are almost 10 years old, and they could focus more on those in need and reflect more fully their emphasis on tackling information poverty and social exclusion. This could be the case for other public libraries in other contexts, which could embrace the need to target social and digital exclusion in their vision and mission statements.

Library usage in Northern Ireland and the challenges of addressing nonlibrary use is discussed next.

2.5 LIBRARY USAGE IN NORTHERN IRELAND

To be more effective at addressing information poverty, public libraries need to encourage more people to use their services. As of March 2014, Libraries NI had 795,026 registered library users and 292,702 active members.[3] With a total of 292,702 active users (2014), and based on a population of 1.83 million in Northern Ireland in June 2013, according to Northern Ireland Statistics and Research Agency statistics (2014), the data indicate that around 16% of the population in Northern Ireland are actively using libraries. Based on the same population figure, this indicates that, with 795,026 registered users (2014), 43.4% of the population in Northern Ireland are registered users. Hence there is a large gap between those who are members of libraries and those who are active users. Furthermore, the figures for active members suggest that around 84% of the population are not active library users. One macro-level interviewee acknowledged this

---

[3] Data obtained from the Library Management System, supplied by a statistician from Libraries NI, September 2014.

disparity. For this interviewee, information poverty was connected to nonuse of libraries. They stated that while Libraries NI do "a lot" to address information poverty, they serve:

> ...at best guess...30 percent of the population...in terms of registered and active users...under 20 percent of the population. That is a huge percentage of population who were paying through their taxes for a library service that they are not using...I think we aren't doing enough to address those issues.
>
> *LI1*

As the previous comment indicates, in Northern Ireland a large proportion of the population is unable to avail of government-funded public library services. Interestingly, the findings of the latest annual report (October 2015) related to the Continuous Household Survey (CHS), which looks at adult public library usage in Northern Ireland, revealed that 'Just under three out of every ten (29%) of the adult population had used the public library service within the previous year' (Continuous Household Survey, 2015). The low level of library usage was noted by another interviewee who commented that 'there are more non-users out there than we have users' (LNI8). Likewise, another interviewee stated that the library service 'is actually less used than any other library service in the UK or possibly Ireland' (DCAL1). Yet another interviewee highlighted fears over decreasing library usage, arguing that 'a big management failing' was 'not giving the information down to [the] front line' (LNI7). This person argued that libraries have 'great repeat customers', but there are not enough new people coming in to sustain it for the future. There could be many reasons for this, for example, they have no tradition of library use, they have no need because they may have access to books or the Internet at home, or, quite possibly, they view libraries as having no connection to or relevance in their lives. So, the acknowledgement by DCAL and some senior library staff that libraries are not as well used as they should be – and therefore are not having as significant impact as they could have – is important and needs to be addressed through proactive engagement, communication and promoting what library services can offer. When Libraries NI was set up in 2009, it seems that an opportunity was missed to design and develop a library service with a vision for community engagement and with strategies and staffing structures in place that have at their core the targeting of local communities and identified groups. As is evidenced in later chapters, Libraries NI's recent temporary community engagement strategy, Targeting Social Exclusion, can have an impact, but as yet no long-term strategy for community engagement has been put in place.

The report titled *A New Chapter: Public Library Services in the 21st Century*, written by MacDonald (2012) for the Carnegie UK Trust, also revealed that Northern Ireland was below the average United Kingdom and the Republic of Ireland (ROI) library usage level, and 'those in semi or unskilled occupations were most likely to feel that libraries were not important to them'. The *New Chapter* report found that library usage was lower among those over 55 years old (30%), a growing age group, which was less than the average of 40% from other jurisdictions. Please replace this with 'the average of 40% of over 55s from the other four countries which participated in the report'. As well as targeting people older than 55 years and those who are retired, Libraries NI should be doing more to increase overall levels of library usage. A Carnegie UK Trust (2012) factsheet, based on the findings of a survey of 1009 participants in Northern Ireland, revealed that 'Two fifths of respondents (40%) had used a public library in the previous 12 months', which was 'lower than any other jurisdiction comparing with 61% for Scotland, 51% for Ireland, 50% for England and 45% for Wales'. Key findings of the Carnegie UK Trust (2012) report various demographic statistics about library usage in Northern Ireland:

- Usage was lower among men (35%) than women (45%).
- Usage was low (30%) among those older than 55 years, compared with 62% in Scotland to 41% in Wales for this demographic.
- Usage was particularly low (27%) among retired people, compared with 61% in Scotland and 53% in Ireland.
- Usage was higher (42%) among people living in urban areas than those from rural areas (35%).
- People in social group B (middle managers) (60%) were most likely to have visited a library, whereas those in social group E (68%) were least likely.

These data illustrates the worrying trend of declining library usage in Northern Ireland and the challenges facing library strategists to come up with innovative ways of improving usage. The Carnegie UK Trust (2012) report indicated that library usage in Northern Ireland was lower among men (35%) than women (45%); therefore public libraries in Northern Ireland need to be more effective at targeting men. This was acknowledged in interviews with community engagement staff who noted that men's groups – especially those aged between 40 and 60 years – could be better targeted.

Interestingly, the study found that in Northern Ireland 30% of the population never or rarely reads books, which is the highest rate among United Kingdom countries, although Wales was comparable with 29% (Carnegie

UK Trust, 2012). While the Carnegie UK Trust report does not provide detailed analysis of the disparities in library use between the regions surveyed, they do highlight the key factors that have an impact on library use: for example, valuing libraries, socioeconomic barriers, geography, age and reading habits. The 2012 report indicated that in Northern Ireland reading habits were particularly lower than in other regions and lower among men. The reading culture in Northern Ireland could be improved by developing literacy levels, promoting reading and more successfully marketing library services. This is not an issue that can be addressed solely by public libraries; it could be addressed by other organisations and at various levels, for instance, within schools, and possibly with a national marketing campaign to promote reading. Evidently, the low levels of library use in Northern Ireland, as evidenced in the Carnegie UK Trust report, need to be addressed, and I believe that focussing on attracting nonusers should be the key priority of libraries.

Because library usage in socially deprived areas is low, DCAL wants Libraries NI to focus on these areas; DCAL has a 'greater requirement to reach out into' the communities that could benefit most from library interventions (DCAL2). Both DCAL interviewees asserted that deprived areas have 'the greatest need' and that library services should be marketed and promoted more effectively within these areas (DCAL1 and DCAL2). Furthermore, DCAL was 'prepared to invest more money to get less output in areas of social need because they need them the most' (DCAL1). Significantly, an interviewee explained that libraries need to get into 'the areas of deprivation', 'get under the skin' and ascertain, first, why people are not using them, and second, what libraries could do to bridge the gap and 'make them usable' and 'accessible' (DCAL2). One interviewee claimed that if they want to increase library usage they could focus on affluent communities that understand the value of libraries, reading and education, but 'the challenge' for libraries is that these communities do not represent 'the type of person' they want libraries 'to focus their attention on' (DCAL1). Similarly, a source from Libraries NI recognised that the library service 'is well used' and 'much appreciated by the middle-class in much the same way as [it] probably benefits from the health service more than perhaps the disadvantaged do' (LNI5). Moreover, tackling disadvantage is where libraries can make the biggest impact, as asserted in this comment:

... where is it we are going to make most impact on people's lives? That has to be people who are suffering from some disadvantage, educational and social disadvantage. It is the second chance for many people as far as education is concerned. It is for people who are socially disadvantaged...That is where [libraries] can make a big contribution to the future.

LN16

Notably, while libraries must also deliver a comprehensive service, it is in areas of social need – for the educationally and socially disadvantaged – that public libraries can have the largest effect. The strong message in the quotation previously mentioned – that libraries can have the 'most impact' for the 'socially disadvantaged' – is similar to DCAL's requirement to target those in 'greatest need'.

While there was general consensus among Libraries NI that libraries were originally established to address educational and social disadvantage, there was no consensus around their educational and social role today. Twelve of the 15 Libraries NI staff at the macro level felt that libraries had a responsibility to address educational and social disadvantage. One source posited that Libraries NI has a responsibility to provide a 'universal service', but that it could have the largest effect by targeting those who are educationally and socially disadvantaged (LNI6). Another interviewee felt they were never 'doing enough' to address educational and social disadvantage because they 'are restricted' by their 'funding' and 'meeting all the other legislative requirements' and 'other demands in the service' (LNI1).

While there was general agreement on the role of libraries in lifelong learning, two interviewees were sceptical about the educational link. For instance, one was 'wary' about the 'formal education' link, which they claimed could, for some people, be a barrier to accessing libraries (LNI7). This interviewee commented that libraries 'have a responsibility for the social disadvantage', but they were 'not so sure about the educational', arguing that the library is 'not an educational organisation' (LNI7). While admitting that libraries 'promote lifelong learning', this interviewee asserted library staff do not 'teach it as such'; rather, they 'facilitate it', making 'information' and 'services available' that 'allow people to develop themselves' (LNI7). Hence, while libraries give people 'some basic skills', LN17 concluded that it is not the library's 'role or responsibility to address educational disadvantage': 'there is an education department for that'. Another respondent asserted that they were 'not sure about the responsibility' for education, asserting that the term 'responsible' suggested 'formal' learning (LNI4). This interviewee claimed that a library's responsibility was 'to provide a space that people feel comfortable' in to facilitate 'informal learning' (LNI4).

There were clear inconsistencies among senior library staff regarding addressing educational and social disadvantage and agreement about where libraries could make the most impact. However, the role of libraries in promoting literacy was re-affirmed by one participant who quoted from the Libraries Act (2008), which states that libraries 'have a duty . . . to promote literacy . . . digital literacy as well as textual literacy' (LNI5). Moreover, 'promoting literacy and lifelong learning' is stated in the Libraries Act 2008, which clarifies the educational role of libraries (Libraries Act, 2008: 2). The conflicting views on the purpose of libraries can arguably be restricting Libraries NI in its capacity to effectively address poverty and social exclusion and to increase library usage in socially deprived areas. Evidently, improved leadership, communication and agreement on the purpose of libraries, and having a vision of how libraries can target services to those who could benefit most from them, are fundamental. Key to this is being aware of the information needs of various groups within socially deprived areas.

As is revealed in the findings chapters, Chapters 6–10, marketing must improve through community engagement, especially in socially deprived areas where library usage is low.

2.6 LIBRARY USAGE IN SOCIALLY DEPRIVED AREAS

The annual CHS, administered by the Central Survey Unit of the Northern Ireland Statistics and Research Agency, is designed to provide information on a wide range of social and economic issues. The CHS is one of the largest continuous surveys conducted in Northern Ireland and is based on a sample of the general population residing in private households. The CHS collates information on public library usage and attitudes toward libraries. Every year, DCAL includes in the CHS questions related to culture, arts and leisure to provide data that can help inform future policy. The CHS (2012/2013) revealed that there is a lower proportion of people who live in the most deprived areas who visit a library at least once a year (30%) compared with those who live in the least deprived areas (36%).

The CHS 2012/2013 survey noted that there were differences in library usage between those living in the most deprived areas compared with those living in the least deprived areas. For instance, 23% of those in the most deprived areas used libraries to access the Internet, compared with 9% in the least deprived areas. Similarly, 21% in the most deprived areas used libraries to use a computer, compared with 12% in the least deprived areas (CHS, 2012/2013: 13). Evidently, the need to use libraries for Internet and computer access is greater in deprived areas where home computer and Internet ownership is significantly lower. Pateman and Williment (2013: 184–185) also observe that findings of the Libraries Omnibus Survey (Ipsos MORI, 2009) revealed that computer usage in libraries 'reduces as income rises, suggesting that this provision is serving the lower-income members of the community'. As noted earlier, public libraries seem to play a fundamental role in providing computer/Internet access for those without the financial means to pay for it. Likewise, a DCAL report titled "Impact of Poverty on Attendance at Libraries in Northern Ireland" (2013) found people in the most deprived areas were more likely than people in the least deprived areas to attend a library several times a week. This could be because those without home Internet/computer access are more reliant on libraries for access than those from the least deprived areas. This is perhaps because their need is greater – they may be unable to afford books or newspapers or may not have home access to technology or the Internet. The report concluded that 'there is a link between attendance at libraries and poverty in Northern Ireland' (Impact of Poverty on Attendance at Libraries in Northern Ireland, 2013: 22). The analysis revealed that people who have never worked, people with a low income and people with no qualifications were less likely to attend libraries (Impact of Poverty on Attendance at Libraries in Northern Ireland, 2013: 22). Among adults who had never worked, attendance rates were 10% below the Northern Ireland average. The CHS survey also found that awareness of public libraries declined within deprived areas. The levels of awareness about library services in deprived areas needs to be addressed through proactive marketing, promotion, community outreach and targeted programmes to encourage usage. Active targeting of the unemployed and those in lower-paid/lower-skilled occupations, who could potentially benefit most from library services, is clearly needed. People without educational qualifications were less likely than people with qualifications to attend libraries. Libraries need to target people with no/limited qualifications to address this gap. Further, libraries have a role to play in providing access to information and support for unemployed people, and they could make a greater contribution to building workforce skills by thinking of imaginative ways to promote and deliver services.

A report by Ipsos MORI (2014) revealed that those from the lower socio-economic groups C2DE[4] groups were less likely to read regularly. The research, based on ≥1000 interviews with adults, investigated the reading habits of library users and non–library users in Northern Ireland. The study found that two-fifths read books at least once a week, but one-third never read books. Also, there were notable differences between social grades:

---

[4] § D Semi-skilled and unskilled workers
   § E Casual workers; those with no income other than state benefits

- 27% of social grade higher socio-economic groups ABC1[5] read two to three times per week or at least once a week.
- 16% of social grade C2DE read two to three times per week or at least once a week.
- The 32% who said they never read tended to be male, ≥65 years old, and C2DE.

One-third of those surveyed read e-books and tended to be from the ABC1 group. Those who have never used an e-book tended to be male and from the C2DE group. In addition, 43% of those who read said they borrowed books from the library. Those who borrowed from the library tended to be female and ABC1. Those who never borrowed books from libraries were usually male and from the C2DE group.

Library attendance in England decreased between 2009 and 2012 among people living in the least deprived areas, and it stayed the same in the most deprived areas during the same period. According to the *Taking Part* report (Department of Culture, Media and Sport, 2013), in the year ending June 2013, 36.2% of adults in England reported using a library service in the past 12 months, a significant decrease from 48.2% in 2005/2006 and 38.8% in 2011/2012. While library attendance has declined in England, it is still more than the 31% of adults who used library services in Northern Ireland reported in the CHS 2012/2013 survey. Similar to Northern Ireland, in England adults in the 'upper socio-economic groups (38.3%) had a higher rate of library attendance than people in lower socio-economic groups (33.3%)' (Department of Culture, Media and Sport, 2013: 26).

In 2011 in Scotland there was a 12% difference in library attendance between the most and least deprived areas. Library attendance has remained similar since 2007 among people living in the least deprived areas. It initially decreased in the most deprived areas between 2007 and 2009. However, the 2011 attendance rate in the most deprived areas is similar to that in 2007 (DCAL, 2013: 21).

While comparable trends exist in library usage in England and Scotland, there are limitations when comparing deprivation and library attendance rates in Northern Ireland with those in other countries because data definitions, collection methods and base populations differ (DCAL, 2013: 19). Library attendance rates are captured in each country using different survey tools, methodological procedures and definitions of library attendance;

---

[5] § A Senior managers and professionals
    § B Middle managers
    § C1 Junior managers; small traders with staff and premises

therefore researchers in Northern Ireland need to be cautious when trying to compare figures. Nonetheless, it is important to highlight the challenges facing public library services in other regions and to place this book within the context of wider public library debate.

2.7 CONCLUSIONS

This chapter began by looking at the historical role of public libraries in addressing educational and social disadvantage. As the chapter progressed, it focused specifically on Northern Ireland and presented poverty statistics to give readers a sense of the context upon which the book is based. It then focused on Libraries NI and the challenge of addressing low levels of library usage in Northern Ireland. The statistics indicate that Libraries NI needs to target more effectively specific sections of the population. This could be achieved by engaging with nonusers, improving marketing and raising awareness of services. Libraries NI's current community engagement strategy to develop stronger links with socially deprived areas, called Targeting Social Exclusion, is examined further in Chapters 6–10.

The next chapter looks more closely at what information poverty is, the United Kingdom government policies to improve access to information and the role that public libraries play in this.

CHAPTER 3

Developing an Understanding of What Information Poverty Is

3.1 INTRODUCTION

This chapter allows for a deeper understanding of what information poverty is and the role that public libraries play in alleviating it. Since public libraries have a role in facilitating information access and reducing educational and social disadvantage, understanding how information poverty manifests is essential if public libraries are to find ways of tackling it. To understand information poverty, we need a clear understanding of what 'information' and 'poverty' are, and of the relationship between these two terms (Britz, 2007: 3). The chapter begins by discussing what information is and its importance for personal fulfilment, then what poverty is, before considering how the two terms are combined in the phrase 'information poverty'. To highlight the factors creating information poverty, I have integrated the responses from the study discussed in Section 1.7 of Chapter 1, with the previously published information poverty literature. In doing so, this chapter reinforces an understanding of information poverty concepts and how they can be applied to libraries. There then follows a discussion of the United Kingdom government policies to facilitate information access and to tackle social exclusion.

3.2 CONCEPTUALISING 'INFORMATION'

Understanding the multifaceted concept of 'information' – how people interpret and value information – is crucial to understanding information poverty. Conceptualising information is also important for library and information professionals. The concept of information continues to evolve, and our understanding of, and need for, different types of information develop as society changes. Early studies of information poverty articulated the complexities of defining information. Childers and Post (1975: 13) defined information as 'that which can be communicated either orally or in written form'; it is 'the raw material that is used in knowing, making

Overcoming Information Poverty
ISBN 978-0-08-101110-2

decisions, taking action, thinking and learning…discrete pieces of meaningful data'. Dervin (1977: 18) views information as a 'valuable and useful' tool to help people 'cope with their lives'; it 'can be whatever an individual finds "informing"' (Dervin, 1977: 22). Dervin distinguishes between objective information 'external reality' (data) and subjective information 'internal reality' (how people give meaning) (Dervin, 1977: 22). Information can be identified by the senses: touch, smell, taste, hearing and sight. Moreover, information can be used to gain knowledge and to change someone's perception of the world; it can inform decision making and act as a conduit to cope with life's circumstances.

Buckland (1991: 351) further identifies three meanings of information: 'information-as-process', 'information-as-knowledge', and 'information-as-thing' (the attributive use of 'information' to denote things regarded as informative), echoing Dervin's earlier comment that information is whatever an individual finds informing. As opposed to 'information as knowledge' (knowledge) and 'information as process' (becoming informed), which are intangible, 'information as thing' is tangible. According to Buckland, 'information-as-thing' is 'evidence' that exists in many forms, including traditional sources such as data, books and documents, and non-traditional sources such as events and objects. Buckland suggests that whatever one might learn from can be called information (Hayter, 2005: 13). The meaning of information and how we interpret information is an important feature of Library and Information Science (LIS). Thus 'information as thing' is applicable to LIS because it views information as a resource, a document that can be used to create knowledge. The definition of 'information as thing' is important. First, it relates to the information, in print and electronic formats, provided by library and information services. Second, it suggests that libraries, by providing access to information, can have an impact on developing the knowledge base of society, communities and individuals.

The meaning of 'information' and how we interpret information is an important feature of LIS. Information can mean different things to different people, and information context is important. Information can be interpreted differently depending on the context in which information is received, the person receiving the information and who presents it. Dervin (1977: 23–27) posits that any two people looking at the same piece of information can interpret it differently, and that the 'same person in the "same" situation on two different days will not see that situation the same'. Dervin's person-centred view of information is echoed in the subsequent information poverty literature (Buckland, 1991; Lievrouw and Farb, 2003; Hayter, 2005;

Britz, 2004, 2007; Bates, 2008). For example, Britz (2004: 196) echoes Dervin's earlier work, noting that two people in the same situation might apply appropriate meaning to information differently. The subjective nature of information therefore makes it more difficult to define. Information context is important to our understanding of information and information poverty. Hayter (2005:14) considers information context as a barrier to access, stating that the 'lack of consensus' in defining information 'stems not only from varying philosophical arguments but also from the fact that information can have different meanings in different circumstances at different times'. A continuation of theory in information poverty studies is evidenced here. Information context and timing are important, and each person interprets information differently depending on the context in which it is received. While information poverty can be the result of no available information, it can also arise when information is available but people cannot understand it or apply value to it. The individual information context can be a cause of information poverty.

In addition, information can be defined and interpreted by social context: the social norms, worldviews, values and the small worlds in which people live (Pendleton and Chatman: 1998).

...information must be understood as information in something. In the cultural sense, we mean that information is in the definition of how practical lives are played out. It is in the act of forming a world view that determines what is important in a world and what is trivial.

Pendleton and Chatman, 1998: 749

As evidenced here, an individual's social environment affects how they understand, use and value information, make sense of their surroundings and perceive the world. This quotation highlights the need to understand information access from a social perspective. Capurro and Hjørland (2003) traced the historical roots of the word 'information' and considered the challenge of defining information for Information Science and other fields. They also comment that 'Meaning is...determined in social and cultural contexts'.

the most important distinction in the concepts of information is the distinction between information as an object or a thing (e.g. number of bits) and information as a subjective concept, information as a sign, i.e. as depending on the interpretation of a cognitive agent.

Capurro and Hjørland (2003)

The multifariousness of information means that defining it is 'problematic' (Weller, 2008: 11). This has been noted by Hayter (2005), Britz (2007),

Bates (2008), Jaeger and Burnett (2010) and Floridi (2011). The current meaning of 'information' in dictionaries describes 'information as a process in which something is communicated and/or someone is informed' (Britz, 2007: 34). Information as an act of informing, however, is not the same as knowledge, which is the act of learning that comes from understanding obtained information. Information access and knowledge acquisition are central foundations of the library and information profession.

> Within LIS, knowledge is usually understood to be formed through information acquisition, understanding, and use. It is a capacity within individuals and derived from education, reading, and experience.
>
> **Bates 2008: 35**

It is through information provision that public libraries can contribute to developing the knowledge base, education and information richness of societies, communities and individuals.

Having considered the various definitions of information, I have created my own original definition:

> Information can be anything that is communicated orally or physically (print or online media), which subsequently influences and motivates an individual's ability to make decisions and take action. Information can be understood in external and internal terms. It is external matter which individuals absorb and process internally to enable them to learn and progress. Information can be physical, which we can touch and feel or from the senses, hearing, sight and smell. Information can be the internally generated thoughts that individuals have which enable them to form opinions.

My definition considers information as both objective and subjective, and in terms of the physical and virtual environment in which we live and the environment in which library and information systems currently operate. The following section considers the importance of information. Following this, I discuss what poverty is and the link between poverty and no or limited access to information.

3.2.1 The Importance of Information

Information is necessary for existence, whether it is basic information needs (obtaining food) or higher-level needs (education, personal and professional fulfilment). Information is needed from birth and throughout life to understand our environment, stimulate our thoughts and motivate our actions. Information enables citizens to make decisions, act on these decisions and move forward; information is therefore needed for any change in life circumstances to occur. Furthermore, people need information for their 'emotional' and 'physiological well-being', 'to make sense of their surroundings, to participate in society, to fulfil personal goals, and to cope with various day-to-day situations' (Bates, 2008: 1–2). In essence, access to information is needed (Britz and Lor, 2010: 17):

- for survival and can be 'equated to fresh air';
- for all human activities;
- for education, political and cultural participation; and
- to enable us to make choices and have a voice.

Britz (2007: 102) posits that information is a 'fundamental human right' and that access to information is 'at the heart of an information-rich society'. As well as a right to access, people need 'the ability to benefit from the use of the information that has been accessed' (Britz, 2007: 71). Britz (2007: 71) cites Article 19 of the Universal Declaration of Human Rights (United Nations, 1948):

Everyone has the right to freedom of opinion and expression; this right includes freedom to hold opinions without interference and to seek, receive and impart information and ideas through any media and regardless of frontiers.

Britz (2007: 122) further observes that the right to access information and participation is an ethical issue, which was included as Article 4 of the Declaration of Principles, developed at the Geneva Summit of the World Summit on the Information Society, 2003. Feather (2011: 77) confirms that access to information is needed for 'cultural, economic, educational, political and social participation'. Not having access to information can lead to 'information poverty', which ultimately affects an individual's ability to develop, succeed and participate in society. Furthermore, information poverty refers to '*particular* information…that can (add value)' and improve lives (Pollock, 2002). Feather (2013: 133) concurs, stating that information poverty can be 'a disadvantage when it deprives its victims of information which could be of benefit to them'. Public libraries can play an integral role in providing access to the information that people need in order to progress in society.

3.3 POVERTY AND INFORMATION POVERTY

There are varying degrees and manifestations of poverty, ranging from absolute to relative and chronic. It is a 'complex phenomenon and its causes are multi-dimensional' (Britz, 2007: 25). Britz (2007: 25) notes that poverty is 'the direct opposite of wealth', which is 'generally linked to concepts such as abundance, status and high quality'. Poverty, then, suggests an absence of or the possession of a resource. Britz observes that poverty is 'linked to people's inability to provide for their basic needs' (Britz, 2007: 16). Poverty can be viewed as a continuum ranging from access to no access to material resources and essential services. UNESCO recognises that 'poverty is a multi-dimensional phenomenon' and offers the following definition of human poverty:

> ...poverty is a denial of choices and opportunities, it is a violation of human dignity. It means lack of basic capacity to participate effectively in society. It means not having enough to feed and clothe a family, not having a school or a clinic to go to, not having the land on which to grow one's food or a job to earn one's living, nor having access to credit. It means insecurity, powerlessness and exclusion of individuals, households and communities
>
> **UNESCO, 1998**

The aforementioned quotation captures the factors of poverty. Information is fundamental to provide access to opportunities for participation and to avoid social exclusion. Britz (2007: 33) states that 'information poverty is one of the manifestations of poverty', which can subsequently accentuate and reinforce 'poverty in general' (Britz and Blignaut, 2001: 63). Bradshaw et al. (2007: 8) concur that information poverty exacerbates and 'maintains other types of poverty'. Moreover, Britz (2007: 75) claims information poverty is 'an instrumental form of poverty because it can affect all aspects of people's lives'. Sinnamon (2009: 213) explains that 'poverty becomes, not so much a condition, but a state of being, where its many effects and impacts form a web of interconnected barriers that are difficult to escape'. Similar to poverty, there are various degrees, levels and manifestations of 'information poverty' (Britz, 2007: 77). While poverty is multidimensional, information poverty is one component subsumed within the broad poverty spectrum. Like poverty, information poverty is complex and can be viewed as a spectrum or continuum ranging from plentiful information access and understanding to limited/no information access or understanding (see Figs 4.2 and 4.3 in Chapter 4).

Thus, two complex and significant concepts in contemporary society – information and poverty – are 'united' in the term 'information poverty' (Haider and Bawden, 2006: 371). In this process of 'discourse synthesis', whereby two concepts are combined to create a new concept with a different understanding, information and poverty are combined to form a new concept: information poverty (Haider and Bawden, 2007: 535). In uniting these concepts, the importance of information in the modern society is elevated (Haider and Bawden, 2007: 535). Moreover, information, as the 'dominant resource to define contemporary society', is now used to describe the society in which we live: an information society (Haider and Bawden, 2006: 371). The information society describes 'the shift from an industrial society to one based on the importance of information and knowledge' (Burkett, 2000: 680). Access to information, information and communication technologies (ICTs) and the Internet, and the ability to use these, are prerequisites in an information society; they are necessary for personal, social and economic advancement and are vital to escape economic and social poverty. Hence, information poverty has been described as '*the* new form of poverty in the information society', whereby the lack of access to ICT and the Internet are 'seen as an additional facet of being poor in today's world' (Wilson, 2003). The pitfalls of the information society, however, are noted by Martin (2005: 5), who suggests it can 'widen the gap between information *haves* and *have-nots* and maintain existing socio-economic disparities'. Groups without access to information and, importantly, access to ICTs/Internet, and without the skills for access seemingly are at risk of information poverty and other forms of poverty: social and digital exclusion. Therefore, to understand information poverty, 'a multidimensional view of information access' is needed (Thompson, 2006: 69) because it is the result of multiple interconnected barriers to information access: social, cultural, educational and intellectual.

The following section considers how the terminology of 'information poverty' and the 'information poor' originated.

3.4 ORIGINS OF THE CONCEPTS OF 'INFORMATION POVERTY' AND THE 'INFORMATION POOR'

The terms 'information poverty' and 'information poor' were first used in the United States in the 1970s to describe the barriers that societies, communities and individuals face when attempting to access information (Thompson, 2011: 131). However, a tendency to stigmatise information-poor individuals was noted as far back as 1947 by Hyman and Sheatsley, who referred to 'the chronic know-nothings' (Sligo and Williams, 2002: 4). With the change from an industrial to an information society as a result of the increasing importance of information, sociological researchers in the United States in the 1960s and 1970s began to explore the link between poverty and information (eg, Dervin and Greenberg, 1972). Subsequent studies by Childers and Post (1975), Chatman (1991, 1996, 1999), Britz (2004, 2007), Hayter (2005), Thompson (2006) and Bates (2008) highlight the link between poverty and access to information. Thompson et al. (2014: 18) assert that 'the concept of "information poverty" grew from the American dialogue during the second half of the 20th century when serious attention was given to poverty and information'. Therefore, with an emphasis on access to information, 'information poverty' emerged as a new dimension on the poverty spectrum, primarily as an acknowledgement of the disadvantages of not having access to information. The concept of information poverty, however, and the 'experience of being information poor [are] not new'; throughout history 'peoples and societies have lacked in some or another way material and other resources as well as the skills to satisfy all their information needs' (Britz, 2004: 192, quoting Lievrouw and Farb, 2003).[1]

In 1960, the American sociologist Daniel Bell noted that information was having an increasingly significant role in the post-industrial society (Thompson, 2006: 2). Michael Harrington's book, *The Other America: Poverty in the United States* (1962), began to look at poverty 'through a cultural/behavioral lens' (Thompson, 2006: 2–3). Harrington cited the idea of a 'culture of poverty', first presented in the 1959 book by the social anthropologist Oscar Lewis, titled *Five Families: Mexican Case Studies in the Culture of Poverty*. Lewis's and Harrington's writings encouraged social research that looked beyond the infrastructural/economic causes of poverty to focus on the 'culture or behaviour of marginalised groups of individuals' (Thompson, 2006: 6–7). Within this culture of poverty research, a 'lack of motivation to change is a common theme' (Thompson, 2006: 7). Roach and Gursslin (1967), however, subsequently challenged Lewis's work on the culture of poverty, which blamed 'the victims of social disparity rather than work to ameliorate unequal socioeconomic opportunities' (Thompson, 2006: 7). The 'culture of poverty' that places the blame on the poor themselves and implies they cannot escape poverty, rather than seeks resolutions to alleviate poverty, has been challenged in the literature (Bates, 2008: 21).

The elevated status of information was re-affirmed by the economist Fritz Machlup (1962), who 'described the increase in information-related employment as the "knowledge society"', sowing the seeds of what we now know as the information society (Thompson, 2006: 8). Flor (2001: 3) asserts that,

> ever since Machlup and Porat introduced the "information society" concept in the seventies, the correlation between access to information and poverty has been widely acknowledged. The main propositions given were as follows: information

---

[1] Lievrouw and Farb (2003: 499) comment that 'Throughout human history some people have been more educated, better connected, more widely travelled, or more well informed than others'.

leads to resources; information leads to opportunities that generate resources; access to information leads to access to resources; and access to information leads to access to opportunities that generate resources.

This quotation primarily illustrates the cumulative process of access to information, in that the more information you possess, the more 'opportunities' you will have to 'generate resources' and, consequently, advance and create wealth. Furthermore, those without access to information are unable to generate resources to escape poverty. Feather (2013) uses the analogy of a farmer to explain information poverty and richness. The farmer is information rich in that he understands the irrigation patterns enabling him to grow crops to feed his family, but if he wants to improve his crop yield and finances, he needs more information resources. Without access to essential information, the farmer 'becomes a victim of information poverty, and will suffer in comparison with those' who have access to information (Feather, 2013: 120). The importance of information for development, progress and improvement is evident in this instance. In essence, the process of information awareness, availability, acquisition and use provides individuals with the necessary tools for personal advancement and to escape poverty.

Within the emerging 'information society', new terms were used to describe how people could access, retrieve and use the information available in society. The terms 'information poor' and 'information rich' were first used by Edwin B. Parker in 1970 to highlight his concerns about the growing information gap which new ICTs might bring (Parker, 1970: 53). In 1972, the sociologist James S. Coleman used the terms 'information poverty' and 'information poor' to describe 'a structural difference between the modern information environment and the information environment of 100 years prior' (Thompson, 2006: 8). Early approaches to addressing information poverty, from the 1960s to the 1980s, were mainly 'categorical', whereby 'certain socio-economic sections of society' – the elderly, the economically poor, the disabled, ethnic minorities, single parents, rural people, the homeless – were deemed to be the information poor (Yu, 2006: 231). Also considered to be prone to information poverty were the working class and the unemployed (Haider and Bawden, 2006: 535).

A seminal study by Childers and Post (1975: 78) identified the following groups as constituting the 'information-poor' in America: ethnic minorities, poor black Americans, poor farmers, migrant workers, elderly, prisoners and those with physical, visual or hearing disabilities. The influential book resulting from that study, titled *The Information-Poor in America* (1975), articulated the information environment of disadvantaged Americans and influenced much of the subsequent information poverty research. Childers and Post discovered that disadvantaged populations lived in an 'information void' and a 'culture of information poverty' (Childers and Post, 1975: 32–33). Their research looked at the information-poor lifestyles that exist within socially disadvantaged sections of American society. Lievrouw and Farb (2003: 507) note that Childers and Post's (1975) book found that information poverty was very often 'associated with economic and social disadvantages' and was the result of the information-poor lifestyle that exists among specific groups in the American society. In their book, 'disadvantaged' 'means to be lacking in something that the society considers to be important' (Childers and Post, 1975: 10). They identified three characteristics of information poverty:

Low information processing skills:
- poor literacy, language ability, physical disability (hearing, sight), under-educated, few communication skills

Sub-cultural behaviour/limitation:
- living in an information ghetto that may be rich in internally generated information, yet deficient in the information shared by wider society
- the information universe is a closed system, harbouring unawareness and misinformation (myth, rumour, folklore)
- information contacts are often one-way information flows, via the mass media
- a 'reliance on television' and 'entertainment rather than information'
- seeking information from the informal network

Personal attitude/predisposition:
- unwilling to change the condition of their lives or to see information as an instrument of their salvation
- fatalistic, sense of helplessness (Childers and Post, 1975: 32–35).

The characteristics of information-impoverished communities described by Childers and Post are arguably still applicable today. Indeed, their study resonates in contemporary society; more recent research conducted in the United Kingdom by Hayter (2005) also noted a sense of fatalism among the population described in her book. Furthermore, the factors creating information poverty based on the study in Northern Ireland described in this book echo Childers and Post's early work: for example, low educational attainment, poor literacy and limited motivation to access information. Another similarity with the current study is how the community and environment can reflect, first, how people value and use information; second, how they value learning; and third, how localised environments can influence their attitudes towards learning, libraries and information providers. The distinct difference of this study from studies such as that by Childers and Post is the emphasis on having and being able to use information and communication technologies, the need for information and digital literacy skills and having Internet access, which are major factors creating information poverty in contemporary society.

Fig. 3.1 outlines some of the groups who are presented in the literature as often being at risk of information poverty.

Information poverty can be viewed from global, national, social, cultural and personal perspectives. On a global scale, Britz (2004, 2007) considered information poverty from a wider social justice and information inequalities perspective that exists within developed and developing countries. Studies by Childers and Post (1975) and Chatman (1991, 1992, 1996, 1999) argued from a sociocultural perspective that the restrictive information behaviours within groups create information poverty. While I have been influenced by the previous information poverty studies, this book is to my knowledge the first to explore in depth how information concepts can be applied to highlight what public libraries can do to alleviate it.

The following section discusses how the concepts of information poverty and information poor have been used within LIS, often as a means of justifying library services.

Figure 3.1 Groups at risk of information poverty.

3.5 INFORMATION POVERTY AND THE INFORMATION POOR IN THE LIS DISCOURSE

The concept of information poverty has been noted in the LIS literature since the 1970s (Lloyd et al., 2010: 46) to define the role of the library and the responsibility of the librarian. Haider and Bawden's (2006, 2007) discourse analysis examines the language of information poverty and challenges conceptualisations of information poverty and the information poor in the literature. It is argued that the 'information poor' are sometimes a 'constructed' group in the institutional discourse and deemed to be in need of assistance by the library profession (Haider and Bawden, 2006, 2007; Bawden and Robinson, 2009). Haider and Bawden (2006, 2007) questioned whether 'information poverty' has been adopted by library and information professionals as a self-serving construct to promote their status within society and justify their information services. Hence, the 'construction of the information poor' can be interpreted as serving an almost strategic purpose aimed at strengthening the profession's role' within the fabric of society and elevating the librarian's status (Haider and Bawden, 2007: 551).

Haider and Bawden (2007) based their study of information poverty on 35 English-language journals from 1985 to 2005, retrieved from the Library and Information Science Abstracts and Library Literature and Information Science Full Text databases. Throughout these journals are references to the educational, historical and traditional roles of libraries. There were recurring themes and topics (543–548):

1. economic determinism: where economistic rhetoric pervades the concept
2. technological determinism: the need for ICT access and digital literacy skills
3. a tendency to historicise the 'information poor', invoking the roots of the (public) library
4. the (library) profession's responsibility and moral obligation.

That the information poor are portrayed as the information profession's core clientele is of further interest (Haider and Bawden, 2007: 542–543) and are often identified as those who suffer from a 'lack' of information, poor literacy and information literacy skills (Haider and Bawden, 2007: 547). They dismantle the notion of information poverty, exposing and challenging some of the 'underlying assumptions' in LIS that infer the potential for library services to alleviate information poverty by targeting groups deemed to be information poor (Haider and Bawden, 2007: 535). The concept of information poverty confers a role to the information profession, and attributing groups as 'information poor' suggests the ability and obligation to target services towards specific groups. The concepts of information poverty and the information poor, then, have often been used in the LIS literature to legitimise and consolidate the library's status within contemporary society. Information poverty is used to confirm and consolidate the librarian's and the library's roles in addressing social inequalities, and it therefore comes across as a constructed concept used to justify the existence of libraries.

The remedial potential of libraries and librarians in alleviating information poverty is noted by Haider and Bawden (2007: 544). They explain that in the literature they examined, medical metaphors are often used to describe society. For example, they cite Diener (1986: 73) who commented that,

> ...information poverty is not simply a malady for the economic poor or the politically disenfranchised. It affects us all. As a societal pathology of our modern times, its cure lies in improved information management, the establishment of information utilities staffed by competent, knowledgeable professionals.

In this way, information poverty is used to evoke the librarian's ethical responsibility to address information inequalities and improve the health of those without access to information. Haider and Bawden (2007: 544) refer to Foucault's concept of pastoral power, which institutions such as public libraries, schools/colleges and hospitals possess, to depict the library and librarian as saviours and 'agent(s) of salvation' to the disenfranchised within society (Haider and Bawden, 2007: 549–551). According to Foucault (2000: 333), pastoral power is 'salvation-oriented', a 'special form of power' that 'looks after not just the whole community, but each individual in particular, during his entire life'. By facilitating access to information and learning throughout life, public libraries are arguably institutions with pastoral power, and libraries and librarians are portrayed as having the information resources, expert skills and strategies to alleviate information poverty (Haider and Bawden, 2006: 379). This 'sense of ethical concern and righteousness' suggests that a connection 'exists between the conceived needs of the "information poor" and the profession's possibilities' to alleviate their information deficiencies (Haider and Bawden, 2007: 549). Similarly, Yu (2006: 912) observes that radical constructionists claim that 'information poverty and the information poor are no more than a mere academic construction'. For example, Bawden and Robinson (2009: 181) also suggest that the 'information poor' have been identified in the LIS literature 'more by anecdote and opinion than by research and systematic book' and 'more often simply by assertion than from any evidence, and always in the context of their needing the services of library/information professions'. The argument that information poverty is an artificial construct and, furthermore, created and used by library professionals to further their aims, is important to this book, which details what information poverty is, the impact of information poverty and the ways it can be addressed by public libraries.

3.6 INFORMATION POVERTY: PERSPECTIVES FROM POLICY MAKERS AND LIBRARY STAFF

Public libraries have a role to play in reducing poverty within society by providing access to information resources, both in print and online, and developing the literacy and digital literacy skills of citizens. Information poverty theories enable library and information professionals to understand the multiple barriers to information access. For public libraries to be effective at addressing information poverty, library strategists and managers need to understand what it is, what causes it and how it can affect communities and individuals. Further, library staff need to know how libraries can address information poverty and recognise the important role that public libraries play in overcoming it.

Both interviewees from the Department of Culture, Arts and Leisure (DCAL) believed that addressing information poverty was fundamental to alleviating poverty and social exclusion and should be a priority for public libraries. Interestingly, one-fifth of the 15 Libraries' NI staff interviewed at the macro level were not familiar with the term 'information poverty', but they were aware of the concepts around it and the role libraries played in tackling it. Information poverty as a concept is seemingly understood, as is what libraries do to address it, but the terminology was not used by or familiar to all library policymakers in Northern Ireland. Three interviewees admitted looking up the term 'information poverty' online because they were previously unfamiliar with it. I question whether this term is widely used in other parts of the United Kingdom, Republic of Ireland, or even farther afield. If the term is not used and understood, then this book can add to the knowledge of and discussion on the concept. At the meso level, the three community engagement staff were aware of what information poverty was and, with their first-hand experience, were able to articulate how information poverty affects people living in socioeconomically deprived areas. Also, the survey of branch library managers revealed that 68.2% of respondents ($n = 15$) knew what information poverty was in general terms, whereas

31.8% of library managers ($n = 7$) saw it as a new concept. Moreover, the library managers in the 10% most socially deprived areas acknowledged that addressing information poverty should be a priority and highlighted the positive role libraries can play in people's lives and in building communities. As with the macro-level data, most library managers were familiar with what information poverty was, but the actual terminology was not known to some.

A DCAL interviewee stated that 'Information poverty affects everybody', and consequently, 'information poverty and disability' are also DCAL priorities (DCAL2). Another DCAL interviewee explained that DCAL addresses information poverty 'through the library service' (DCAL1). One interviewee described information poverty as part of 'a family of issues' that Libraries NI was 'trying to address' (LNI5); however, opinion was divided among interviewees as to whether information poverty should be a priority for libraries. Two interviewees from Libraries NI suggested that while libraries have a part to play in addressing information poverty, it is not solely their responsibility. For instance, one commented that they did not have a responsibility to address information poverty but thought they could 'assist' the 'government achieve targets of it' (LNI3). This interviewee concluded that it was something that should be addressed initially by schools. One interviewee from Libraries NI thought that addressing information poverty was important: 'it's part of the bigger picture of addressing social exclusion' and 'should be on a par with some other aspects'; however, this person asserted that they would not place information poverty 'as the number one priority over and above everything else' (LNI8). As this book demonstrates, information poverty is a problem within society, and the macro–meso–micro framework presented in this book demonstrates that public libraries have a vital role to play in reducing it. Furthermore, library leaders need to understand what information poverty is, recognise the role they have in addressing it and develop strategies to tackle it.

For public library services to be successful in addressing information poverty, they need clarity on what their purpose is; specifically, they need to be aware of how poverty manifests and the issues affecting people in socially deprived areas: poverty, educational underachievement and deprivation. Public library staff need to be aware of how information poverty manifests if they are to develop strategy and services that can enable them to tackle it effectively and to contribute to government priorities to alleviate digital and social exclusion. For instance, one interviewee commented that 'we don't have the poverty here that you are seeing in parts of England' or

Scotland (LNI3). As the statistics presented in Chapter 2 confirmed, however, the poverty figures for Northern Ireland reveal that it is arguably more disadvantaged than other regions in the United Kingdom.

Other library staff were more aware of the reality of poverty and were in touch with the issues facing many people during economic downturn. One commented that with the 'recession' there is 'a lot more poverty' and more people who are 'not working' (LNI12). This interviewee was aware of the stark realities of those affected by increasing austerity where fuel poverty is now a problem for many who were faced with the dilemma of 'heat or eat' in the previous 'winter' (LNI12). Arguably, those making decisions about libraries are often far removed from the lives of those who could benefit most from library services. Library staff at all levels need to understand the circumstances and the needs of the socioeconomically disadvantaged if they are to successfully alleviate poverty and social exclusion. Furthermore, they need to keep in touch with the information and communication needs of those facing educational and social disadvantage, who often compose the communities that could benefit most from libraries.

I acknowledge that public libraries are often constrained in their capacity to alleviate information poverty by their resources (staffing and financial), but I believe that those designing library strategies and policies need to be aware of what information poverty is and the instrumental role that libraries have in reducing it. I argue that public library strategists need to be aware of statistics on poverty, digital inclusion and educational attainment if they are to address information poverty effectively or poverty in general. Importantly, library policymakers and strategists need to have a strong grasp of the issues affecting people in socially deprived areas: poverty, educational underachievement and deprivation. This will enable them to develop policy that improves skills and learning and encourages social participation and library usage within these communities.

The next section considers the link between information poverty and social exclusion using both the empirical data gathered in this study and the previous literature.

3.7 INFORMATION POVERTY AND SOCIAL EXCLUSION

Communities and individuals affected by information poverty are often at risk of social exclusion as a result of not having access to information or the skills to access information when it is available. Pateman and Vincent (2010: 90) assert that public libraries need to 'engage with all sections of their local communities, particularly non-users, the socially excluded and those who are at risk of exclusion'. Public libraries can play a role in making the socially excluded part of the community and wider society. When public libraries target the socially and digitally excluded, they can thereby be instrumental in creating a more inclusive society. In doing so, the marginalised in society – such as the homeless, travellers, the disabled (mentally or physically), ethnic minorities and the elderly–can be included in mainstream society.

Both interviewees from DCAL claimed that tackling information poverty was part of the bigger picture to alleviate poverty and social exclusion. Importantly, one interviewee viewed information poverty as 'the inability to make the most of your life' and one of a range of constraints, such as health or education, that can hold 'back you or your family's ability to achieve and attain as much as you can' (DCAL1). This comment stresses that information poverty constrains individuals from achieving their potential and echoes the UNESCO definition of poverty cited earlier: that poverty is a 'lack of basic capacity to participate effectively in society'. It was argued that access to information enables the most disadvantaged to develop the self-confidence, knowledge and skills needed to 'move themselves out of poverty' (DCAL1). Information poverty can seemingly affect an individual's ability to improve his or her social and personal circumstances. In essence, access to information is essential to lift people out of poverty and reduce social exclusion.

An interviewee asserted that 'libraries have always worked with people who have been excluded for whatever means in society' (LNI4), thus reaffirming the historical roots of libraries in targeting the most disadvantaged and marginalised in society. The following quotation articulates the link between social exclusion, information poverty and libraries:

> The whole rationale for libraries is to address social exclusion and those with information poverty are excluded socially. It follows, if you have information poverty you are pretty much are excluded from a lot of things in this life
>
> **LNI7**

Lloyd et al. (2010: 46) concur, explaining that 'information poverty is closely related to social exclusion', since limited access to information and the skills for access 'limit the capacity of individuals to fully participate in society and to make informed decisions', which subsequently,

> ...can affect the ability to extend social networks, to gain employment, maintain health, and improve educationally, thus creating a cycle of alienation from mainstream society and continued marginalisation and disenfranchisement of sectors of the community.
>
> **Lloyd et al. (2010: 46)**

Being without access to necessary information means that individuals are often excluded from other educational, cultural and social benefits that information can bring. Moreover, with new information and communication technologies becoming increasingly prevalent, the need to be online and to be communicating with family, friends and community means that those who are not online are often at risk of being marginalised from the wider society.

The link between access to information, social exclusion and information poverty has been noted by Lloyd et al. (2013: 140), who refer to 'social exclusion as an information problem', whereby poverty is connected to the concept of information poverty, which they describe as 'an inability to recognise viable sources of information, to access information that is circulated and distributed'. For Lloyd et al. (2013: 140) 'approaching the concept of social exclusion from an information perspective' is fundamental because it 'acknowledges that the ability to become socially included is predicated on the ability to connect and engage with the information of a community'.

Clearly, being without access or being unable to access available information exacerbates information poverty and can subsequently lead to exclusion from wider society. Social exclusion, a concept that 'arose in France', highlights the importance of 'citizenship and social cohesion' (Vinson, 2009: 1). It is described as 'a process that directly reduces people's capacity to participate in society' (Kennan et al., 2011: 191). Having examined the various definitions of social exclusion from European Union (EU) policy documents, Vinson (2009: 6) declares that they generally 'contain common elements of "lack of connectedness"'. One result of social exclusion is limited social networks, or 'network poverty', which is a barrier to the 'social support and informal help' that everyone needs 'to take part in community life' and 'enjoy the standards of living shared by the majority of people' (Vinson, 2009: 7). Yu (2011: 667) concurs, affirming that limited social networks can create 'network-based information poverty'. People may not have access to a computer or have within their own social network people who have a computer.

Consequently, not having access to information can restrict individuals socially and limit their capacity to participate in their communities. As well, information poverty can restrict a person's ability to participate fully in society – to access government information, financial information or access the information they need to vote – and can ultimately socially exclude people. For instance, one source declared that 'Information is power' (LNI4).

Another interviewee highlighted the importance of 'learning and knowing about things'. which can enable you to:

> ...talk to people because you have maybe read about something and you have access to information and...you wouldn't feel excluded because you didn't know about something. You know sometimes someone is sitting and everyone is talking about the latest film and that person doesn't know about it...you don't feel empowered to participate, so that is you excluded
>
> *LNI3*

This confirms what Lloyd et al. (2013: 123) observed earlier: 'A lack of access to information creates conditions and barriers that prohibit full participation in education, work, and every-day life'. People are at risk of exclusion by not using the Internet to access citizenship information (benefits, entitlements, public services, health information) or information that can help solve educational, employment or financial problems. Information poverty, therefore, can restrict an individual's ability to improve his or her life chances and participate fully in his or her community and wider society. In an information society, access to the Internet and computers is increasingly important for 'economic success and personal advancement' (Martin, 2005: 5) and for 'social engagement' (Jaeger et al., 2012: 5). By providing free access to ICTs/the Internet and information and digital literacy support, public libraries can be instrumental in contributing to digital and social inclusion.

3.8 UNITED KINGDOM GOVERNMENT: ACCESS TO INFORMATION AND PUBLIC LIBRARIES

Thus far, this book has noted the importance in modern society of having access to information for social inclusion and the role public libraries play in this. The following sections consider how the successive United Kingdom governments have prioritised improving access to information and the evolving role public libraries have been given. I begin here by detailing various policies for social inclusion in the United Kingdom.

Hayter (2005: 1) observes that the United Kingdom government believes 'more effective access to information' will 'contribute towards eradicating social exclusion'. As well, information access can develop literacy and learning within disadvantaged communities and can contribute to social inclusion, 'social cohesion and social capital' (Hayter, 2005: 6). From the early 1990s, successive United Kingdom governments have placed improving information access at the 'heart' of government initiatives to alleviate social inequality (Hayter, 2005: 5). In addition, 'there has been ongoing government support for public libraries to play a role in addressing social exclusion' (Hayter, 2005: 7). Muddiman et al. (2000: 22) state that 'public library attempts to address disadvantage and exclusion' were 'at a low ebb by the early 1990s', and with the election of the Labour Party in 1997, 'the public library policy environment began to change'. McMenemy (2009: 6) explains that libraries were now 'on the political agenda' and that the Labour Party 'identified early on' the role of libraries in 'combatting social exclusion'. In December 1997, the Labour government launched the Social Exclusion Unit, which focused on regenerating deprived communities in England. There were 'parallel initiatives' in Scotland, Wales and Northern Ireland (Pateman and Vincent, 2010: 39). The New Targeting Social Needs strategy was launched in Northern Ireland in 1998 to target social exclusion and social need (Pateman and Vincent, 2010: 39). It replaced the Targeting Social Need strategy in 1991, which had previously been adopted by the public library service in Northern Ireland to target information services towards those in need. Subsequently, Lifetime Opportunities (2006) became the government's Anti-Poverty and Social Inclusion Strategy for Northern Ireland (Lifetime Opportunities, 2006: 55).[2] Social justice is at the heart of these government policies to address poverty and is cited as a key priority in Lifetime Opportunities (2006). It was recognised that by offering a 'universal service', public libraries 'provide equality of opportunity and assist in combating social exclusion' (DCAL, 2006).

The Labour government's Our Information Age (1998) policy was an early government policy to introduce citizens in the United Kingdom to ICTs (Buckley-Owen, 2011: 72–73). The argument was made that ICTs 'could improve educational effectiveness, combat social exclusion, improve individuals' economic position and facilitate the smooth running of democracy through e-government services' (Goulding, 2006: 167). The People's Network, commissioned by the Department of Culture, Media and Sport (DCMS), was launched in 1999 as the United Kingdom's solution to Internet connectivity, with the goal of ensuring the all citizens had access to technology (Feather, 2011: 76). The People's Network was one of the United Kingdom government's initial policies to bridge the digital divide and the means to fulfil wider European agendas to embrace digital inclusion (Sinclair and Bramley, 2011: 1). The People's Network was implemented in

---

[2] See Office of the First and Deputy First Minister, 2006. Lifetime Opportunities: Anti-poverty and Social Inclusion Strategy for Northern Ireland. Available from:
http://www.ofmdfmni.gov.uk/antipovertyandsocialinclusion.pdf.

Northern Ireland through the Electronic Libraries for Northern Ireland project, from 2002, which was subsequently replaced by the e2 Project in 2013, which provides the library ICT infrastructure.

By the end of 2002, as a result of the People's Network, all of the United Kingdom's 4000 public libraries had access to the Internet. This enabled libraries to contribute towards broader policy objectives for social inclusion and lifelong learning, providing access to those who could not afford the technology or did not have the skills to use it (Big Lottery Fund, 2004). Hence, it represented a major shift in the role and purpose of the public library service in the United Kingdom, changing the library landscape from a traditional book-lending focus to one in which ICTs and the Internet were prominent. Public libraries now have a major role to play in reducing information poverty and in providing access to information and support so that socially and digitally excluded members of society can become included and participate.

Goulding (2006: 184) notes that official statistics presented by Brophy (2004) confirm that the People's Network had an impact on 'combating the digital divide', helping people to gain qualifications online and achieve enhanced access to job-seeking information. Pateman and Williment (2013: 105), however, argue that 'the biggest failure of the People's Network' was that there were few attempts to target ICT initiatives 'more closely at excluded groups and communities'. They aver that providing access to technologies is fundamental, but public libraries must guard against 'the tendency to believe that it (ICT) can be a panacea or "silver bullet" which can solve all of the library's problems', and by simply providing the technology libraries will be 'more inclusive' (Pateman and Williment, 2013: 101). Moreover, they suggest that public libraries should use ICT in a more effective and strategic way to address social exclusion (Pateman and Williment, 2013: 105). Public libraries in the United Kingdom have witnessed many changes since the People's Network, including changes in how societies and libraries facilitate and support digital access, which have become core features of library services. In the future library staff will need to be prepared for more change, to keep up to date with the changing information and communication needs of users and to adapt roles and services accordingly. Furthermore, library staff will need to cope with financial budgets that will undoubtedly continue to affect how libraries operate in the future.

As well as the People's Network, other United Kingdom government initiatives highlighted the role of public libraries in mitigating socioeconomic disadvantage and promote lifelong learning. The government's 'The

Learning Age: A Renaissance for a New Britain' (1998), was one of the first policies to influence the growth of lifelong learning (McMenemy, 2009: 99). The new 'national policy guidance on social exclusion was provided via "Libraries for All: Social Inclusion in Public Libraries" (DCMS, 1999)' (Pateman and Williment, 2013: 127). Caidi and Allard (2005: 317) explain that the 'Libraries for All' document identified the following barriers to the use of libraries by socially excluded groups:

- institutional barriers (opening hours, staff attitudes, rules and regulations)
- personal/social barriers (basic literacy skills, low income, and low self-esteem)
- environmental barriers (physical access, remote areas, isolation)
- perceptional barriers (sense of isolation, educational disadvantage, relevance of libraries to one's needs, awareness of facilities and services)

These barriers to information access and to libraries are similar to the factors that create information poverty. Understanding the various personal, institutional and social barriers to public libraries can enable library and information professionals to build better relationships with library users and potential users and to improve their library services. These barriers are discussed in detail in this chapter and in Chapter 4.

Among the guidelines contained in the 'Libraries for All' report was the recommendation that 'social inclusion should be mainstreamed as a policy priority within all library and information services' (Birdi et al., 2008: 581). Similarly, the Open to All study, conducted by Muddiman et al. (2000: 581) between October 1998 and April 2000, 'investigated the capacity of the public library to tackle social exclusion'. The findings of the Open to All survey, based on public library authorities (PLAs) in the United Kingdom, revealed that 'only one-sixth of PLAs' had a 'comprehensive model of good practice for social inclusion', and that 'most PLAs (60%)' had 'no comprehensive strategy' and only 'intermittent activity' to deal with social exclusion (Muddiman et al., 2000: ix). Open to All found that public libraries 'have service priorities and resourcing strategies which work in favour of existing library users rather than excluded or disadvantaged communities or groups' (Muddiman et al., 2000: xi). Muddiman et al. (2000: 59) concluded that,

...the public library will need to become a far more proactive and interventionist public institution, with a commitment to equality, education and social justice at its core. Only then...will marginalised and excluded communities be returned to the mainstream of the library world. Only then will public libraries be truly open to all.

Open to All was an 'important early study' (Gehner, 2010: 41) of public libraries and social exclusion. The writer can see how his book on information poverty and public libraries is linked to the study by Muddiman et al. (2000) and adds to the existing understanding of public libraries in facilitating access to information and addressing social exclusion.

The subsequent report 'Framework for the Future: Libraries, Learning and Information in the Next Decade', published in 2003 by the DCMS, was an attempt by 'national government to formulate a long-term strategic vision for public library services in England' (Goulding, 2006: 54). As one of the Labour government's key social policy areas, social exclusion–along with books, reading and ICT–formed the main themes contained in the 'Framework for the Future' (DCMS, 2003: 7). Birdi et al. (2008: 582) explain that 'Framework for the Future' 'defines the potential role of public libraries in developing social capital, including learning activities, digital citizenship and community and civic values'.

A report by PricewaterhouseCoopers (2008: 46–48) in Northern Ireland contends that there are wide differentials between public library authorities in the United Kingdom in terms of activity relevant to social inclusion:

- Only one-sixth of public libraries demonstrated a comprehensive model of good practice for social inclusion.
- Targeting of disadvantaged neighbourhoods and social groups was used comprehensively by only approximately one-third of public libraries; and
- There is currently a dearth of studies that have examined the economic and social benefits of public libraries in Northern Ireland.

The PricewaterhouseCoopers report notes that there was 'less evidence of quantifiable social inclusion benefits' of public libraries and that the identified gaps in libraries contributing to social exclusion and social cohesion needed attention. This book demonstrates, I hope, how the three-level information poverty framework is an effective way of assessing the impact of public libraries in addressing both social and digital inclusion.

The current government in the United Kingdom claims that tackling poverty, disadvantage and social exclusion is a key part of their Big Society agenda. The British Prime Minister, David Cameron (2010), commented, 'If Big Society exists for any reason it must be to help the most disadvantaged'. The *State of the Nation report: Poverty, worklessness and welfare dependency in the UK* (2010) highlights the multiple forms of disadvantage which the government's Big Society agenda is trying to address, such as intergenerational disadvantage, income poverty, poor housing, poor health, unemployment and having no qualifications. A theme of the United Kingdom government 'is that of localism and the Big Society' (Casselden et al., 2014: 4); the underlying feature of Big Society and localism is that communities and individuals – rather than the government and the state – should take responsibility for public services. Thus, the Big Society approach suggests that there is a personal responsibility, rather than a societal responsibility, to address social problems. The Big Society agenda has had an impact on public libraries in England through community-managed libraries run by a mix of professional staff and community volunteers.

The Big Society approach has implications for how information poverty could be addressed, as it places responsibility on communities and individuals themselves, rather than on the central government. While Big Society policies have not had as big an impact on public libraries in Northern Ireland, Libraries NI's Business Plan for 2014/2015 (Libraries NI, 2014: 11) indicates its intention to 'develop and implement an employer-supported volunteering policy'. Volunteers could have implications for how information poverty is addressed: for instance, when ensuring staff have the appropriate skills to support library users with ICT/the Internet and when seeking information, as well as the fear that volunteers could replace staff and lessen the quality of service.

3.9 CONCLUSIONS

This chapter has articulated the value of information in contemporary society and how a lack of information access can lead to information poverty and social exclusion. It began by considering what information is, its importance within society and how those without access to information can be socially excluded and are at risk of poverty. It then looked at what information poverty is, the origins of the concept and how it has been presented in the LIS literature. It linked the concepts of poverty and information poverty. Following this was a discussion of the link between information poverty and social exclusion. I examined the understanding of information poverty as detailed by experts and elites in Northern Ireland, thereby gaining a deeper insight into the strategic thinking of DCAL and Libraries NI.

Public library strategists and policymakers should have a strong grasp of the issues affecting people in socially deprived areas: poverty, educational underachievement and deprivation. This will enable them to develop policy that improves skills and learning and encourages social participation within these communities. To address information poverty, those designing public library services and strategies should understand what information poverty is and its effects, understand how poverty manifests itself and have library staff in community engagement roles to proactively engage with communities and ascertain what groups want from libraries. Public libraries, therefore, need to recognise the role libraries play in tackling information poverty so that they can be more successful in meeting government requirements to create a socially and digitally inclusive society.

To further illuminate what information poverty is and how it can manifest, the next chapter focuses on the factors that lead to information poverty, both as discussed in the literature and that emerged from the data gathered from library policymakers, community engagement staff and library managers working in the most socially deprived areas in Northern Ireland. It specifically considers measuring the impact of library services and how information poverty indicators are a useful tool for evaluating library impact. It presents a model of information poverty indicators. While these indicators can be applied to Libraries NI, their application is not specific to the Northern Ireland context; these indicates are a generic model that can be adapted to suit any public library setting. Then, Chapters 5–9 consider how the macro-, meso- and micro-level indicators can be addressed by public libraries.

CHAPTER 4

Factors Creating Information Poverty

4.1 INTRODUCTION

This chapter continues the discussion from Chapter 3 and considers the multidimensional range of factors that can exacerbate information poverty. A range of interconnected economic, educational, social and cultural factors can prevent equality of information access, constrain information use and sharing, and contribute to information poverty. As noted previously, information poverty can manifest in, and accentuate other forms of, poverty. The conceptualisation of information poverty is distilled here to present a macro-, meso- and micro-level framework of indicators, which can be used to measure how information poverty could be addressed with library interventions. For instance, the indicators can be used by library and information professionals to measure the impact of their services in developing literacy, information literacy and information and communication technology (ICT) skills. In addition, the importance of measuring the impact of library services is discussed.

4.2 FACTORS CREATING INFORMATION POVERTY

Understanding the factors that lead to information poverty can enable organisations such as libraries and schools to address it more successfully. Typically, the interviewees and the survey respondents quoted here were aware of the financial, educational and personal factors creating information poverty and the role that libraries play in alleviating it. One interviewee cited 'educational', 'social', 'economic', 'cultural', 'historical', 'geographical' and 'political' factors, as contributing to information poverty (Department of Culture, Art and Leisure [DCAL] 2). This interviewee observed that the social and economic factors that lead to information poverty 'are the same factors that lead to unemployment, ill health, poor lifestyle' (DCAL2). The three community engagement staff (through the Targeting Social Exclusion [TSE] program) cited the following factors

Figure 4.1 Factors creating information poverty.

leading to information poverty: financial poverty, disability, lack of access to information, lack of Internet access, ICT ownership, limited ICT and literacy skills and information awareness. The cyclical nature of information poverty, whereby not having access to information or the skills to access information can affect an individual's capacity to succeed socially and to make informed decisions, was evident in the interview and survey data.

Fig. 4.1 presents some of the factors creating information poverty that are discussed in the sections below (see also Appendix 3).

4.3 PHYSICAL ACCESS TO INFORMATION: INFRASTRUCTURAL APPROACHES

Physical access to information/ICTs may be available, for example, in countries or areas where there is good public provision. Access to information, ICTs and the Internet, however, is not enough to overcome information poverty; individuals also need to be willing to access information and the skills to use that information once it has been accessed. When the information infrastructure is plentiful and information technologies are available, users need to have the information processing skills to use the technology. This claim is supported by Britz (2007: 84), who notes that the provision of information infrastructure, ICTs and the Internet does not guarantee information access and use; for example, if a person is uneducated, illiterate or information illiterate, 'access to such a well-developed information infra-structure is of no or little use'.

Information poverty at the macro level was described by one Libraries NI (LNI) interviewee as 'not having the infrastructure' to 'access information' (LNI6). Similarly one source explained that information poverty was "not being able to afford ICT infrastructure" and "ICT equipment" (LNI8). Interestingly, another interviewee highlighted the differences in the information infrastructures between developed and developing countries when they commented that 'if you are in Malawi or somewhere you are not going to have same access to information in quite the same way as we would in the UK' (LNI5). The 'absence of a well-developed information infrastructure' is noted in the information poverty literature (Britz, 2004: 194), in which studies of information poverty are primarily focused on information poverty in the context of developing countries. A lack of information infrastructure, a poorly developed infrastructure or, indeed, a poor public library system can be a macro-level indicator of information poverty. Public libraries, as part of the information infrastructure of countries, play a major role in tackling information poverty. Britz (2007: 216) comments that 'libraries can and should play a leading role to address information poverty' and improving education and that a 'lack of libraries, can be seen as a manifestation of information poverty'.

Physical access to information is essential to overcome information poverty. Physical approaches to information poverty are often discussed in terms of the digital divide and the inability to participate within the information society because of a lack of access to computers, the Internet, information, books, documents, journals and other information resources. In addition, physical information access can be both in the physical and the virtual environments (Burnett et al., 2008: 57). Infrastructural approaches that focus mainly on the distribution of information technology (Thompson, 2006: 29) are the most popular way of looking at information poverty. Thompson (2006: 16) identifies three complementary features needed for physical access:

- an environment with an infrastructure supporting information access
- tools necessary for information communication and retrieval
- skills or ability to navigate the information environment to obtain needed information.

When the information infrastructure is plentiful and information technologies are available, users need information-processing skills to use technologies. If a person is uneducated, illiterate or information illiterate, 'access to such a well-developed information infrastructure is of no or little use' (Britz, 2007: 84). While physical access to ICTs and an information infrastructure is fundamental, it is not 'sufficient to eliminate information poverty' (Thompson, 2006: 25), since 'factors beyond infrastructure affect one's information poverty or richness' (Thompson, 2006: 27). At the macro level, the infrastructural approach to information access and information poverty has its limitations, and we must look beyond this to the sociocultural and personal aspects of information poverty. Sociocultural factors such as the environment, which encourages learning how to share and use information, is important. Other factors such as personal interest, motivation and attitude can become barriers to accessing information. These factors are further developed later in the chapter.

The next section briefly considers information poverty from a social perspective: the meso level.

4.4 SOCIAL FACTORS CREATING INFORMATION POVERTY

The findings of this study found similarities with previous studies of information poverty in other countries. Even though a society or region may be information rich in terms of infrastructure/ICT, other social, cultural and behavioural factors may prevent information access and use. Social information access can be determined by the environment in which an individual resides – that is, whether it values learning and education, for example. Information poverty studies at the meso level examine the perceived 'culture of information poverty' within communities and small-world environments, and are valuable for public libraries when engaging with communities and excluded groups. Meso-level information poverty studies include a study by Childers and Post (1975) that articulated the information environment of disadvantaged Americans and influenced much subsequent research. Social constructivist studies (Childers and Post, 1975; Chatman, 1996, 1999) argue that information poverty is a product of the information behaviours that exist within a group or community, rather than simply the result of a lack of access to information. These approaches developed new ways of looking at the information needs and behaviours of the disadvantaged by examining the cultural constraints that prevent information acquisition and sharing. By developing an understanding of information behaviours within small groups, information poverty theories at the sociocultural level can enable library and information professionals to understand how people value information, learning, libraries and information providers. From the social perspective, information poverty is often determined by the 'environment in which an individual resides' (Thompson, 2006: 41), and it is often the shared values and behaviours emanating from where people live that determine their information wealth or poverty.

Understanding the social factors that exacerbate information poverty – how communities interact and value information and learning – is important for public libraries when trying to target library services to specific communities and groups. The sociocultural factors creating information poverty (for example, small-world information behaviour, strong ties/weak ties theories and limited social networks) are explored in detail in Chapters 7–9 to demonstrate how earlier information poverty theory can be applied in a public library context when developing effective community engagement interventions for use in disadvantaged communities.

4.5 AWARENESS OF INFORMATION

Information poverty can be caused by a lack of awareness of available information within communities. One interviewee explained that not being 'aware of the range of information' available in libraries was a factor that could contribute to information poverty (LNI2). Public libraries can make a difference by more successfully promoting the benefits of quality information and their valuable resources. Another source suggested that people in socially deprived areas might not know what information is freely available, their 'benefits and entitlements' or their rights (LNI11). For instance, the comment was made that information poverty was linked to awareness of financial entitlements: 'not taking up benefits' (DCAL1). Typically, the inability to access information as a result of a lack of awareness, or not known where to go to get needed information, was noted at each stage of the investigation. In an earlier information poverty study, Yu (2006: 234) noted that information poverty is usually 'characterised by the lack of information awareness, lack of motives for information access and inadequacy in information skills'. These factors were reflected in the current study. For instance, one survey respondent asserted that

> *People need to be aware of the resources available to them to better inform their choices, and improve their lives, whether it be through reading, for leisure, study, to avail of computers and the Internet, to get advice on finances, health, all things which can have a positive impact on their lives*
> **Branch Library Manager (BLM) 10**

Again, this reiterates the need for libraries to increase information awareness and access to resources that can improve lives. One source emphasised the library's role: 'it is our job to get out there and let them know' (TSE1). The research presented here adds to the earlier information poverty literature but connects information poverty to public libraries in an original way.

As noted above, raising the awareness of library services and available information is fundamental to address information poverty. Public libraries have a significant role in addressing educational and social disadvantages by developing, improving and promoting their information services to socioeconomically deprived areas. Ongoing promotion, marketing and outreach to groups within communities are essential. The interviewees indicated that libraries need to promote their services more within deprived areas, through targeted interventions to specific groups. Outreach needs to improve to change the perception of libraries within disadvantaged communities, and also to raise awareness of library services. This outreach must involve communication with hard-to-reach groups to ascertain what services they want their local library to provide and what skills they need library staff to help them develop. Typically, interviewees at the macro and meso levels believed that libraries can address information poverty by raising awareness of the information resources available. Libraries therefore need to be more proactive in how they market their resources and services. Continuous community engagement and proactive marketing are key to this.

4.6 FINANCIAL FACTORS CREATING INFORMATION POVERTY

While information poverty is a multifaceted concept that exists in any social status within society, it is arguably more likely to affect the socioeconomically disadvantaged, who may not have the financial means to access information or a cultural environment that encourages information access and learning. Both the macro- and meso-level interviewees acknowledged the link between Internet access, the skills needed for access and the financial means to pay for access, and information poverty. One interviewee cited 'actual poverty' as a factor exacerbating information poverty, as well as a lack of literacy and ICT skills (DCAL1). Consequently, it can be inferred that information poverty can be caused by 'actual poverty' and at the same time reinforce poverty. People living in areas of high deprivation, in isolated rural areas, elderly people, those with 'some sort of disability' and 'ethnic minorities…because of language issues' were deemed to be at risk of information poverty (LNI6). Examples of library outreach to marginalised groups are provided in Chapters 8 and 9.

Economic factors leading to information poverty were cited by most of the interviewees; the inability to afford access to the Internet was mentioned specifically. For instance, one interviewee suggested that a factor creating information poverty was the large percentage of the population who cannot afford computer and broadband access, or mobile phones with Internet access (LNI7). In addition, the 'unemployed', with limited resources, may be at risk of information poverty because they may be unable to afford a computer or broadband since their limited funds are being prioritised elsewhere:

If you are unemployed and you have to use your [money] to feed your family, pay your rent…can you really afford [a] broadband connection? Can you afford to have a computer? No

LNI6

Feather (2011: 76–77) explains that while information poverty is not solely an economic issue, the socioeconomically disadvantaged have been 'disproportionately deprived of their capacity' to have home Internet access and 'the skills and culture to make use of public access'. Reflecting on their experience working within socially deprived areas, one of the community engagement staff explained that 'The big thing is poverty', and there is a 'belief that everybody' has computers and the Internet 'at home' (TSE2). This interviewee stated that parents in groups they attend 'would say that very few of them have a computer at home and probably none of them have Internet access' because it is 'very expensive' (TSE2). Crucially, the cost of home broadband is outweighed by the 'main focus', which 'is trying to put food on the table and keeping the place warm' (TSE2).

Other financial factors creating information poverty could manifest in an inability to afford books, newspapers, home computers and Internet access or transport to information providers. Typically, survey respondents also viewed information poverty as being linked to financial poverty; one was 'aware of the lack of resources in a lot of homes in the area due to financial deprivation' (BLM17). Another stated that 'it's fairly logical that people with less disposable income will have less access to information' (BLM5). Public libraries have an important role to play in mitigating socioeconomic disadvantage by providing access to information resources (books, ICTs, free Internet, printers, scanners, photocopiers, fax machines, newspapers and magazines) to those with lower incomes. In doing this, libraries can have a significant levelling role in narrowing the gap between low-income and more affluent communities in terms of providing access to information and developing the skills needed for access.

Lievrouw and Farb's (2003) vertical perspective on information poverty highlighted the socioeconomic approach of information access and use. The vertical dimension views information as a commodity and is similar to the information rich–information poor dichotomy, whereby a 'person's information access and use' is determined by his/her 'demographic traits, economic resources, and social status' (Lievrouw and Farb, 2003: 527). The vertical approach implies that information equity 'can be best achieved by an even distribution of resources and technologies across different social groups' (Lievrouw and Farb, 2003: 527). Lievrouw and Farb (2003: 503–504) describe information equity as 'the fair or reasonable distribution of information among individuals, groups, regions, categories' to provide the opportunity 'for effective personal achievement and social participation'. Access to and the ability to afford information resources, however, do not guarantee that individuals will benefit from it, as the ability to 'benefit from a resource' depends 'on people's skills, experience, and other contextual factors' (Lievrouw and Farb, 2003: 514). Alternatively, Lievrouw and Farb's horizontal perspective emphasised the capacities of people to benefit from information and use it effectively (Lievrouw and Farb, 2003: 514–515), rather than 'by the redistribution of material resources-information services and systems-alone' (Lievrouw and Farb, 2003: 516). The horizontal perspective views information access 'as subjectively and context dependent', that a 'person's access and use' depends on his/her 'capacity to understand and benefit from information and information technology in a particular situation' (Lievrouw and Farb, 2003: 527). This echoes the information context approach to information poverty, mentioned earlier. Lievrouw and Farb (2003: 527) concluded that to achieve information equity, 'both the vertical and horizontal dimensions of access and use must be considered'. Furthermore, the 'distribution of resources and systems…should be complemented by efforts to foster social and human capital and capacities' (Lievrouw and Farb, 2003: 527). They posit that information equity is 'best achieved' by 'assuring that all individuals have the background and skills to use information effectively for their particular ends and purposes, and that essential types of content remain freely available to everyone' (Lievrouw and Farb, 2003: 527).

Clearly, it is important to stress that information poverty should not be viewed in solely economic terms – between those who can and those who cannot afford access to ICTs and the Internet – because it involves other factors such as a lack of awareness of information, the skills to access information, personal attitudes and the ability to understand information in a source. Bates (2008: 22) notes that 'anyone can experience information poverty', but 'certain societal groups have been identified as being more susceptible'. Socioeconomic disadvantage contributes to information poverty, yet it is not always the result of economic poverty: 'an individual can be relatively well off in economic terms yet have little or no interaction with sources of information' (Bates, 2008: 41–42). Bates (2008: 44) further comments that while 'concepts such as "information poverty" and the "digital divide" serve an important purpose, it is important not to over simplify the situation by categorising individuals, households, communities (and, indeed, countries and regions) as either "haves" or "have-nots". Moreover, categorising individuals implies they are unable to 'move beyond the limits of the label that has been applied to them' (Bates, 2008: 42). Sligo and Williams (2002: 4) also conclude that binary approaches to information poverty are 'exclusionary', leading to 'stereotyping' and 'categorising' the subjects 'into what may be convenient but ultimately invalid and unhelpful groupings'. Such negative categorisations – the 'information poor', 'haves and have-nots' – can be unhelpful for library and information professionals when attempting to address information poverty. The polarities of the terminology found in the literature indicate that a more embracing approach would be to describe information poverty within a continuum, which is considered in Section 4.13.

Because public libraries play a significant role in reducing the disparities in information access among lower socioeconomic groups and ensuring that information resources are distributed equitably, library and information professionals can learn from the horizontal and vertical approaches, first, to provide equitable information access, and second, to promote the individuals' development of capabilities through literacy and digital and information literacy skills training.

4.7 EDUCATIONAL FACTORS CREATING INFORMATION POVERTY

While information poverty can be a consequence of having limited financial resources, it can also be linked to low educational attainment. Typically, the macro-level interviewees stated that educational factors – poor literacy and ICT skills – determined information poverty. For instance, one interviewee commented that being 'uneducated or lacking in education' was a factor creating information poverty (LNI11). A DCAL interviewee observed that 'long term failure of the State' and the education system, 'which doesn't seem to work for everybody', were factors creating information poverty (DCAL1). This interviewee questioned 'to what extent our education system is actually addressing' low levels of literacy and ICT skills (DCAL1). This point was reflected in the following comment:

> ...people with a negative educational experience who don't have any educational qualifications and therefore they don't have the confidence perhaps or the skills to access the information they would need to enhance their own careers
>
> **LNI7**

Having a 'negative educational experience' can affect multiple aspects of people's lives. For example, it can hinder opportunities for employment, the communication skills required to succeed socially and the confidence to pursue further education beyond the compulsory level. The comment highlights the vicious circle that is perpetuated as a result of underachievement in education and also highlights the role that public libraries can play in supporting informal adult learning. A failure in the education system was noted by another interviewee, who posited that information literacy was not 'well taught in schools' and that many people leave school without formal qualifications (LNI8). One source further detailed this vicious circle: 'people leave school' without the ability to 'read, write or access information' (LNI3). Levels of education can exacerbate information poverty, and this highlights the vicious circle that can exist, whereby the socioeconomically disadvantaged are more likely to suffer educational disadvantage.

4.8 THE SKILLS NEEDED TO ACCESS INFORMATION

While information poverty can be a result of a scarcity of information in societies or communities, it can also occur in a situation where information is available but people cannot access it because they do not have skills to do so. Hence, if people cannot use information 'appropriately', they cannot exercise their 'democratic rights' and play a 'part in the community' (LNI6). As Thompson (2006: 16) confirms, information poverty is about the democratic right to information access. Yu (2011: 667) concurs that 'lack of information access inevitably hinders people's social and democratic participation'. As well as the need for information to be available, people also need a range of literacy, numeracy and ICT skills, as well as information literacy skills to interpret and evaluate information sources and apply them appropriately.

Because illiteracy and a lack of computer skills can contribute to information poverty, developing skills to enable access can help overcome it. To meet most information needs, people need technical, literacy, numeracy and information literacy skills, together with cognitive capabilities to process information and physical abilities to access information. The lack of these skills and an inability to develop these competences can lead to information poverty. Bawden and Robinson (2012: 244) note that lacking the basic education or the information literacy skills necessary to use a range of information resources is a factor leading to information poverty. One interviewee in this study used their first-hand experience in engaging with communities to support their understanding of information poverty and asserted that information poverty has 'a lot to do with Internet access' and the difficulties accessing online information because of a lack of ICT and literacy skills:

I think...a lot of people...don't know how to use computers properly or access information on computers properly. From what I see from going out I think there are a lot of people who don't know of a lot of services that there are because (a) they don't know how to look it up online and most of it is online and (b) they maybe have problems with their literacy and can't read or they don't read very well

TSE2

The importance of being online and being able to access online educational, community and government services is evident here. For information access, content must be available, but information literacy skills are also critical to enable citizens to obtain and use the 'most appropriate and reliable' information needed 'to make decisions about their lives' (Buckley-Owen, 2011: 151).

The term 'information literacy', first used in 1974 by Paul Zurkowski (Gigler, 2011: 7), refers to 'a person's ability to collect, process, evaluate, use and share information with others within her/his own socio-cultural context' (Gigler, 2011: 15). Critical thinking skills – the ability to judge and critically evaluate information sources, either in print or online, needed to solve problems and influence decision making – are key components of information literacy. Information literacy is about developing the information processing skills to critically use information and empowering citizens to make informed life choices and decisions (Lloyd et al., 2010: 46). It is acknowledged that individuals who lack information literacy skills are at risk of information poverty and ultimately exclusion from mainstream society. For instance, Lloyd et al. (2013: 124–125) highlight the 'strong relationship' in the literature 'between information literacy, information poverty, and exclusion': 'limited access to information and associated information skills restricts the capacity of individuals to participate' in society. Indeed, information literacy skills are needed for citizenship and are a 'prerequisite for full participation in the modern, digital world' (Britz and Lor, 2010: 11). Furthermore, developing it is the 'duty of the state to ensure that all citizens become information literate' (Britz and Lor, 2010: 18–19).

Purchasing goods online or concert tickets is an example of when information and digital literacy skills are needed. The skills required to move through each stage of the purchasing process, for example, to understand what to click next, can sometimes be difficult for even the most computer literate person. Think of how difficult these tasks would be for someone with no ICT skills and poor literacy or language skills – this gives you an idea of how information poverty can manifest itself. Moreover, if the individual who is struggling to access the information he/she needs has poor communication or limited English language skills, he/she is in a frustrating situation, not only for himself/herself but also for the library staff member who is trying to support him/her in accessing the information he/she needs. Understanding these barriers to accessing digital and printed information are at the core of this book, which illuminates a major problem for many people in contemporary society.

It is important to stress that while information poverty and information literacy are linked, they are not the same. Information poverty discourse focuses on those with restricted access to information, 'whereas those with poor information literacy skills have access, but don't use information properly' (Putkey, 2009). Moreover, information poverty is not just about having access to large amounts of information; it is the capacity to understand and use this information effectively. In essence, information literacy skills are needed to reduce information poverty and to ensure that individuals are able to access, understand and use the information that is made available to them. I therefore argue that information literacy is one component within the broader concept of information poverty.

Chapter 6 looks more closely at how information literacy and digital literacy skills are increasingly important in modern society and are becoming a major priority for public libraries.

4.9 BARRIERS TO LIBRARY USAGE

Institutional barriers can lead to information poverty; for example, people may not want to approach information providers because of a fear of bureaucracy or a lack of trust in outside sources. Similarly, they may have negative perceptions of libraries and librarians. Public libraries need to get rid of some of the bureaucracy in libraries – for example, an insistence that library users show identification or that they have their library cards to borrow a book or to use a computer – which can be a barrier for access for some people. It is important for public library staff to recognise these institutional barriers in order to create an inclusive library service. A study by Hayter (2005) revealed that there are many constraining factors that prevent those in a disadvantaged community from using information providers such as libraries. She found that institutional barriers, such as formal language and bureaucracy, often prevent people from using libraries. Public libraries need to promote their services more effectively and to change the perceptions of libraries and library staff within local communities.

Interviewees from Libraries NI specifically mentioned current focus group research that their marketing team was conducting with non-library users. One interviewee explained that there is a 'barrier that exists for people to come into a library', especially in 'areas of high deprivation', where people, 'to some degree, associate the library with formal education' (LNI6). This source noted that their research revealed that those from the 'lower socio-economic groupings' (skilled manual workers, semi-skilled and unskilled workers) often said they associated the library with school (LNI6). This research found that 'people who were in those groups who came from the Cs and Ds, the lower socio economic groupings', 'didn't like school', 'found school difficult' and felt that 'the library and the school seemed to be almost linked' (LNI6). This participant believed that there was a need to remove the 'shush culture' from libraries and make them more accessible and appealing for those with negative educational experiences (LNI6). Another interviewer noted the importance of 'giving people the confidence to come into libraries because' entering a library building may be a barrier for them (LNI1). Another commented that people sometimes see libraries as the 'keep quiet' place, and it is important to change this perception (LNI12). Likewise, an interviewee from DCAL highlighted the need to remove the 'dusty and silent' library and stereotypical librarian perception (DCAL2).

Relaxing attitudes and removing the perception of formal education are key to improving accessibility and attracting nonusers. Importantly, public libraries need to promote the value of learning in a way that does not associate libraries with formal learning. One source confirmed that while efforts were made to brand the service, they need to do more to 'alter the image in the public's head of what libraries are' (LNI13). Another claimed that 'changing the image of the library service' was their 'big challenge' (LNI7). Some people still maintain a perception of public libraries as intimidating, old-fashioned places. Their preconceptions of librarians might be of someone with a stern, unapproachable disposition, constantly demanding silence. Moreover, they might see libraries as somewhere only academic people go, a place where underachievers will not fit in. Changing the perceptions of people in socially deprived communities regarding libraries and library staff is an important part of this. There was a realisation among macro- and meso-level interviewees that more should be done to improve the image of libraries and librarians. One interviewee commented that libraries need to be more involved in their communities and 'have to change the image of the library from that old stuffy image' (TSE2). Another argued that the image of the library can be a contributing factor that prevents library usage and can lead to information poverty:

> … the libraries have not got a great image amongst the local community. We are still a bit middle-class and a bit intimidating and not the sort of place they would be going…I think in terms of the TSE [agenda]…with us going out and talking to people and…letting them see that libraries and librarians are just normal people… it is a normal place…not somewhere fancy or special
>
> **TSE1**

This quote indicates that the community engagement staff can see the impact of their engagement to change perceptions of libraries and librarians. The interviewee believed that the outreach work of the TSE team and the BLMs 'will hopefully get rid of' the 'stuffy image that seems to still perpetuate, even though we are all trying really hard to let people know we are not like that, they still imagine that we still are' (TSE1). Because the community engagement staff have direct engagement with deprived communities, they are aware of how libraries and librarians are perceived. They acknowledged that 'changing people's perceptions of libraries would take time and that this change should start with library activities to young children', for example, bringing them to libraries for programs such as Rhythm and Rhyme and instilling positive memories of the library as a 'fun place', which their parents maybe had not experienced (TSE2). This interviewee believed they were 'working in the right direction' to change the negative 'perception of libraries' and that the stereotypical librarians 'doesn't exist anymore' (TSE2). They suggested that because some people may never have been in libraries 'they automatically assume we all have horn rimmed glasses and buns', and people may 'be amazed when they go to a library that it is just normal people like them that work in libraries' (TSE2). This interviewee posited that it was the 'whole media perception of a librarian' that creates a barrier to library use (TSE2). Similarly, Pateman and Williment (2013: 142) observe that the 'common perception of public libraries' is of 'quiet oases of intellectual and academic endeavour' and the 'stereotypical image of a librarian is of a shy and retiring' character 'who dresses conservatively and wears thick glasses (if a man) or a pearl necklace (if a woman)'. Evidently, library outreach needs to improve to change the perception of libraries within disadvantaged communities and also to raise awareness of library services.

In addition, interviewees commented that libraries need to change people's preconceptions about what libraries have to offer, that 'it is more than books' (TSE3), and that they are not places where people had to be quiet (TSE2). They suggested that it can be 'daunting' for people who have not been used to coming into a library or have not been brought up going into libraries (TSE3). One interviewee observed that libraries were viewed as 'a learning institute in that you have to go in with a purpose…that you want to find out something or you want to learn something or do research' (TSE2). From their experience working in deprived areas, two community engagement staff described how the library was perceived as a 'middle-class' place (TSE1 and TSE2). Interviewees noted that they often get the response, 'Oh, I wouldn't be going to the library. That isn't for me that is too high brow for me' (TSE2). Even though libraries are often situated in deprived areas, two interviewees concluded that a barrier exists for people who think the library is 'not for them' (TSE1 and TSE2). One interviewee suggested that their outreach was enabling community engagement staff to break down the barriers to accessing libraries and the 'preconceptions' that people have of libraries and librarians (TSE3).

The above comments made by the three TSE interviewees reinforce the data from the five-point Likert scale in the BLM survey, which queried 22 respondents. The 12 Likert scale statements on why people in socially disadvantaged areas may not use libraries came from the macro-level interviews and the information poverty literature. These data are important in understanding what factors may lead to nonuse of libraries and potentially perpetuate information poverty within deprived areas. The Likert scale is 'a bipolar scaling technique, which allows a respondent to select a choice that best demonstrates their levels of agreement with a given statement' (Pickard, 2013: 213). McMillan and Weyers (2007: 113) point out that Likert scale questions 'are useful for assessing people's opinions or feelings'. Using indicators as statements of behaviour and measuring the responses with a Likert scale were appropriate here to ascertain the survey respondents' views on the barriers to library usage in socially deprived areas. These data are based on just 22 responses, and it must be noted that these findings are not widely generalisable because of this small number. They do, however, provide some indication of the reasons why people in socially disadvantaged areas may not be using libraries. Table 4.1 presents the statements and responses.

The Likert scale data revealed that 95.5% (21 of 22) of the survey respondents felt that people in deprived areas do not think libraries provide information that is relevant to their needs. The results show that people in socially disadvantaged areas may not be using libraries because they are not aware of the range of resources and services available. Moreover, the data confirmed that BLMs believe that people in disadvantaged areas are not using libraries because they feel that libraries are only for educated, middle-class people – 59% either agree or strongly agree with this. This reinforces the comments by interviewees that people in disadvantaged areas see libraries as 'not for them' (TSE1 and TSE2). Removing the perception people have of libraries and librarians and making them more accessible for everyone are essential.

The Likert scale data revealed that 68.2% of library managers either agree or strongly agree that people in disadvantaged areas are not using libraries because they see libraries as being like formal education/school. As mentioned earlier, a bad experience of formal education can potentially discourage people from using libraries if they see a connection between the two. By focusing on image, changing people's perception of libraries being like school and making libraries accessible for everyone, they could improve and thus further enhance their capacity to address information poverty. Therefore changing the library 'brand' and the image of the stereotypical librarian is fundamental. Seemingly, there was an agreement between what macro-level interviewees stated and what library managers and community engagement staff believed were the barriers to library use, with an acknowledgement that marketing and promotion of library services need to be improved.

This study has similarities with the findings detailed by Pateman and Williment (2013: 70) in the Working Together Project (WTP), which explored 'the impact that the existing public library image has on socially excluded members' use of libraries.' They discussed how community development librarians in the WTP asked 'library staff about their perceptions of why socially excluded community members do not use public library services' (70). Pateman and Williment comment that 'librarians in the WTP study found that the socially excluded did not use libraries because they did not know 'what the library has to offer' (70). They recommend similar ways of addressing these barriers, by marketing 'existing services better' (70). Engaging with communities and finding out what they want can enable libraries to provide relevant services and attract more users.

Table 4.1 Branch library managers' perceptions on why people in socially disadvantaged areas may not use libraries (n = 22)

In socially disadvantaged areas people may not use libraries because they…:	Likert scale responses				
	Strongly disagree, % (n)	Disagree, % (n)	Unsure, % (n)	Agree, % (n)	Strongly agree, % (n)
Do not think libraries provide information that is relevant to their needs	0.0 (0)	4.5 (1)	0.0 (0)	**95.5 (21)**	0.0 (0)
See libraries as being like formal education/school	0.0 (0)	9.1 (2)	22.7 (5)	**54.6 (12)**	13.6 (3)
Have low self-esteem and lack self-confidence to come in to the library	0.0 (0)	4.5 (1)	9.1 (2)	**77.3 (17)**	9.1 (2)
Get the information they need from within their own social networks (friends, family and neighbours)	0.0 (0)	13.6 (3)	13.6 (3)	**72.7 (16)**	0.0 (0)
Have poor literacy and limited education	0.0 (0)	13.6 (3)	22.7 (5)	**54.6 (12)**	9.1 (2)
See libraries as dusty and silent places	0.0 (0)	27.3 (6)	22.7 (5)	**31.8 (7)**	18.2 (4)
Use the Internet for their information needs	0.0 (0)	18.2 (4)	31.8 (7)	**45.4 (10)**	4.6 (1)
Are not aware of the range of resources and services available in libraries	0.0 (0)	0.0 (0)	4.6 (1)	45.4 (10)	**50 (11)**
Feel that libraries are only for educated, middle-class people	4.6 (1)	13.6 (3)	22.7 (5)	**40.9 (9)**	18.2 (4)
Have negative images of library staff; they feel that staff are patronising and elitist	13.6 (3)	27.3 (6)	**36.4 (8)**	18.2 (4)	4.6 (1)
Find the library layout/signage confusing and not accessible to them	4.6 (1)	**45.4 (10)**	31.8 (7)	18.2 (4)	0.0 (0)
Are not interested in education or do not see the value of lifelong learning to improve their life chances	4.8 (1)	**33.3 (7)**	**33.3 (7)**	28.6 (6)	0.0 (0)

The factors that prevent access to information are not always socioeconomic or educational; they also include intellectual and attitudinal factors. The following section considers the personal factors that can lead to information poverty.

4.10 PERSONAL FACTORS CREATING INFORMATION POVERTY

A factor that can prevent access to information is individuals deliberately choosing not to use or purchase ICT, the Internet or mobile phone technologies. This was noted in the macro-level interviews, with one participant explaining that 'there is a significant amount of' people without home Internet access 'who just don't want to have the Internet' at home 'not because they don't have the means or the ability to get it' (LNI15). This comment echoes the previous information poverty literature (Anderson, 2005) that describes 'Internet poverty'. Anderson (2005: 353–354) describes this as 'ICT poverty', 'Internet poverty' or 'mobile poverty'. In addition, Van Dijk and Hacker (2003) outline other barriers that can impede the use of ICTs:

- *Psychological access*: lack of interest; computer fear (for example, if you have never used a computer it may seem challenging and daunting); and unattractiveness of the new technology (for example, it may not engage an individual's interest)
- *Material access*: no possession of computers or network connections
- *Skills access*: lack of digital skills caused by inadequate education or social support
- *Usage access*: lack of opportunities or perceived value of the above three in furthering an individual's aspirations

The assumption that everyone can afford access to the Internet and is computer literate is often made. Likewise, it is often assumed that everyone wants to be online or even *needs* to be online.

As noted above, motivation for information access and learning is important. Van Dijk (2006: 226) argues that as well as physical access there needs to be motivational access, the will to have a computer and associated Internet connections and an understanding of its potential contribution to the individual's life. He suggests that in relation to ICT and Internet access 'it appears that there are not only "have-nots", but also "want-nots"' as a result of 'Computer anxiety and technophobia' (Van Dijk, 2006: 227). Likewise, Selwyn (2003: 104) describes these as information 'refusniks', who choose not to engage with ICT. De Beer (2007: 201) concurs that for ICT access individuals need 'an intellectual willingness or proneness, a keenness to know'. So, people may have ICT and Internet access but decide not to use them as a matter of personal choice, not solely because of a lack of financial resources (Jaeger et al., 2012: 14). Lack of interest in information can contribute to information poverty. Lack of interest in information can contribute to information poverty. Sweetland (1993) provides the example of watching television news reports repeatedly: the repetitive exposure to superficial summaries of news/information and the assumption that such exposure may be increasing or deepening the individual's information richness, is information poverty. Thus, the problem with too much information either on television (news) or the Internet is that we could miss the important elements (Sweetland, 1993). Information poverty, then, does not solely affect the economic poor as individuals need the skills to access information, motivation for access, the intellectual capital to process information and the physical capabilities to get to information sources and providers. So, at the individual level, personal choice can contribute to information poverty, 'when people choose not to learn, not to discover new knowledge' (Britz, 2007: 95), or to be engaged with and absorb the information they have access to. Information poverty, then, does not solely affect the economic poor: individuals need the skills to access information, motivation for access, the intellectual capital to process information, as well as the physical capabilities to get to information sources and providers.

At the individual level, personal choice can contribute to information poverty, 'when people choose not to learn, not to discover new knowledge' (Britz, 2007: 95). The need to access information (its value to an individual and to his or her world), the value it is perceived to have in the individual's community and, of course, the extent to which the information can further the individual's aspirations are possibly a product of the environment. This can lead to a rejection of information because of a lack of trust of outside information or outsiders and a lack of belief that information is actually useful to meet personal information needs (Thompson and Afzal, 2011: 32–33).

4.11 INTELLECTUAL AND COGNITIVE FACTORS CREATING INFORMATION POVERTY

Information poverty can also result when individuals do not have the cognitive skills, abilities, capabilities or competences to process information and use it effectively to improve their social and personal conditions. Interestingly, one interviewee compared information poverty to teaching children to read, specifically the need for 'phonic skills' to decipher a word and interpret information (LNI9). Information poverty was also described as not having the skills to 'find the information' they need nor 'having the skills to apply' information 'to their own situation' (LNI6). Britz (2004: 199) describes information poverty as a 'lack of an intellectual capacity to filter, evaluate and benefit from information'. Burnett et al. (2008: 58) assert that in addition to the physical (macro) and sociocultural (meso) aspects of information access, the 'intellectual aspects' must be considered. Intellectual access involves the ability to understand how to get to and, specifically, how to understand the information itself once it has been physically obtained. Intellectual access 'is often not equally available' as the result of factors such as 'information seeking behaviours', 'education', 'literacy', 'technological literacy' and 'subjective views' (Burnett et al., 2008: 58). According to Burnett et al. (2008: 58) there are three elements to intellectual information access: first, knowledge of the value of the information; second, knowledge about how to get it and third, knowledge about what to do with it when it has been retrieved.

The inability to ascertain the value and usability of information is important; for instance, if individuals and communities cannot see the value of information and how it can be used, then the information itself will be meaningless and useless to them. As Jaeger and Burnett (2010: 63) observe, 'information value can lead a community to limit access to some information simply because it defines that information as of being of little importance'. Furthermore, not valuing information can arguably lead to not valuing libraries. Similarly, intellectual access could possibly prevent individuals from entering libraries; for instance, if they have poor literacy or ICT skills, they could be intimidated by the library environment. Understanding intellectual access is important for libraries in all sectors when attempting to make information more accessible and presentable, especially to those with disabilities, learning difficulties and literacy problems. It indicates that library staff need to be aware of intellectual factors that prevent information access and perhaps contribute to the nonuse of libraries.

In addition, at the personal (micro) level, information poverty has also been approached from a cognitive science perspective (Yu, 2006: 234). Cognitive capabilities are required to access information and develop information richness, and they are not determined by socioeconomic status. Cognitive science approaches (Grabe et al., 2000) examined individuals' learning processes and discovered that individual learning differences can result in information poverty largely because of 'inherited qualities which has little to do with the socio-economic stratification' (Yu, 2006: 232–235). While an individual's cognitive capabilities may be inherited and are not related to 'socio-economic stratification', an individual's cognitive world can be shaped by family, friends and community. Cognitive development is likely to increase in an environment with plentiful information (books, ICT, Internet, television). Thus the information environment in socially deprived areas, in which people may not have access to the Internet, books or newspapers, may be less stimulating than that of more affluent areas. The role of the public library is to provide a stimulating environment for learning and opportunities to access quality resources to improve cognitive abilities. Awareness of the cognitive barriers to information access are therefore important for library and information professionals, other government and community agencies and schools that are trying to address poverty and social exclusion and to improve literacy and ICT skills within deprived communities.

Having examined the factors creating information poverty, I have created two diagrams as a means of understanding the varying degrees of information poverty.

4.12 VIEWING INFORMATION POVERTY AS A CONTINUUM

Based on a combined reading of the literature and my own understanding, I developed two diagrams to illustrate a continuum approach to information poverty (see Figs 4.2 and 4.3). It is important to acknowledge that the template for Fig. 4.3 has been adapted and modified from the Continuum of Deprivation model described by Gordon (2008).[1]

Having outlined the factors which create information poverty, the next section discusses the process of developing information poverty indicators.

4.13 INFORMATION POVERTY INDICATORS

As noted previously, information poverty is multidimensional and complex, and consequently a range of quantitative and qualitative indicators are needed to measure it. I define an indicator as 'a short description of a particular state of something'. 'Measure' suggests the act of determining the quantity of something, which implies a dimension to ascertain its size, amount, value or effect. Indicators can be used as a measurement tool to assess the performance of an intervention. Vinson (2009: 12) recommends that indicators should 'identify the essence of the problem', 'be robust,

[1] See Gordon (2008). Measuring Child Poverty and Deprivation. Available from:
http://www.southampton.ac.uk/ghp3/docs/unicef/presentation4.1.pdf.

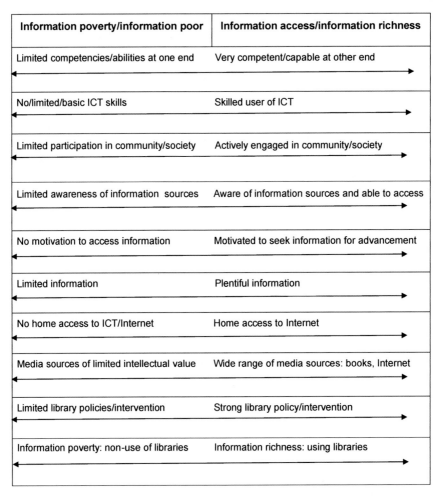

Information poverty/information poor	Information access/information richness
Limited competencies/abilities at one end	Very competent/capable at other end
No/limited/basic ICT skills	Skilled user of ICT
Limited participation in community/society	Actively engaged in community/society
Limited awareness of information sources	Aware of information sources and able to access
No motivation to access information	Motivated to seek information for advancement
Limited information	Plentiful information
No home access to ICT/Internet	Home access to Internet
Media sources of limited intellectual value	Wide range of media sources: books, Internet
Limited library policies/intervention	Strong library policy/intervention
Information poverty: non-use of libraries	Information richness: using libraries

Figure 4.2 A continuum of information poverty comparing information poverty (information poor) with information access (information rich). *ICT*, Information communication and technology.

statistically validated and measurable' and 'responsive to effective policy interventions.' Indicators provide the evidence that a change has occurred, for example, improved ICT skills gained by participation in a library program. As mentioned earlier, access to computers and the Internet is an important factor that creates information poverty, but also was mentioned that information poverty is about much more than a technological divide: it involves skills, motivations for digital access and intellectual and social factors. This is important for public libraries to acknowledge when seeking strategies to address it.

Continuum determining information poverty or richness			
Absence of IP	**Moderate level of IP**	**Severe IP**	**Extreme IP**
Home access to ICT	Access to ICT within their social network - use libraries	Basic ICT skills	No ICT skills, not using public libraries for access or support
Access to information at home (printed sources)	Some access to information (printed sources) – use libraries	Unable to read information (printed sources)	Illiteracy
Social networks	Some access to other social networks	Unable to develop social networks	Social isolation, marginalisation, exclusion
Information awareness Awareness of resources – where to access benefits/entitlements	Some awareness of information resources within the community	Unaware of resources available within the community	No information access leading to social exclusion
Information literacy skills	Some ability to locate, evaluate and use information effectively	Unaware of how to obtain information or how to evaluate it when it is obtained	Information illiterate (possible reliant on other people to access and interpret information)
Digital literacy skills	Some ability to use a PC and access the Internet. Basic skills	Can use a mouse and has basic typing skills, but needs support from friends or library staff	Digitally illiterate, have never used a PC or accessed the Internet

Figure 4.3 A continuum determining information poverty (IP) or richness, based on the Continuum of Deprivation model described by Gordon (2008). *ICT*, Information communication and technology; *PC* personal computer.

Traditionally, information poverty has been measured quantitatively, in terms of the digital divide, using the statistics that account for telephones at home, mobile phones, number of personal computers and access to the Internet within specific areas (Britz, 2007: 86). However, measuring information poverty is more than simply measuring the digital divide between those with access to technologies and those without. Thompson (2006: 67) avers that the 'narrow focus' of the digital divide constrains the measurement of information poverty. Quantitative indicators can be used to measure infrastructure, for example, the number of ICTs/libraries within areas; however, Britz (2007: 87) argues that 'statistical measurements have limitations' because they cannot measure 'attitudes towards information and levels of intelligence'. Because information poverty is a 'more complex phenomenon including issues such as socio-cultural and language diversity, different levels of education', 'the ability/inability to access, use and benefit from information', its measurement should not be 'only about statistics' or 'restricted to a technology/digital divide' (Britz, 2007: 89). Measuring information poverty is 'problematic' (Britz, 2007: 25); to understand its 'true complexity', we need qualitative and quantitative indicators (Britz, 2007: 86). There are 'degrees and levels of information poverty' (Britz, 2007: 119), and to measure it Britz (2007: 215) proposes a quantitative and qualitative index that can be used within a community, region or country (Britz, 2007: 215):

- information infrastructure
- quality of available information
- physical infrastructure
- human capacity

Britz (2007) suggests that two very important information poverty indicators, access to the Internet and level of literacy, can be quantified. Because there is a 'close relationship' between 'lack of education and information poverty', educational attainment and skill levels can indicate those who are perhaps more likely to experience poverty (Britz, 2007: 28). By mapping levels of educational attainment and ICT/Internet access figures, public libraries can ascertain which areas and groups might benefit most from library services. Access to the Internet and low educational attainment are often lower in socioeconomically deprived areas than in more affluent areas. The statistics for Internet access and educational attainment within the Northern Ireland context are presented in the next chapter, which outlines the macro-level indicators and how these can be addressed by libraries. The information poverty indicators can be used to provide evidence of the impact of library services within socially deprived communities where educational attainment may be low, computer/Internet ownership may be limited and attitudes towards learning and libraries may be negative.

While ICT access and use are contributing factors to information poverty, they are not the only factors: people's awareness of information and their ability to use and evaluate it is fundamental. Qualitative indicators can examine the information behaviours of individuals by measuring various factors (Britz, 2007: 90):

- how people value and react to information
- the ability to understand their information needs
- knowing where to obtain needed information
- the ability to evaluate information and use it effectively
- the ability to communicate and share information

Information poverty is multifaceted, with a range of factors contributing to it; therefore a multilayered approach to measure and address it is appropriate. Taking a macro, meso and micro approach to information poverty enables us to understand the concept from multiple viewpoints and how it may be addressed at various levels.

4.14 INFORMATION POVERTY INDICATORS AND PUBLIC LIBRARIES

For public libraries to be effective at measuring their impact in reducing information poverty, they need quantitative and qualitative measures. A combination of quantitative data (statistics on book issues, registered users, participation in events) and qualitative data (focus groups, questionnaires) can enable library services to measure their impact on users. Markless and Streatfield (2006: 65) assert that indicators should be tied to service objectives, be seen in the context of what the library service is trying to do and give clues about the difference it is making. Indicators should be

- directly linked to what the library service is trying to achieve
- clear, understandable and valid
- informative, providing significant information
- as few in number as possible.

The process of developing information poverty indicators began by analysing and synthesising the information poverty literature. I gathered a wide spectrum of indicators and began categorising them into themes, for example, education (literacy, ICT skills); attitudes towards information (behaviours, interest, value); affordability (ownership of, and access to, technologies). Next, I began listing the indicators, calculating which were cited most based on how frequently they were referred to in the literature, to thus enable me to attach an appropriate weight to each one. The indicators were arranged according to the factors that contributed to them, for example, physical, educational, intellectual, economic, social, cultural, geographic and political.

This process of listing and categorising indicators was fundamental to the development of the framework in Table 4.2. As well, it added to my understanding of information poverty, which proved valuable when analysing and discussing the research findings (see Appendix 4).

4.15 MEASURING THE IMPACT OF PUBLIC LIBRARY SERVICES

To evaluate library services, we need to have an understanding of *impact*. Impact creates a change in society, community or individuals. Assessing the impact of public libraries can help library leaders to secure future funding as it can illustrate how the library is fulfilling government priorities. Impact assessment has become important for libraries because they are now tied into government agendas for lifelong learning and digital and social inclusion. Measuring precisely the public library service's impact at societal, community and personal levels is challenging; it requires a 'wide range of methodologies' to 'gather both qualitative and quantitative data, so as to paint an accurate picture of the difference' that the library service makes (Brophy, 2006: 72–73). Brophy (2005: 44) defines 'impact' as 'any *effect* of a service, product or other "event" on an individual or group'. He asserts that the 'aim of impact assessment' could be to 'influence policy-makers' at various levels:

* national government, when highlighting the role of public libraries in 'delivering on social inclusion or lifelong learning agendas'
* local government, when emphasising the 'positive impacts' of library services on local communities
* potential collaborators (other educational institutions), to persuade them of the value of joint service delivery.

In addition, measuring impact can influence strategic management: to 'understand better where impacts are being made (or failing to be made) so as identify areas for improvement and then plan strategically for future investment', and to check whether 'past decisions are having the anticipated results and to adjust plans and planning processes accordingly' (Brophy, 2005: 45). Measuring impact can influence operational management to 'develop insights into the different responses and needs of different user groups' and to 'provide comparative data with which to monitor the effect of changes in the service'. In essence, measuring library impact is crucial to demonstrate value, improve services and secure future investment. The above comments by Brophy (2005) are relevant to this book, which uses information poverty indicators to measure the impact of public libraries.

Similarly, Town (2011: 305) points out that 'evaluation and measurement' are used and have influence at three levels:

1. internal library operational management
2. advocacy, strategy and understanding of the library and its services within its governance or organisational frame
3. a broader justification for the role of the library or libraries within communities or societies

Consequently, to secure government funding public libraries need to be accountable, to be able to show how they are making a difference and to demonstrate the impact they are making on society, communities and individuals. As well, libraries need to produce evidence of the 'impact' they 'have on communities', demonstrating their contribution to alleviating poverty and social exclusion and to promoting lifelong learning (LNI6). There are various challenges to making this vision a reality, for example, addressing declining library usage and continuous reduced funding. Libraries will undoubtedly continue to face financial challenges – government budget cuts will mean less funding for libraries – and it will be increasingly important to demonstrate the impact of library services on society, community and individuals.

The challenges of measuring the impact of library services were noted by the interviewees at the macro level. Interviewees typically emphasised the difficulty in measuring the impact that library services have on people's lives. One interviewee professed that they wanted to be able to demonstrate that libraries 'make a difference in people's lives' (LNI6). Thus, 'measuring the impacts' of their services was important so Libraries NI could demonstrate these impacts to DCAL (LNI15). One source admitted that libraries cannot 'measure everything' because so much of 'people's reactions' to library services are 'anecdotal and you can't measure that' (LNI13). Both DCAL interviewees highlighted the importance of measuring impact and the challenges involved. One explained that they 'can measure activity', 'how many people are going' to activities/events and the number of active members in deprived areas, but questioned whether there was 'any way of measuring over fifteen or twenty years whether or not engagement with the library services actually improves your educational performance' and 'your ability to find' work (DCAL1). The challenge for DCAL, therefore, is 'being able to demonstrate that it makes a difference on the ground' (DCAL2). So, to measure the impact of library services, both quantitative and qualitative indicators are needed. These indicators need to be long-term and measured against various library activities aimed at different groups.

The macro-, meso- and micro-level framework of information indicators presented in this book provides public libraries with a schema to measure the effectiveness and impact of their information services. Indicators can have quantitative measures of impact – for example, books borrowed from libraries, participation in events, registered users, computer access, requests – or they can have qualitative measures of impact, such as descriptions of desirable conditions and characteristics obtained from focus group research. Pateman and Williment (2013: 181) point out that public libraries are now 'moving away from statistical quantitative indicators and towards those which measure quality, satisfaction, impact and outcomes'. They add that public libraries should have 'performance indicators and targets' to measure their success 'in their attempts to tackle social exclusion' (Pateman and Williment, 2013: 199). The three-level framework of indicators (see Table 4.2) can be used to align information poverty indicators with library services at strategic, community and personal levels. The following section looks at the information poverty indicators that I derived from the literature.

4.16 A THREE-LEVEL MODEL OF INFORMATION POVERTY

The indicators in Table 4.2 can be used by public libraries to demonstrate how they are addressing information poverty. The indicators are designed to be approached in a flexible way and can be modified to suit any context or culture.

Appendix 5 provides a condensed version of this framework that could be adapted and used in other settings. In Section 6.6 of Chapter 6, the information provision and services that enable Libraries NI to tackle information poverty are mapped against the information poverty indicators.

In essence, with the three-level model I have developed an innovative way of looking at public library activities. It is important that the three tier approach to understanding information poverty and the indicators is robust enough to be transported to other settings. Significantly, this framework could be applied in other library settings and organisations to measure how they address information poverty at various levels. For instance, a government in any country could take the framework and assess how their library services address information poverty at macro, meso and micro levels. In addition, an individual library – whether a public, school or academic library –

Table 4.2 Information poverty indicators framework

Macro-level indicators of information poverty

1. Physical access to information
   - Lack of access to information infrastructure
   - Lack of access to ICTs/PCs, Internet/broadband, information resources and services
   - Lack of accessible information in different media formats (physical/electronic)
   - No access to quality-assured information
2. Digital inclusion: E-government, Digital by Default
   - No strategy for digital inclusion
   - No ICT/broadband infrastructure for digital inclusion
   - No human support to assist with digital inclusion
3. Educational attainment (literacy, information literacy and ICT skills)
4. Poverty and social exclusion
   - High levels of poverty
   - Sections of marginalised and hard-to-reach groups within communities

Meso-level indicators of information poverty

5. Access to information services in areas of social deprivation
   - No local libraries
   - No community centres with information services available
   - Limited ICT and basic skills support within communities
6. Social participation
   - Lack of empowerment and knowledge to participate
   - Limited participation in local library
   - Little participation in community activities
   - Limited weak ties needed for political and social participation
   - Limited social networks
   - Small-world mind-set, not valuing use of libraries, not valuing education or learning for advancement.
7. Community information access
   - No or limited availability of community information
   - Low levels of home PCs in area/Internet, ICT resources in communities
   - No or limited community ICT/skills and basic literacy training and support
   - No people in social networks to assist with PC/Internet
   - No access to information that is relevant to communities
8. Educational attainment
   - Qualification levels within an area
   - ICT qualifications
   - Basic adult literacy/numeracy/ICT skills within area
   - Limited participation in part-time higher education courses within areas

Continued

Table 4.2 Information poverty indicators framework—cont'd

   9. Ethnic groups/minorities in area
   - Poor language skills (not speaking English or the language in which information is available)
   - Limited communication barriers
   - Cultural barriers

Micro-level indicators of information poverty

10. Skills and knowledge deficits
   - Poor literacy
   - Unable to read
   - Limited information literacy
   - Limited digital literacy (computer/ICT skills)
   - Poor communication skills

11. Information literacy deficits
   - Limited ability to evaluate and use information to improve one's situation
   - Limited ability to interpret the quality of information
   - Limited ability to use information appropriately to benefit from it to improve one's life

12. Technical skills
   - Limited ability to use mouse/keyboard
   - Limited ability to use a computer
   - Limited ability to use the Internet
   - Lacking awareness of and the skills required to use social media

13. Disabilities
   - Physical
   - Visually impaired/blind
   - Hearing impaired/deaf
   - Intellectual (cognitive abilities, learning disabilities)
   - Autism

14. Information affordability
   - Lack the capacity to buy books, magazines, newspapers
   - Unable to get library or information service providers because of financial constraints
   - Unable to afford home PC/laptop/broadband connection
   - Not owning a mobile phone with Internet access

15. Information behaviour
   - Lack the information seeking skills to find the information one needs
   - No value placed on access to information
   - No value placed on access to libraries and using libraries
   - Fear of the technology, using PCs
   - No interest/desire to get the Internet at home
   - Choosing not to learn, use information
   - No interest in reading
   - Limited/low aspirations, expectations, ambitions

Table 4.2 Information poverty indicators framework—cont'd

16. Information awareness
- Not knowing where to find information
- Not knowing why and how to access online government services
- Limited awareness of library services
- Limited awareness and understanding of health information (health literacy)
- Limited awareness and understanding of financial information (financial literacy and benefit information; ability to manage personal finances)

17. Institutional barriers
- Not wanting to approach information providers; fear of bureaucratic institutions/negative perceptions of libraries/librarians
- Lack of trust in information channels (in information providers)
- Not using libraries
- Language being presented in a bureaucratic way that prevents access

could, for example, apply the micro-level indicators to examine how they are developing information and digital literacy skills. Similarly, other public libraries could use the meso-level concepualisation to engage with the communities surrounding their libraries and ascertain those communities' information needs.

I can envision multiple ways in which this unique framework of information poverty indicators could be used to measure the impact of library services. So, while the indicators presented here are generic, they could be used and modified to suit the location, culture or context to:
- measure information access and design public library services at a national level
- plan community outreach to ascertain the information needs of specific demographic groups
- be used at an individual level to measure information and digital literacy skills.

Moreover, this original information poverty framework has validity beyond the public library service and could be used in other settings when measuring how poverty, social exclusion and skills are addressed at government and community levels.

4.17 CONCLUDING THOUGHTS

This chapter has developed a multidimensional analysis of information poverty and has identified the main factors creating information poverty: infrastructural, financial, social, educational and personal. As well as providing viewpoints from library policymakers, strategists and library staff, the previous literature has been integrated with the current study to conceptualise information poverty from a public library perspective. The subsequent chapters focus more closely on the public library's role in addressing this form of poverty. In addition, this chapter has discussed the importance of measuring a library service's or an individual library's impact. Measuring more precisely the impact of library services in addressing information poverty – what they do for the society, communities and individuals – is challenging. The chapter presented a model of information poverty indicators that can be used to demonstrate the impact of public libraries. The framework can be adapted and applied in other library settings at all levels or at each level individually.

Thus far, the book has set up the theoretical framework and contextual background. To understand and gain evidence of these indicators in practice, the three-level framework is used to apply the methodology, which seeks to understand how information poverty can be addressed at strategic, community and personal levels. Chapters 5–9 present the macro-, meso- and micro-level findings.

CHAPTER 5

Investigating Information Poverty at the Macro Level: Part 1

5.1 INTRODUCTION

This first 'findings chapter' considers the macro (strategic)–level approaches to addressing information poverty. It looks at how public libraries provide access to information through their infrastructure (information and communication technology [ICT] facilities, library buildings, staff) and can contribute to alleviating information poverty by developing strategies to create a more socially, culturally and digitally inclusive society. The UK government's digital inclusion strategies and the burgeoning role that public libraries are expected to play in supporting digital access are discussed. Current UK Internet usage statistics are presented. To give the reader an idea of the issues that public libraries are trying to address, Internet access and poverty statistics for Northern Ireland are outlined briefly. Following this, I discuss how public libraries contribute to government priorities to alleviate poverty and social exclusion, and look at Libraries NI's current community engagement strategy, Targeting Social Exclusion (TSE).

5.2 MACRO-LEVEL APPROACHES TO INFORMATION POVERTY

Macro-level approaches to information poverty examine a broad spectrum of societal, economic, infrastructural, technological, social justice and political concerns that can determine information poverty. At a macro level, the ethics and social justice approaches (Lievrouw and Farb, 2003; Britz, 2004, 2007; Lor and Britz, 2007; Bradshaw et al., 2007) suggest that information inequalities exist as a result of an 'imbalanced distribution of information-related rights' (Yu, 2006: 232). The idea of information poverty as social justice and a moral concern is exemplified in the writings of Britz (2004, 2007), whose studies of information poverty focus primarily on information poverty in the context of developing countries.

Overcoming Information Poverty
ISBN 978-0-08-101110-2

The macro-level approaches include studies examining globalisation and the information divide that exists between the developed and developing world. These approaches are evident in studies that discuss the political economy–based interpretation of the information divide, in which information inequality is associated with capitalism, class struggle and geopolitics (see, e.g., Britz, 2004, 2007). These studies argue that governments need to bridge the gap between the information rich and poor (Yu, 2006: 232). On the macro scale, information poverty can be viewed as an ethical issue, 'a serious moral concern and a matter of social justice' (Britz, 2004: 192), created by the growth of the Internet and the information society. Britz's (2004, 2007) social justice approaches to information poverty argue that governments and education systems have an ethical responsibility to address it.

I want to stress that it is beyond the scope of this book to discuss information poverty from an international perspective, or to draw comparisons between developing and developed countries. The macro-level focus on information poverty is discussed in relation to how public library services operate within broader strategies to facilitate access to information and digital and social inclusion. Public libraries have the potential to address social (in)justice by targeting excluded groups and addressing the social and educational inequalities within society. Thus, at a societal level, public libraries can contribute to social capital, social cohesion and social inclusion. Considering public library services at the macro level enables information professionals, library strategists and researchers to examine how effective public libraries are in delivering government strategy for digital inclusion, ameliorating social exclusion and promoting lifelong learning.

At the macro level, information poverty is also about the democratic right to information access (Thompson, 2006: 16). Thompson (2006: 28) notes that 'equality of opportunity is the first step to information access'. Public libraries provide opportunities for information access and knowledge acquisition, especially to the socioeconomically disadvantaged in society who may not have the financial means to afford it. Indeed, a core value of the library profession has always been to ensure 'equality of access' for all (Clarke et al., 2011). In bridging the information gap public libraries 'have the potential to be powerful forces in the fight for social justice' (Pateman and Vincent, 2010: 141–42). By addressing information poverty, public libraries can play a role in addressing the social justice issues around information access and equity.

5.3 DIGITAL INCLUSION: THE DIGITAL BY DEFAULT AGENDA

The macro-level approach to information poverty is a prerequisite for physical access to information, since the decisions and priorities of a government at a political level determine the information infrastructure, information policies and public library provision within a country. At the heart of any understanding of macro-level information poverty is the analysis of how infrastructure – including political decision making, allocation of societal resources and the distribution of wealth – contributes to information poverty. Infrastructural approaches to understanding information poverty are one component of the broad, macro-level approach to it. At the macro-level, government priorities to support access to information and to tackle poverty and social and digital exclusion provide public libraries with an enhanced role within society to support the needs of the most educationally, financially and socially disadvantaged. The macro-level information poverty indicators, such as a poorly designed information infrastructure and not having an ICT/broadband infrastructure, can be used to ascertain whether a region is well designed to support digital inclusion. In addition, they can be used to examine whether a country has a digital inclusion strategy or has the human support to assist with digital inclusion.

At the macro level, the European Union has developed information society strategies, such as the eEurope 2002 objectives and the eEurope 2005 Action Plan. Martin (2005: 8) observes that the European Union recognises the need to confront the digital divide and social exclusion and is now interested in skills development, e-business and e-government. The European Union's e-learning initiatives promote digital literacy as one of the basic skills of all Europeans (Davies and Butters, 2008: 137–138). Europe's information society policies acknowledge the role ICTs play in modern society and has at its core 'E-inclusion', which looks at the ability of ICTs to contribute to wider inclusion objectives. E-inclusion aims to promote the use of ICTs to overcome exclusion, create employment opportunities and facilitate social participation; it features in the Digital Agenda for Europe (European Commission, n.d.). This Digital Agenda focuses on developing digital literacy, skills and inclusion, and it proposes a series of measures to encourage the take-up of digital technologies by potentially disadvantaged groups, such as the elderly, less-literate and low-income persons and the disabled. EU countries are encouraged to develop strategies to reduce poverty and exclusion, to improve the skills of citizens and to create a more inclusive society. Hence, European agendas to develop skills for inclusion are reflected in UK government policy and in the Northern Ireland government's lifelong learning agenda.[1]

Digital inclusion initiatives from Europe filter into UK initiatives. The UK government's Digital Inclusion strategy, outlined in the 2009 'Digital Britain' report, emphasised the need for digital inclusion. The report defined digital inclusion as the 'best use of digital technology, either directly or indirectly to improve the lives and life chances of all citizens, particularly the most disadvantaged' (Buckley-Owen, 2011: 76–77). The United Kingdom's *Government Digital Strategy* (Great Britain Cabinet Office, 2013) was introduced more recently to promote digital inclusion. The government's Digital by Default agenda was announced in 2010 (Great Britain Cabinet Office, 2010) in response to a report by Lane-Fox (2010), titled *Directgov 2010 and Beyond: Revolution Not Evolution*, which argued that 'in order to 'empower' citizens and make 'life simpler' public services should be delivered online'. The government argues that Digital by Default could save the government money, and it 'estimate[s] that £1.7–£1.8 billion of total annual savings could be made by shifting the transactional services offered by central government departments from offline to digital channels' (Great Britain Cabinet Office, 2013). As well, it is claimed that, while '£1.1–£1.3 billion of these savings will be saved directly by the government', the rest would be 'passed on to service users through lower prices' (Great Britain Cabinet Office, 2013).

Recent figures from the Office for National Statistics (ONS) (2015) reveal that 5.9 million adults (11%) in the United Kingdom have never used the Internet. Figures confirm that, by region, Northern Ireland the lowest usage (80%) (ONS, 2015). Table 5.1 presents the current ONS statistics on Internet use.

As the UK government moves to Digital by Default, the ONS statistics are used to help the government, researchers and academics build a picture of who is and who is not online. In doing so they help to inform the 'wider debate about social and digital exclusion' (ONS, 2015). The ONS Internet Access: Households and Individuals figures from August 2015[2] reveal that the Internet was accessed every day, or almost every day, by 78% of adults (39.3 million) in Great Britain in 2015, compared with 35% (16.2 million) in 2006, when directly comparable records began. In the United Kingdom

---

[1] See Department of Employment and Learning (2012a) *Graduating to Success: A Higher Education Strategy for Northern Ireland*, Available from: http://www.delni.gov.uk/graduating-to-success-he-strategy-for-ni.pdf.

[2] See Office for National Statistics (2015), *Statistical Bulletin: Internet Access: Households and Incomes 2015*. Available from: http://www.ons.gov.uk/ons/rel/rdit2/internet-access-households-and-individuals/2015/index.html.

Table 5.1 ONS statistics on internet use
ONS statistics Q1 2015

- 44.7 Million adults (86%) in the United Kingdom had used the internet in quarter 1, an increase of 1% since the quarter 1 (January–March) 2014.
- Of adults, 11% (5.9 million) had never used the Internet, falling by 1% since quarter 1 (January–March) 2014.
- The percentage of adults who have never used the Internet has decreased from 17% in quarter 1 (January–March) 2011 to 11% in quarter 1 (January–March) 2015.
- In quarter 1 (January–March) 2015, almost all adults aged 16–24 years were recent Internet users (99%), in contrast with 33% of adults aged ≥75 years.
- While recent Internet use is notably lower among the older age groups, the proportion of adults aged 75 years and over who had never used the Internet decreased from 76% in quarter 2 (April–June) 2011 to 61% in quarter 1 (January–March) 2015.
- The South East had the highest proportion of recent Internet users (90%); Northern Ireland had the lowest (80%).

Internet Access Quarterly Update Q1 2015 (see Office for National Statistics, 2015. Statistical Bulleting, Internet Users, 2015 Available from: http://www.ons.gov.uk/ons/rel/rdit2/internet-users/2015/stb-ia-2015.html?format=print (accessed 28.09.15.).).

in 2015, 86% of households (22.5 million adults) had Internet access, up from 57% in 2006. These statistics reveal that people are increasingly using the Internet on a daily basis for social networking, shopping online and accessing newspapers; the most common activity is emailing: 76% of adults used the Internet for this purpose (ONS, 2015: 5). As noted in the previous chapter, individuals are at risk of exclusion if they are not online. The following quotation highlights the disadvantages people face economically and socially when they are not online:

> I am aware that parts of our society do not have access to information which would inform their decisions on i.e. [the] job market, cheap shopping, benefits available… With so much information online, there are parts of society which do not find this easy to access.
>
> **BLM1.**

In essence, decision making is restricted if individuals cannot access information online or interpret the information available. The need to have access to the Internet and the skills to used computers is evident, and this supports the role that libraries play in providing free access and support.

Fig. 5.1 shows the daily computer use by age group in 2006 and 2015 (ONS, 2015: 5). Interestingly, 'Internet use for reading or downloading

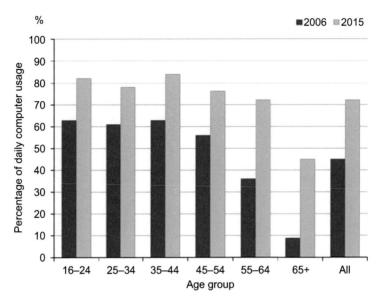

Figure 5.1 Daily computer use in the United Kingdom by age group in 2006 and 2015 (ONS, 2015: 5).

newspapers and magazines' shows the 'largest rise'; over half of all adults (62%) used the Internet to read or download the news, newspapers or magazines in 2015, compared with only 20% of adults in 2007 (ONS, 2015: 5–6). Computer usage among adults >65 years old remains lower than the other age groups and is an area that needs to be addressed. Public libraries have a key role to play in this (this is discussed in Chapter 8).

The statistics also indicate that in 2015, 22.5 million households in the United Kingdom (86%) had an Internet connection, up from 84% in 2014 and 57% in 2006 (ONS, 2015: 12).

Interestingly, of the 14% of households in the United Kingdom without Internet access, the majority (53%) stated they did not need a connection. Many households without the Internet are actively choosing not to subscribe, whereas a large and important minority state that other barriers prevent them from connecting to the Internet; for instance, 31% reported that this was the result of a lack of skills. Further barriers reported included equipment costs being too high (14%) and access costs being too high (12%) (ONS, 2015: 13). The barriers to home Internet access reflect many of the factors that create information poverty (financial, personal choice and skills); these were discussed in Chapter 4.

5.3.1 Digital by Default and Public Libraries

The digital agenda can exclude those without the financial means to pay for the technology or the skills to use it. Consequently, the digital agenda has the potential to exacerbate information poverty and exclude citizens who could benefit from accessing information. At the macro level, public library priorities and strategies are often aligned to government agendas to improve access to information and to alleviate poverty and social and digital exclusion. Society is now more dependent on access to the Internet and the ability to use it, and therefore public libraries have a pivotal role in delivering the UK government's Digital by Default agenda and supporting digital participation.

With this Digital by Default agenda, public libraries will increasingly be expected to work in partnership, to provide support for those without access or the skills for access and to deliver digital inclusion. 'Digital inclusion' is the term governments and information access providers use to describe how they provide access to digital technologies. Digital inclusion encompasses those outreach activities, strategies, training and services targeted to the digitally excluded, which narrow the digital divide and increase digital literacy (Jaeger et al., 2012: 3). One interviewee commented that with the Digital by Default agenda there was a 'push by government to get people to apply for whatever, digitally rather than having staff in their office' (LNI4). In addition, an interviewee commented that information poverty,

could be knowledge, that's educational knowledge … around access to information of government services, so increasingly the emphasis is on [the] government to provide services online and remove [the] human interface … so … you could be excluding…people from access to those services or from information about how to access those services.

DCAL2.

This is an important comment because it highlights the government's focus on Digital by Default and the challenges some people might face when accessing essential information: they may not be aware that the information is available or of how to get to it and may not have the skills needed for access. Public libraries are continually evolving in response to cultural and societal trends, government agendas and new ICTs. Government agendas for digital and social inclusion, lifelong learning and tackling poverty shape the role of public libraries. It is important to stress that at some point most people in modern society will need to use the Internet, and this is where public libraries can provide the resources and the skilled staff to assist

with these information needs. Tackling social exclusion and providing facilities and support to encourage digital participation will increasingly be key
features of public libraries in the 21st century. This was recognised by Buckley-Owen (2011: 266), who avers that public libraries should have a 'greater
role' in 'providing help to those who did not have the necessary access or
skills to use online services', and that as government strives to 'move citizens
over to accessing government services electronically', public libraries are
'well-positioned' to provide support to 'people without the skills to use the
services or whose needs are so complex that they require personal attention
and help' (Buckley-Owen, 2011: 260).

5.3.2 Public Libraries and Supporting Digital Inclusion

In the digital age, public libraries have the potential to address information
poverty and support digital inclusion, especially for those who cannot afford
technologies and those without the skills for access. Thus public libraries
bridge 'educational divides' (Harle and Tarrant, 2011: 121), bridge financial
divides by providing free access to ICTs/Internet and bridge the digital gap
by enabling participation and inclusion (O'Loan and McMenemy, 2005: 8).
Specifically, public libraries have a key role in providing access and support
to those without access to technologies or the skills for access so they can
use government services, such as applying for and renewing driving licences
and applying for Ministry of Transport (MOT) and vehicle insurance tests;
access online banking services; seek housing benefits; pay bills; access commercial services and recreation such as travel; and access health information
and pensions entitlements,. A survey respondent recognised a 'levelling' role
for libraries (BLM22), and another explained that 'libraries are in a position
to guide' individuals with limited ICT skills 'through the Internet to look
for jobs, apply for a passport' (BLM1).

By providing free access to ICT and the Internet, public libraries have a
significant role in closing the gap between those who can afford technology
and those who cannot. In addition, libraries can have a significant supporting role in developing the ICT and information literacy skills of citizens
through one-on-one and group training. Jaeger et al. (2011: 9) also note the
ability of public libraries to 'address gaps in access and technological literacy
through not only the provision of information, but also through education
and training that link patrons to socioeconomic and employment opportunities'. With more information online, public libraries are a place where
people can get the support that is not available in their own small worlds/
social networks. Johnson (2012: 53) states that, by providing to the

socioeconomically disadvantaged access and support that may not be available within localised social networks, public libraries 'contribute to social capital'. The next section looks at digital inclusion within Northern Ireland, presenting the statistics for home ICT/Internet access, before taking a closer look at public libraries in Northern Ireland, which were used as a basis to investigate information poverty at the macro, meso and micro levels.

5.4 NORTHERN IRELAND HOME ICT AND INTERNET ACCESS

The Northern Ireland Statistics and Research Agency (NISRA) and the Office of Communications (Ofcom)[3] statistics can help us gauge levels of ICT/Internet ownership and usage in Northern Ireland. NISRA statistics for home Internet access reveal that 37% of people in the most deprived areas do not have home Internet access, compared with 19% in the least deprived areas. Further, in the second most deprived wards, 32% do not have home Internet access, compared with 25% in the second least deprived wards (see Table 5.2). Leith (2012: 106–7) argues that a digital divide exists in the United Kingdom, stating that the 51% of those with only a basic secondary school education were digitally excluded, and that people earning over £40,000 per year were more than twice as likely to be digitally included as those earning less than £12,500 per year.

Public libraries have the potential to address this marked difference in levels of access in deprived areas and lower-income groups by targeting services to those in need of free computer/Internet access. Possible reasons for the disparity in numbers of those who have access in socially disadvantaged areas could be not having the skills, affordability, or lack of interest in owning a home computer or Internet connection (as mentioned earlier).

As with other parts of the United Kingdom, there were differences in broadband take-up in Northern Ireland by age, socioeconomic group, and household income (Office of Communications, 2015: 69). For example:

- Adults aged 65 and over were less likely to have broadband (32%) compared with those aged 16–34 years (82%) and 35–64 years (81%).
- Broadband take-up was 25% higher among ABC1 (higher socioeconomic group) households in Northern Ireland (86%) compared with C2DE (lower socioeconomic group) households (61%).

[3] Ofcom is the 'independent regulator and competition authority for the UK communications industries, with responsibilities across television, radio, telecommunications and wireless communications services' (Buckley-Owen, 2011: 17).

Table 5.2 Home Internet access by multiple deprivation measure
Continuous household survey 2011/12 (Q, Quintiles)

All households (by quintile)	Total		Yes		No	
	Valid cases	Row (%)	Valid cases	Row (%)	Valid Cases	Row (%)
Total	2780	100	1981	71	799	29
Q1 (most deprived wards)	571	100	361	63	210	37
Q2	572	100	389	68	183	32
Q3	565	100	396	70	169	30
Q4	553	100	413	75	140	25
Q5 (least deprived wards)	519	100	422	81	97	19

NISRA; data provided by a statistician at the Central Survey Unit of the Department of Finance and Personnel Northern Ireland (DFPNI).

- Similarly, there was a 35% difference in broadband take-up between households with an income below £17.5k (57%) and those with a household income above £17.5k (92%) in Northern Ireland.

According to the Ofcom 2015 report, ICT, tablet and smartphone ownership, and home Internet connections, are increasing in Northern Ireland. For example, at 45%, Northern Ireland, along with Wales, has the highest rate of tablet ownership in the United Kingdom, up from 29% a year ago and 9% in 2012. Likewise, smartphone ownership has risen from 45% to 55% in the past year, with the biggest increase recorded in rural areas. In addition, 8 in 10 households (80%) have access to the Internet; slightly lower than the United Kingdom average, whereas Northern Ireland still has the highest availability of fibre broadband in the United Kingdom, with 95% of premises being served by next-generation networks compared with the UK average of 78%. The Ofcom (2015) report also revealed that people in lower-income households in Northern Ireland (C2DE social groups) are less likely to have broadband than those in social groups ABC1. For example, among the C2DE group, 64% had broadband in Northern Ireland against a UK average of 65%, whereas in the ABC1 group, 84% had broadband in Northern Ireland against a UK average of 87%. Again, the disparity between those who can afford Internet access and those who cannot is evident in these figures.

The next section looks at how Libraries NI's infrastructure, strategic partnerships and its strategic priority of 'access to information' enable it to alleviate information poverty.

5.5 ACCESS TO INFORMATION: INFRASTRUCTURE

At the macro level, public library infrastructure consists of staff, catalogues, collections, technology and facilities (Hernon and Matthews, 2013: xii). This infrastructure enables public libraries to play a major role in facilitating digital inclusion. Their infrastructure comprises their buildings, ICT systems, strategic policies for digital and social inclusion, free access to the Internet and information provided in print and electronic formats; these allow them to play a leading role in addressing information poverty. Libraries NI's infrastructure consists of 96 libraries, 2 specialist libraries and 26 mobile libraries across Northern Ireland.

The government has invested £26 million in the ICT infrastructure (e2) for libraries in Northern Ireland, with the aim to 'greatly improve digital access' (DCAL2), and has given Libraries NI a key role in facilitating digital inclusion. With a new modern ICT infrastructure, public libraries in Northern Ireland now have improved broadband, Wi-Fi in all libraries (which is free to library members), and radio identification frequency (RFID) (self-service machines) in the 20 largest libraries. In addition there is a Virtual Learning Environment, where library users can 'engage' with some 'learning from home'. All these improve online access for people who may never come to a physical library (LNI9). Along with the technological infrastructure, public libraries have the facilities and knowledgeable staff to support information access.

A future challenge for public libraries is deciding how services will be delivered and how to re-design the library space to accommodate changing service priorities. As noted earlier, RFID machines have been installed in larger libraries. This brings further challenges for staff and for library users, and undoubtedly can have both negative and positive impacts on the delivery of library services. Macro-level interviewees explained that RFID would free staff from issuing books, enabling them to spend more time assisting the public on computers and do more activities like Rhythm and Rhyme. Typically, the interviewees outlined the potential of RFID to remove barriers to library use; for example, no one will know what customers are borrowing. One interviewee acknowledged the social barriers and 'social norms' that could lead to 'social information poverty' (LNI1). This interviewee explained that the library service had 'representations from the gay and bisexual community about accessing' books and information, especially the difficulties 'for young teens, for children who are exploring their own sexuality and they want to read about what is happening elsewhere or what is happening to other people' (LNI1). Thus it was argued by Libraries NI Senior staff that RFID could break the barriers people may face when accessing books, such as health or basic literacy issues. Such comments confirm previous studies of social information access, such as the Theory of Normative Behaviour proposed by Chatman (2000), which illustrated how the social norms and worldviews with which people live affect their information access. Interestingly, a meso-level interviewee questioned senior management's motives for RFID: 'they keep saying it won't reflect on staffing levels but how can they say that really? It has to have some kind of impact' (TSE2). As the quotation suggests, the emphasis on the advantages of RFID could be a senior management agenda to save on other costs, such as staffing. I can see both the advantages and the disadvantages of RFID: on the one hand, it can improve access to books and information for those who may not want library staff to see what they are borrowing, and it can free up library staff time for other activities. On the other hand, however, there is a fear that RFID may remove the human element, which is needed to support the public. What is important is that there is a balanced approach to public library services when new processes are introduced, but that the traditional personal touch remains in place for those who prefer social interaction with library staff.

5.5.1 Access to Information: Strategic Partnerships for Digital and Social Inclusion

Strategic partnerships can enable public libraries to work collaboratively with other government bodies to deliver government priorities for digital inclusion in a cost-efficient way. In Northern Ireland, having one library authority makes it easier to develop strategic partnerships. Interviewees from DCAL indicated that libraries are increasingly viewed by the government as vital to delivering digital inclusion and supporting access to e-government. Public libraries are therefore viewed as key players in enabling the government's Digital by Default agenda. One interviewee explained that 'government service deliverers' are seeking partnerships with Libraries NI to facilitate information access and to provide ICT support for 'people who don't have computers at home' or 'broadband' (DCAL1). In Northern Ireland, government agencies such as the Department of Agriculture and Rural Development (DARD) have reduced the number of their offices and staff, and are cutting costs by working with libraries and using library facilities and support from library staff (DCAL1). One interviewee described how universal credit and 'changes to the welfare system' – with government 'targets' to have about 80% of the population doing 'benefits online' by 2017 (LNI6) – can have an impact on those without home computers or the skills for access. As well, people in socioeconomically deprived areas may not have the support from within their own social networks to help them and provide assistance with ICT. Consequently, libraries will increasingly have a role in supporting online access by the digitally excluded, who may not have computers or the skills to use computers, enabling them to access online government services (LNI6). Another source explained that, based on their experience of government, Members of the Legislative Assembly (Northern Ireland government) are aware of the 'underlying issues' facing many people when trying to access online information, and that they understand both the role and the importance of library services in supporting information access (DCAL1). The interviewee detailed how Members of the Legislative Assembly from isolated rural areas were aware that people cannot 'get broadband', and they would emphasise the importance of being connected to the Internet since government services are increasingly being provided online (DCAL1). Being without broadband, for instance, in remote rural areas can exacerbate digital exclusion. Macro-level interviewees articulated the changing role of public libraries, which are now key players in supporting the government's Digital by Default agenda and therefore have been given a fundamental role in alleviating information poverty. So, with the changing information and communication environment, public libraries must be prepared to change, adapt and re-think how they promote and deliver their services to improve literacy among, and the information and digital literacy skills of, citizens.

5.5.2 Strategic Partnerships to Address Information Poverty

First, strategic partnerships can raise the profile and perceived value of public libraries among the government and broader society. Second, they can increase participation in library services among those members of the population who may not have thought of using libraries before. Third, partnerships enable libraries to contribute to wider government agendas to reduce digital and social exclusion. The macro-level interviewees outlined the partnership with DARD and the importance of improving information access for farmers and rural dwellers. Government departments such as DARD now see the potential for the network of 96 public libraries throughout Northern Ireland to deliver the government's digital agenda (LNI4). One interviewee commented that the large network of libraries, ICT access and skilled staff can address information poverty in rural areas, especially among farmers who 'are not necessarily the most technically literate in the world' (LNI5). People are increasingly expected to access government services electronically, and farmers are expected to complete online Single Farm Payments, assist forms for cattle movement and their grant applications. The information packs distributed by DARD to 38,000 rural businesses about Single Farm Payments specify that farmers can fill in the online application farms 'in the local library free of charge' (LNI8). This working partnership demonstrates the benefits of government departments 'working together' to deliver services and improve access to digital information (LNI12).

When public libraries develop strategic partnerships with other organisations and government agencies, they can seemingly be more effective at achieving similar aims and provide a smoother transition towards the government aim of 'digital by default'. One interviewee stressed that strategic partnerships are fundamental to addressing social deprivation because 'these are long-term issues that need holistic approaches across organisations' (LNI6). This interviewee asserted that while public libraries make a contribution to address poverty and social exclusion, they were 'only one element', and that there needs to be 'a whole cross-departmental approach' to address societal problems (LNI6). Libraries, therefore, 'have to work with other people' who are addressing similar issues 'to maximise limited resources' (LNI6). This interviewee stated that 'government departments tend to work in silos', but that to address issues 'like information poverty and social inclusion', a 'joint approach' is needed (LNI6). Clearly, addressing information poverty and digital and social exclusion needs joined-up approaches across government departments.

Another strategic partnership is Health in Mind, a Big Lottery Fund project, in partnership with the Public Health Agency and leading mental health agencies: Action Mental Health, Aware Defeat Depression, CAUSE and Mind Wise, which facilitate access to information. Health in Mind activities in libraries include workshops and the distribution of health information packs aimed at developing health literacy and information literacy skills. As well as developing health literacy skills, the neutral atmosphere of a library is also an ideal place to address financial information poverty. One survey respondent stated that their library 'has an advice group who deal with queries from people regarding their benefits and financial circumstances', which fills a gap for those who find information difficult to find and understand (BLM7). By working in partnership, libraries can offer facilities where financial information poverty is addressed. In partnership with A2B (Access to Benefits), Libraries in Northern Ireland held financial advice sessions (called the Money Advice Service) in nine libraries and Check It Out roadshows in five libraries, providing information on benefits, money and consumer advice for older people (Libraries NI, 2013: 12). As one interviewee explained, financial 'experts' deliver the advice and libraries provide the neutral venue, since:

> *… some people may not want to go into a money advice centre or a mental health centre, they walk into a library and nobody knows what they are coming in for, so we can break down those barriers and [break] down the stigma that nobody knows why you come into a library.*
>
> *LNI4.*

Public libraries can arguably provide a non-stigmatising space for those with poor literacy, few communication skills and lacking confidence. Where possible, public libraries should explore partnership with other agencies to promote access to health, financial and community information. When they do this they can use the neutral library environment to deliver information services and support for people with social, cultural, financial and educational barriers.

5.6 TACKLING POVERTY AND SOCIAL EXCLUSION: THE TSE STRATEGY

Another macro-level indicator of information poverty is high levels of actual poverty within society and communities. At the macro level, it is essential to develop and implement a community engagement strategy to enable public libraries to have an impact in reducing information poverty among marginalised and hard-to-reach groups living in socially deprived areas. Within Northern Ireland, the wider political agenda, which is prioritising tackling poverty and social exclusion, determines and influences DCAL's policy and subsequently the agenda of Libraries NI. Libraries NI needs to be able to provide evidence of how it is supporting government priorities to combat poverty and social exclusion in order to secure future investment.

In 2013, in response to DCAL priorities, Libraries NI developed a community engagement strategy called Targeting Social Needs (TSN), which re-embraced the TSN policy of the 1990s.

This was later changed to 'Targeting Social Exclusion' to reflect DCAL's emphasis on addressing social exclusion. Libraries NI began targeting resources at 28 libraries identified by NISRA as being in the top 10% most socially deprived areas in Northern Ireland. Consequently, they started to focus specifically on tackling poverty and social exclusion, targeting disadvantaged groups and increasing library usage in areas of social need. When it comes to addressing social need, public libraries are often advantageously positioned in areas of high deprivation. This is evident within Northern Ireland, where 28 of 96 libraries across Northern Ireland are located in the 10% most deprived areas, amounting to 29% of libraries being located in socially deprived areas. A DCAL interviewee commented that while Libraries NI was 'playing a good role' in contributing to the government's anti-poverty and social inclusion strategy, with its library infrastructure of 96 libraries, many of which were 'very close' to 'deprived' urban and rural areas, there was 'a lot more they could do' (DCAL2). Specific targets have been set for library managers working in the most deprived areas to increase the number of Rhythm and Rhyme sessions, adult and children's reading groups, community partnerships and participation.

One interviewee acknowledged that 'the political agenda is pushing' libraries to be 'more proactive', and there was a more 'co-ordinated' and 'focused approach' to 'raising the profile of the library' within socially deprived areas (LNI11). With the TSE strategy there is an enhanced focus on community engagement, and it was acknowledged that libraries can no longer be 'passive'; they 'have to work very hard to get people to use the service' (LNI5). To tackle social exclusion in disadvantaged areas, Libraries NI set aside additional financial resources. Two temporary TSE community support officers (one in Belfast and one in Derry/Londonderry) and three temporary TSE community project officers (two in Belfast and one in Derry/Londonderry) were appointed to mentor and support BLMs in their outreach capacity[4]. One interviewee explained that it is hoped that 'additional staffing' would give libraries 'more of an impact' to target poverty and social exclusion (LNI2). A financial commitment is evidence of taking this initiative 'more seriously' (LNI13). It is hoped that by investing more resources to reduce social deprivation through creating partnerships, targeting groups and raising awareness, libraries will be able to penetrate 'deeper into society' than they were (LNI5). Five staff were originally appointed across Northern Ireland on a temporary basis to implement the TSE strategy and support BLMs in their outreach capacity. At the time of writing there is one TSE community project officer and two TSE community support officers.

[4] Derry, officially Londonderry, is the second-largest city in Northern Ireland and the fourth-largest city on the island of Ireland. The names of the city, county and district of Derry or Londonderry are the subject of a naming dispute between Irish nationalists and unionists. Generally, although not always, nationalists favour using the name Derry, and unionists, Londonderry. Legally, the city and county are called 'Londonderry', whereas the local government district is called 'Derry'. See Wikipedia (2014a,b).

As is evidenced in the next chapter, these community engagement roles can greatly reduce information poverty and encourage library usage in disadvantaged areas. Based on the findings of this research, I believe that public libraries need to have more staff in community engagement roles to forge links with local communities and promote library services. This outreach should be taken seriously, with relevant long-term plans drawn up. Indeed, I would argue that stopgap measures to fulfil current government agendas are not the way to address information poverty or to encourage library usage in socially deprived areas. Public library strategists should see community engagement as key to promoting library services and develop long-term strategies for this, with financial resources set aside to support library outreach. Engagement with local communities and collaboration with groups, therefore, should be continuous, and the necessary resources, both financial and human, should be provided.

The next section considers the skills needed by library staff when engaging with socially and digitally excluded individuals.

5.7 STAFF SKILLS TO TACKLE SOCIAL AND DIGITAL EXCLUSION

Importantly, community engagement training was delivered to BLMs to encourage discussion about what social deprivation is, what poverty and social exclusion are and the role libraries can play in disadvantaged communities. This training was primarily to get staff to think about the context of targeting social needs and how to develop local partnerships and share best practices (LNI11). These sessions discussed the barriers that people in deprived areas may face when accessing libraries, as well as possible 'solutions' (LNI11). Interviewees discussed the new skill sets for community engagement: promoting the service, making connections and networking. Interviewees typically commented that library staff should be empathetic, diplomatic and sympathetic, adopt non-patronising approaches to socially disadvantaged groups who may have low literacy, low self-esteem and may never have used a library.

Staff are arguably the greatest asset of the public library service. Developing and training staff can lead to improved services. Appropriate skills are fundamental for staff dealing with excluded groups and working in social deprived communities. Training on how to deal with the socially excluded members of society (the disabled, homeless, travellers, people from multinational backgrounds) should be delivered to public library staff. Pateman and Williment (2013: 226) concur, asserting that staff should 'be trained in the skills required to work with socially excluded communities', including communication, listening and negotiating skills. Understanding what information poverty is and the barriers to accessing libraries for marginalised groups who may have limited ICT skills or poor literacy and communication skills is fundamental. Further, having patience, understanding the barriers to accessing information and having the capacity to empathise and sense the frustration that those with no or very limited ICT, literacy and communication skills may have when faced with new technologies are essential skills for front-line public library staff.

By engaging with the community and delivering library services based on community needs for information and learning, libraries can improve customers' experience. When public libraries reach out to and embrace those most excluded from society, staff need the skills to deal with library users who may have mental health–related issues, drug- and alcohol-related issues and limited social skills. It is evident that training is vital so that public library staff are equipped with the skills to engage with marginalised sections of society. In the future, library staff will need varied skill sets; for example, skills and qualifications to work with youth may be useful for library staff when working with younger adults. In addition, early years qualifications or primary school teaching qualifications may be of use to library staff working with children. As McKeown and Bates (2013) observed, emotional awareness training can provide staff with the skills needed to communicate and interact more successfully with socially excluded groups and those from multicultural and diverse backgrounds. Emotional awareness can improve customer care, allowing staff to identify moods/emotions and to handle situations more successfully. The ability to empathise with library users can also contribute to fulfilling wider library agendas to tackle poverty and social exclusion and to respect multicultural diversity.

Public libraries offer multifaceted services (books; activities; ICTs; Internet; printing, faxing and scanning facilities) and support to develop the literacy and information and digital literacy skills needed for participation in modern society. Increasingly, library staff will need new skills: they will need to balance traditional library services while embracing the challenges and opportunities that new technologies such as iPads, social media and mobile devices can bring. An interviewee commented that information poverty was 'to do with pace of change in Information Technology' (LNI13). This important comment highlights the need for library staff to keep up to date with technology to be able to assist library users and be prepared for the changing ways in which people access and use information. Library staff are expected to assist people who often have varying levels of information literacy and digital literacy skills in a rapidly changing information and communication environment. Providing this support can place a strain on public library staff resources, for instance, when dealing with those with no or very basic ICT skills, where even logging on to a library computer and the basics such as 'Control-Alt-Delete' and using a mouse are a challenge. As well as having up-to-date ICT skills, library staff need 'social skills' and 'book knowledge' (LNI15), and they need customer engagement skills to promote library stock and to be able to help users find the books and the information that they need. Thus, the multifaceted role of library staff at the ground level is changing, which makes understanding what information poverty is and the role public libraries play in addressing it even more significant.

Illuminating the main factors and the changing role of library staff can enable strategists and policymakers to put in place practical measures that can improve library services, for instance, more training to assist library users and awareness sessions so that staff understand how to assist diverse clientele with their information needs. In short, library staff need ongoing training to assist the public in using new technologies – ICT skills; social media (Facebook, Twitter); digital photography; mobile phone technologies; iPads – to equip them with the skills to tackle digital exclusion. Public library staff should also be trained to support learning, for example, a basic level of literacy and information and digital literacy skills. In addition, as public service organisations, libraries rely on customers for survival; excellent customer service and an improved customer experience are therefore fundamental. Libraries need to promote the uniqueness of their services and seek new customers by more effectively promoting awareness and marketing. In essence, libraries need to create a customer experience that makes people choose libraries rather than other information providers.

5.8 CONCLUSIONS

The primary focus of this chapter was to demonstrate how public libraries at the macro level can develop and implement strategies to support government agendas to alleviate digital and social exclusion. Public libraries, which are an important element of a country's information infrastructure, have a key role to play in reducing information poverty. The UK government's Digital by Default agenda to address digital exclusion and the role that has been bestowed upon public libraries to support citizens to access online information was discussed. To enable public libraries to alleviate information poverty, they should work at a strategic level with other organisations and government bodies by developing partnerships and sharing resources to reduce digital exclusion. The examples provided here demonstrated how public libraries in Northern Ireland worked strategically with other organisations and government bodies to develop partnerships to reduce digital exclusion. The data highlighted the role that public libraries play in contributing to government agendas, such as ameliorating poverty and social exclusion. In addition, the skills that public library staff need to engage with marginalised groups within socially deprived areas and to support digitally and socially excluded members of society in their attempts to access information were discussed.

The next chapter continues the macro-level discussion by outlining how public libraries can contribute to wider agendas to support learning and to develop the literacy and information and digital literacy skills needed to participate and succeed in society.

CHAPTER 6

Information Poverty at the Macro Level: Part 2

6.1 INTRODUCTION

Chapter 5 began by discussing how information poverty at the macro level was related to wider ethical, economic, infrastructural, technological and political issues. This chapter considers how public libraries contribute to wider European agendas to support learning and facilitate access to information for social and digital inclusion. The chapter outlines how government agendas for lifelong learning are reflected in public library strategies and services. The role of libraries in developing literacy, improving information and communication technology (ICT) and information literacy skills is discussed.

6.2 LIFELONG LEARNING AND PUBLIC LIBRARIES

Adult learning is firmly on the European political agenda, with a focus on 'raising skills levels, reducing social exclusion, promoting active citizenship and supporting employability' (Davies and Butters, 2008: 137). The European Union's learning strategy emphasises the 'use of ICT for lifelong learning and social inclusion' (Davies and Butters, 2008: 137). Public libraries have a role in supporting strategic agendas for learning and increasing the number of qualified and skilled people in Europe (Davies and Butters, 2008: 139). As Ferguson (2012: 28) confirms, the European Union's Public Libraries in the Learning Society project was 'designed to improve information literacy and active citizenship among adults, especially those in danger of being excluded from the Information society'. Eve et al. (2007: 394) acknowledge that 'lifelong learning has become one of the major policy goals of Western governments'. As part of the European Union's learning strategy, public libraries are seen by governments as important to supporting lifelong learning (Eve et al., 2007: 396). Wider macro-level strategies for learning and for supporting digital and social exclusion are reflected in public library policies and services aimed at facilitating access to information and to developing

Overcoming Information Poverty
ISBN 978-0-08-101110-2

the literacy and information and digital literacy skills of citizens. One interviewee commented that 'lifelong learning is what libraries have always been about' (LNI6). Consequently, public libraries have a key role to play in providing facilities for and developing strategies to encourage learning, reading and literacy skills for all ages and sections of society.

Macro-level interviewees commented that facilitating lifelong learning through early learning activities, school visits, and targeted programmes for adults and the elderly contributes to the learning society and reduces information poverty at various stages of people's lives. Libraries NI was trying to work with families – through outreach and encouraging family reading – to break cycles of deprivation. Moreover, they explained that for those who have had a bad experience of formal education, libraries can fill a gap in their learning because of their informal approaches and their welcoming environment. Typically, interviewees cited strategic partnerships to promote lifelong learning, for instance, with the University of the Third Age for older people. One interviewee observed that this partnership has 'proved a very powerful tool for promoting lifelong learning' (LNI8). This partnership aims to use the shared goals of both organisations to improve access to information and learning for older adults.

As well as having personal computers (PCs) and Internet access, literacy skill is arguably the most influential indicator of information poverty. Improving literacy has always been at the core of public library services, and therefore public libraries have a major role to play in developing literacy skills in society.

6.3 SUPPORTING LEARNING: DEVELOPING LITERACY SKILLS

Key indicators of information poverty are the levels of literacy, educational attainment and ICT skills within countries and communities. Improving literacy skills is therefore fundamental to alleviating information poverty. Literacy involves reading, writing and communicating, and has undoubtedly the greatest impact on information poverty because it is the main factor that seems to affect all others. There was an acknowledgment among the macro-level interviewees that educational attainment and literacy are major factors contributing to information poverty. One interviewee stressed that basic literacy skills were 'a gate-way to other information' (LNI4). Indeed, a lack of literacy skills can lead to poor ICT skills because the former are needed to interpret and understand information and for using a computer: 'if you cannot read and write effectively you cannot use a PC' (Hendry, 2000: 333). Consequently, poor literacy can affect other aspects of people's lives, such as their economic and social circumstances. It is often the case that the poorly educated have poor literacy abilities, which affect their subsequent ability to use and benefit from ICT. Ultimately, illiteracy can affect an individual's ability to fill in printed and online forms, which can restrict his or her capacity to apply for jobs and access online government services, which in turn can restrict their opportunities for employment and social engagement. Poor literacy can also lead to feelings of inadequacy and disempowerment, as well as exclusion from society, and can exacerbate an individual's chances of escaping poverty. Public libraries have always had a traditional role in improving literacy skills among the educationally and socially disadvantaged by providing access to books and printed information. An interviewee observed that a key role for libraries was to 'help the less literate' (LNI5). Importantly, access to information can be prevented because of the complexity of the language used. Therefore public libraries should provide information in a way that individuals who have poor literacy skills can understand.

As is explained in the sections that follow, in modern society the proliferation of ICTs and the Internet means that the development of literacy skills goes hand in hand with the development of other literacies, such as information and digital literacy. The next section considers literacy levels in Northern Ireland to highlight an area that public libraries can contribute to developing.

6.3.1 Literacy Levels in Northern Ireland

In 2011, 24% of usual residents aged 16 years and over in Northern Ireland had achieved level 4 or higher qualifications, whereas – significantly – 29% had no qualifications (Census 2011: Key Statistics for Northern Ireland). In 2013 an Organisation for Economic Cooperation and Development (OECD) survey tested the literacy, numeracy and problem-solving skills of more than 150,000 adults aged 16–65 years in 25 countries. The report indicated that while the percentage of Northern Ireland's adults aged 16–65 performing at level 1 or below in literacy fell from 23% in 1996 to 18% in 2013, literacy rates in Northern Ireland were still below the OECD average. Interestingly, England and Northern Ireland were among the three highest-performing countries in literacy when comparing 55- to 65-year-olds, but they were among the bottom three countries when comparing literacy proficiency among 16- to 24-year-olds (OECD Skills Outlook First Results from the Survey of Adult Skills, 2013). Moreover, it indicates a worrying decline in

Table 6.1 Northern Ireland findings of the Organisation for Economic Cooperation and Development literacy, numeracy and problem solving skills survey (2013)

- The percentage of Northern Ireland adults aged 16–65 years performing at level 1 or below in literacy[a] fell from 23% in 1996 to 18%.
- Overall, the trend between the International Adult Literacy Survey and the International Survey of Adult Skills is more positive for Northern Ireland than for many other countries that participated in both surveys. Only Poland, Italy, Australia and England showed significant increases in literacy scores since 1996.
- Northern Ireland's literacy levels were higher than those in France, Italy and Spain. A number of countries, including England, Denmark, Germany and the Republic of Ireland, had literacy levels that were broadly the same as those for Northern Ireland.
- Those who earn the most in Northern Ireland are also those with the highest level literacy, numeracy or problem-solving skills.
- Those adults with lower levels of educational attainment perform less well on literacy, numeracy and problem solving.
- Northern Ireland's numeracy levels were below the Organisation for Economic Cooperation and Development average; however, they were significantly better than those in the United States, France, Italy and Spain.
- Northern Ireland's performance in problem-solving skills in a technology-rich environment was below the Organisation for Economic Cooperation and Development average.

[a]These are the lowest levels of literacy proficiency; level 5 is the highest.
Adapted from Northern Ireland Executive, 2013. Literacy Levels of Adults Improving in Northern Ireland. Available from: http://www.northernireland.gov.uk/news-del-081013-literacy-levels-in (accessed 13.08.14).

literacy among younger adults, who are entering the job market. Table 6.1 presents the key findings of the OECD survey in relation to Northern Ireland. It clearly demonstrates the need for information poverty indicators to be used not just within the context of public libraries, but at a national level.

The next section considers the importance of reading, which is at the heart of public libraries.

6.3.2 Literacy, Developing Readers and Supporting Families

Public libraries have a key role to play in improving literacy standards across society, and they can support literacy skills development from an early age. To help alleviate information poverty, public libraries should work at a strategic level with other organisations, educational bodies and government bodies to develop partnerships to improve literacy standards. Public libraries could improve literacy rates across society, within communities or among groups by targeting specific areas and groups and developing more services, stock and training tailored to those with basic skills. Typically, interviewees placed a strong emphasis on the importance of reading, the underlying principle behind libraries, in alleviating information poverty. One interviewee claimed that Libraries NI 'want[s] to promote the benefits of reading and information' and 'the role and value of libraries' (LNI5). Furthermore, Libraries NI's Business Plan, 2014/2015 states that 'Reading and the development and enhancement of literacy skills are central' to 'addressing social exclusion' (Libraries NI, 2014: 6). It also notes that 'Support will be provided for those with poorer literacy skills through targeted programmes and specialist reading material' (Libraries NI, 2014: 7). An interviewee noted the therapeutic and educational benefits of reading: 'Reading can reduce stress and it is a very calming[,] relaxing activity. It can still the mind and quieten the mind' (LNI4). In addition, reading improves spelling, grammar, basic literacy and 'world knowledge' (LNI4).

Across all branch libraries in Northern Ireland there is a strong focus on developing library services for children and encouraging library usage and a love of reading from an early age. As part of Libraries NI's strategic priority, 'Support for Learners', early literacy skills are being targeted. Services aimed at children and young people are a core priority because 'early interventions' help improve literacy and break 'the cycle of deprivation and educational underachievement' (Libraries NI, 2014: 4). To develop reading from an early age, public libraries have strategic partnerships with Bookstart[1] and Sure Start for early literacy and reader development. The focus of Sure Start is combating social exclusion and child poverty through partnerships; public libraries play a significant role in this by encouraging a home learning environment (Goulding, 2006: 273). An interviewee from the Department of Culture, Arts and Leisure (DCAL) claimed that Sure Start was a highly 'valued' service in 'difficult to reach communities' (DCAL1). It is argued by library strategists that when public libraries improve the literacy skills of very young children, they start a process that can contribute to the

---

[1] "Bookstart is a national scheme offering free books to every child. The Bookstart baby pack is usually delivered to families by their Health Visitor or other health professional, before the baby's first year. The bag usually includes two board books, a rhyme sheet and a booklet of tips and ideas for sharing books.' Available from: http://www.bookstart.org.uk/about/packs/
Unfortunately, in March 2015 that Northern Ireland government funding would be cut and Book Trust are looking for alternative partners. Northern Ireland is now the only UK region without a bookgifting scheme, but efforts are being made to find alternative funding to ensure that children do not miss out on the benefits that books can bring'. Available from: 'http://www.bookstart.org.uk/about/northern-ireland/

government's anti-poverty strategy. With programmes such as Rhythm and Rhyme, public libraries can introduce pre-school children to the library and a positive learning environment, which can enhance the early cognitive development, language and literacy skills of pre-school children. Regular story time sessions in libraries also encourage learning, reading and the development of literacy skills. One interviewee explained that by developing 'early learning skills' through Rhythm and Rhyme, public libraries begin to 'break cycles of deprivation' (LNI6). Another interviewee explained that with pre-school activities public libraries can introduce children to literacy and information literacy skills, which will, it is hoped, improve their vocabulary when they go to school, and ultimately help children perform better academically (LNI10). Hence, when public libraries aim to develop literacy and information literacy skills among children from an early age, they can make a significant contribution to reducing information poverty during future development.

Interviewees typically noted that outreach and community engagement were necessary to promote library services, promote the positive aspects of reading, increase library usage and encourage family reading. Promoting libraries as informal learning places and changing the 'perception that people have of learning' was fundamental (LNI6). One interviewee made an important comment that through community engagement the library service was trying to support families to address 'that increasing circle where young children who have poor education and life experiences, become young parents who have children who are in that non-ending cycle' of poverty and low educational attainment (LNI9). This cycle can often prevail within socioeconomically deprived communities. The same interviewee argued that it is essential that public libraries provide more support for parents to develop literacy and numeracy skills so that they in turn can 'support their children' to end the 'cycle' of low literacy and low educational attainment (LNI9). This interviewee stated that with library outreach they were trying to break down attitudes and address the poverty of aspiration by 'making reading a family activity' and encouraging library usage (LNI9). Evidently, public libraries have a role in changing aspirations of those in socially deprived communities by promoting the value of informal education, learning and reading and providing the resources and support necessary to access information.

Macro-level interviewees commented that public libraries can make a difference within disadvantaged areas by encouraging usage of libraries and introducing families to the importance of reading and learning. A DCAL interviewee suggested that some parents in socially deprived areas do not understand why reading and learning are 'important' for their children's development (DCAL1). This interviewee asserted that libraries have a role in developing and promoting early education by (1) encouraging learning and improving 'reading and information skills', (2) promoting the value of family reading and library use and (3) 'socialising' pre-school children and acclimatising young children in the learning environment by mixing with other children and responding to authority (DCAL1). Importantly, they observed that libraries need more outreach in 'a more engaged, subtle and sympathetic way' to 'tailor things' to the needs of people living in socially deprived areas (DCAL1). As well as pre-school development, other children's services (e.g. visits to primary schools) allow public libraries to help develop at an early age the information literacy skills needed to search for and use information, as well as a love of reading and an interest in libraries.

While libraries in Northern Ireland have class visit programmes with local primary schools, I have found that it is important to maintain these links with secondary school pupils. Developing links and engaging with the secondary sector to encourage reading and use of libraries among children aged 11 years and older is essential for public libraries. Class visits to post-primary schools, could encourage teenagers to use libraries more and reinforce the value of using library resources. This would enable libraries to continue the contact which they previously established with children when they were at primary school. In addition, libraries could do more to engage with teenagers and support this demographic with reading initiatives, study support and career guidance. This was acknowledged by one interviewee, who explained that libraries 'needed to forge more of a link with secondary schools so students are aware they can come in and do research' and use library resources such as study guides (TSE2). This interviewee stated that there could be more engagement with General Certificate of Secondary Education[2] and A-level[3] students to 'show them what they can do when they come into the library' (TSE2). Public libraries need to engage with secondary school pupils at various times – for instance, in the first year and later stages of their schooling, such as when beginning General Certificate of Secondary Education and A-level exams. These interventions would

---

[2] General Certificate of Secondary Education (also called GCSE) is a qualification received by pupils aged 14–16 years in secondary schools in England, Wales and Northern Ireland.
[3] General Certificate of Education A-levels are qualifications students must achieve to leave school. They are exams taken over 2 years, offered by educational bodies in the United Kingdom, and are usually completed at 18 years of age.

remind them of the benefits of reading and of using their local libraries and the resources available to them. Through continual engagement with teenagers and reinforcing what libraries can do to help them, public libraries may be able to narrow the disconnection this demographic can often have with libraries and reading. Teenagers are in a transitional period when they are either embracing further education or seeking employment, and it is essential that public libraries engage with them, provide relevant resources and create learning and social spaces that welcome them. Arguably, students who leave school could be targeted more successfully by providing support to develop skills and improving stock to obtain jobs or enter further education. This was acknowledged by an interviewee who suggested that those of the 'young adult age', who are 'notoriously difficult to target', were a group that libraries should be looking at more (TSE1).

This was recognised in the BLM survey with 40.9% (9) of respondents citing 'Teenager's as a demographic that could be targeted more effectively. Because of low participation of teenagers, two BLMs considered this group as hard-to-reach. To engage teenagers, one respondent contacted "local schools and community groups" and invited them "to various events in the library" (BLM3). One BLM made a poignant comment about how their library targeted teenagers, specifically in relation to health and wellbeing, and tackling the issue of teenage suicides:

> ...I have delivered a Teenage Health Fair with other partners...targeted at Year 10 + 11's in post primary education to give them health and wellbeing information that they could need in the future and was developed in response to the high teen suicide rate in the area: (BLM7)

Forbes et al. (2012: 7) note that "compared with the Republic of Ireland, England, Scotland and Wales, the suicide rate in Northern Ireland in 2010 was highest for both males and females". Thus, the quotation by the BLM demonstrates how the library's information provision contributes to wider societal benefits and to government objectives to tackle suicide. Developing events which reflect community and societal concerns are paramount to enhance the library's social impact. However, potential exists to do more to engage with teenagers and support this demographic with reading initiatives, study support and careers guidance. Research conducted by Reilly (2012) recommended that a strategy be drawn up specifically for teenagers and a "teen advisory board" should be established, similar to initiatives in the US. Reilly (2012: 83) suggested that "library services and facilities for teenagers need to be marketed specifically to this age group." Furthermore, "marketing" to teenagers could "involve outreach to the places where teenagers already spend time, such as schools and youth centres" (ibid, 83).

Evidence of library outreach to families in socially deprived areas was provided in the data collected from the survey of library managers and in the interviews with community engagement staff, which are discussed in more detail in Chapters 8 and 9.

6.3.3 Supporting Literacy: The Role of Public Library Staff

Public libraries need to be continually adapting and evolving to meet the changing needs of their users and potential users. In addition, they need to channel their resources in the most effective ways so that they can develop the literacy, information literacy and ICT skills of local communities. I believe that in the future public library staff could have a key role in delivering skills training to groups in areas of need, either in partnership with other groups or by trained library staff themselves. The public librarian's role as teacher was debated with library staff in Northern Ireland. While community engagement staff recognised that there was a desire for the library service to provide literacy support for parents, this was not fully supported by the interviewees, who questioned the role of library staff as potential trainers. For instance, one interviewee commented that the leaders of after-school and children's groups wanted them 'to speak to parents to raise their awareness of the library service' and to provide 'some literacy support…for the parents' (TSE1). While library staff can explain what library services are available (books, ICT, Internet), the 'actual literacy thing' is something that the library service currently does not have (TSE1). This interviewee queried why libraries provide ICT skills assistance, but not basic literacy support:

> *It seems strange that we are offering the ICT skills, but not the basic literacy skills. I can understand why we are offering ICT, but that should be alongside the literacy, it shouldn't be on its own[,] the literacy should be in there.*
>
> *TSE1*

Similarly, another interviewee stated that 'quite a few groups' asked 'us about teaching literacy to parents' who 'have very poor literacy skills' in order to improve their ability to assist their children with reading and schoolwork (TSE2). However, this interviewee was reluctant to commit to the library staff's role as teachers of literacy because it would require 'training staff to teacher level', arguing that they 'would be very wary of that' since library staff may not teach literacy correctly (TSE2). The interviewee concluded that they did not think 'staff could be trained' to teach basic literacy to parents of young children, but that the library could sign post people to other organisations that could help to provide basic literacy skills support or that work in partnership with other essential skills providers (TSE2). The responses echoed comments from the macro-level interviewees about what libraries and librarians can and cannot be expected to do. For example, a macro-level interviewee explained that libraries are 'not teaching literacy skills' but were 'sign posting' people to appropriate materials (LNI12). Another observed that, 'when it comes to children', libraries can do a lot, and with adults they can ensure there is 'appropriate stock'; however, it is 'not part of our strict remit' and 'not our core business' to teach basic literacy skills (LNI8).

These responses highlight the challenges facing library staff when considering the changing roles and expectations being placed on them. While basic literacy support was deemed important, the interviewees were not united on Libraries NI's capacity or responsibility to deliver it. What is clear is that there may be a need for public libraries in Northern Ireland to re-evaluate their role, learn from other locations and adapt their services to meet the needs of local communities. A possible answer is that when library staff deliver ICT training, such as the Got IT and Go ON programmes, they coordinate this with information literacy and basic literacy skills development. Thus, to improve their capacity to address information poverty, specific library services could be developed, and existing services modified, to include literacy as well as ICT skills. Moreover, these could be targeted towards specific groups in need of library support.

In the branch library manager survey, literacy was recognised as an area that public libraries could develop more in disadvantaged areas. Library managers were asked to rank (from 1 to 7) the areas they thought libraries should be developing more (see Fig. 6.1 below). By using a ranking question, I was looking for the statistically lowest option, where lower numbers mean higher rank. The most important area was improving adult literacy skills, scoring an average of 3.1. This was followed by improving ICT skills (3.4) and improving information literacy skills (3.6). While these figures illustrate data collected within Northern Ireland, I question whether the responses to a similar survey distributed in public libraries in other countries would be similar.

As the findings of the Northern Ireland study demonstrate, addressing basic literacy skills should be prioritised and developed more within public libraries, which should encourage more strategic and community-level partnerships to target literacy. I believe that public libraries could do more to target those with basic or limited literacy skills and to put more financial and staff resources into this. To tackle poverty and social exclusion

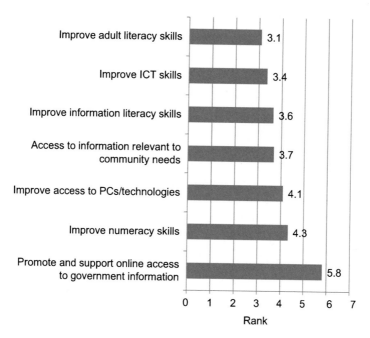

Figure 6.1 Average rankings of skills and access that libraries could develop more in disadvantaged areas. *ICT,* Information and communication technology; *PC,* personal computer.

more successfully, public libraries should develop strategies for reader development, focusing on enhancing the literacy skills of those most in need. For instance, Pateman and Williment (2013: 131) observe that 'reader development provides public libraries with a unique opportunity to tackle social exclusion by enabling people to gain' essential skills. They suggest that book stock should reflect the needs of local communities and excluded people by actively engaging with 'local people, finding out what they want and need' (Pateman and Williment, 2013: 131). In the data from the library manager survey, just over a quarter (27.3%; $n = 6$) cited 'book clubs/reading groups' as an engagement strategy. As part of reader development, reading groups encourage learning and social engagement. Most libraries now have reading groups for adults, children and/or teenagers[4]; however, they need to be promoted more. For instance, the Continuous Household Survey (2013: 18) noted that less than a third of people knew that public libraries provide 'reading groups (30%)' or 'events/exhibitions

[4] Currently, Libraries NI supports over 90 adult reading groups and 62 reading groups for children (Libraries NI, 2013).

(27%)'. Reading groups are welcome, but they generally cater to users who are comfortable reading. Obviously, more time and resources could be distributed to those most in need of literacy, ICT and information literacy support.

While libraries provide basic literacy stock for adults, such as Quick Reads, staff could do more to develop literacy skills. As mentioned earlier, the OECD (2013) survey testing literacy, numeracy and problem-solving skills revealed that, while the percentage of Northern Ireland's adults aged 16–65 years performing at level 1 or below in literacy fell from 23% in 1996 to 18% in 2013, literacy rates in Northern Ireland are still below the OECD average. In light of this report, there are huge implications for public libraries in terms of addressing skills deficits. Specifically, it indicates that public libraries could identify the groups within the population who need assistance with literacy and target them, such as young people in Northern Ireland who need targeted interventions to improve their literacy and ICT skills and their employability skills. I argue that a greater emphasis could be placed on promoting reading for adults with basic skills and designing adult literacy classes, possibly in partnership with other organisations.

The next section discusses language as a factor that creates information poverty and the role that public libraries can play in contributing to more culturally inclusive societies.

6.4 PUBLIC LIBRARIES AND CULTURAL INCLUSION

Language is also a macro-level factor that can impede information access and lead to information poverty. Britz (2004: 196) believes that because most ICT formats and interactions are in the English language, developing, indigenous communities are excluded and alienated from using the information technology; this means that 'these communities are increasingly dependent on the information rich for access to and interpretation of information.' Kim and Kim (2001: 89) state that:

> Language is increasingly becoming a determining factor in the widening information media accessibility gap among non-English speaking countries as well as between information-rich countries and information poor countries.

Language can therefore be a barrier that leads to information poverty in terms of ICT usage, interpretation and application. Language is not only a barrier between countries; it can also be a barrier to accessing information in multicultural societies. For example, language is often a barrier for newcomers or ethnic minorities living within a predominantly English-speaking society, such as ethnic minorities within the United Kingdom and the Republic of Ireland. Furthermore, language can be a barrier to accessing information, since information online is predominantly presented in English. For immigrants with poor literacy, 'language barriers create difficulties in adapting to a new community and new culture psychologically and socially', and the 'role of the library is irreplaceable in welcoming and instructing immigrants and reducing information poverty for marginalised immigrant groups' (Shen, 2013: 6). Thompson (2007: 96) also highlights the librarian's role as gatekeeper, acting 'as a link to the larger information society' by delivering important information to those who do not speak English. By identifying areas where there is a large ethnic mix, public libraries can design services to improve information access for non-English speakers. For instance, Shrem (2012) noted how public libraries in New York developed programmes to target English-language learners.

Importantly, multicultural awareness training is needed for library staff so that they know the barriers customers may face when using libraries (cultural, language, awareness of services) and accessing the information they need. Staff may also need to develop skills to enable them to assist with teaching basic language and literacy; for example, it may be beneficial to consider having basic English classes in libraries to help ethnic minorities. These could be presented by library staff, volunteers within communities or in partnership with community organisations and trainers. In doing this public libraries can play an important role in alleviating the information poverty of minority groups. As well, in predominantly English-speaking societies, public libraries should be equipped with stock to enable minorities to learn English language skills themselves and to help their children learn. Library interventions should be based on identified needs, building the demographic profiles of minority groups and working in partnership with ethnic organisations.

Public libraries have an important role in supporting cultural and social inclusion by providing access to the Internet and printed sources for immigrants, and providing the knowledgeable support to help them seek employment opportunities and access e-government information. As one interviewee explained, ethnic minorities and migrants are increasingly using library services to develop English language skills, taking advantage of 'free access' to ICT and the Internet and 'a link to their homes' (LNI2). With society becoming more culturally diverse, public libraries need to ensure that the information needs of minority groups are met. Furthermore, a challenge for public libraries is encouraging the adults and children with minority backgrounds to use the library to develop English language skills, use library resources and become involved and integrated within local communities.

In 2011 minority ethnic groups made up 1.8% (32,400) of the usually resident population of Northern Ireland, which was more than double the proportion in 2001 (0.8%) (Census 2011: Key Statistics). Ethnic minorities were cited by almost one-third of survey respondents (31.8%; $n = 7$) as a demographic that public libraries in Northern Ireland could target more effectively. Public libraries can engage with ethnic minorities and raise awareness of library services. For example, one interviewee described how they developed a partnership with a local migrant centre; this involved inviting the centre's manager for a library tour and promoting different language books and materials on 'how to learn English' (TSE3). Another initiative with an ethnic minority group set up a reading group to 'learn English' for 'speakers of another language' (TSE3). Similarly, outreach to the Polish community involved going to 'an ethnic mums and tots' group and delivering Rhythm and Rhyme to them which illustrates how libraries can support the development of language and literacy skills (TSE3). This interviewee commented that minority groups were often keen for their children to 'use the library' to develop their English language and literacy skills, but 'maybe not so much for themselves' (TSE3). As society becomes increasingly multicultural, it is important that libraries have the stock to support minorities, for example, appropriate books for children and adults to acquire basic English language skills. Moreover, library staff need to have the listening skills and patience, along with the emotional awareness, to understand the frustration that English language barriers can create for non-English speakers.

Developing information literacy skills for ethnic minorities and migrants is an area in which public libraries have growing role to play. Kennan et al. (2011: 194) state that for newcomers attempting to settle into a new society, information overload[5] – where too much information which is often irrelevant and lacking quality – can 'result in a sense of social exclusion' as a result of the 'overwhelming amounts of unnecessary information'. Information literacy is 'often prescribed as the main antidote to information overload' (Goulding, 2001: 110–11). Because information overload can affect any member of society, people need the information literacy skills to be able to sift through information and evaluate what is important to them. By developing information literacy skills, libraries can provide individuals with the

---

[5] The term 'information overload' 'first came to prominence in the 1990s, with a series of reports showing the waste of time, decrease in efficiency, and even ill-health, allegedly caused by information overload' (Bawden and Robinson, 2012: 243).

necessary skills to evaluate and interpret useful information, and thus reduce information overload. The expected role of public libraries in developing the information literacy skills of citizens is discussed in the following section.

6.5 INFORMATION LITERACY SKILLS AND PUBLIC LIBRARIES

The Alexandria Proclamation (2005), a report that emerged from a high-level international colloquium on lifelong learning and information literacy, organised by UNESCO, the International Federation of Library Associations and Institutions (IFLA) and the National Forum on Information Literacy (Garner, 2005: 1), requested that governments and government agencies, such as libraries, pursue policies and programmes to promote information literacy and lifelong learning (Ferguson, 2012: 27). According to the Alexandria Proclamation, to be information literate an individual must be able to:

- recognise his or her information needs
- locate and evaluate the quality of information
- store and retrieve information
- make effective and ethical use of information
- apply information to create and communicate knowledge (Catts and Lau, 2008: 7).

The Alexandria Proclamation defined information literacy as a human right and essential for social inclusion:

Information Literacy lies at the core of lifelong learning. It empowers people in all walks of life to seek, evaluate, use and create information effectively to achieve their personal, social, occupational and educational goals. It is a basic human right in a digital world and promotes social inclusion of all nations.

IFLA[6]

At a policy and strategy level, information literacy is now a key priority area for the UK's Chartered Institute of Librarians and Information Professionals (CILIP); they are 'committed to promote the importance of 'information literacy and digital inclusion within the learning environment' (CILIP)'The link for this is: http://www.cilip.org.uk/advocacy-campaigns-awards/advocacy-campaigns/information-literacy/information-literacy-project-2013/information-literacy-project-overview'.[7] The important role

[6] See IFLA, 2005. Beacons of the Information Society: The Alexandria Proclamation on Information Literacy and Lifelong Learning. Available from: http://www.ifla.org/publications/beacons-of-the-information-society-the-alexandria-proclamation-on-information-literacy.

[7] See CILIP Information Literacy. Available from: http://www.cilip.org.uk/get-involved/advocacy/information-literacy/pages/default.aspx.

of librarians in teaching information literacy is also highlighted by IFLA (2006).[8] Feather (2008: 185) observes that in recent years the role of the librarian and information professionals, in all sectors, has been in a state of transition, and they are increasingly needed as trainers in ICT and information skills, as well as information providers. In addition to providing ICT access and supporting the development of ICT skills, many authors have noted the public library's role in supporting information literacy (Eve et al., 2007; Haider and Bawden, 2007; Harding, 2008; O'Beirne, 2010; Buckley-Owen, 2011; Lai, 2011; Ferguson, 2012; Crawford and Irving, 2012). Because information literacy is linked to lifelong learning, it can contribute to social capital (Ferguson, 2012: 24): 'the development of information literate communities and the targeting of specific community groups' are 'two specific strategies that are central to the role of public libraries as potential developers of social capital' (Ferguson, 2012: 26). Librarians themselves need an understanding of information literacy (O'Beirne, 2010: 128). Moreover, 'information literacy training skills must be embedded in staff development' (Crawford and Irving, 2012: 88). Lai (2011: 82) concurs that library staff, as well as customers, should develop their own information literacy skills.

To support information literacy, public libraries should work in partnership with other organisations, schools, information service providers and local communities (Lai, 2011: 86). Lai (2011) outlines four important guidelines when developing information literacy training in the public libraries: (1) developing an advanced ICT infrastructure; (2) providing formal information literacy training courses; (3) improving library staff's information literacy and teaching skills and (4) building partnerships with local organisations (Lai, 2011: 86). Furthermore, Lai argues that library staff should see themselves as teachers of ICT and information literacy, and they need to keep their own ICT skills up to date. In addition, information literacy skills are essential to overcome information poverty and to avoid social exclusion. The Libraries Inspire report (2011: 29), which describes the strategic development framework for Welsh libraries, states that the 'levels of information literacy within the population can impact on the economy of a country, the educational attainment of its learners and the social inclusion of its citizens' (Llywodraeth Cymru Welsh Government, 2011: 29). Information literacy is fundamental to educational attainment; therefore public libraries should develop a strategy for information literacy to ameliorate social exclusion. Public libraries need to create strategies that define what information literacy is and how they intend to address it with specific services and training.

[8] See IFLA Information Literacy. Available from: http://www.ifla.org/information-literacy.

If libraries are to be effective in overcoming information poverty, they need to establish strategies to improve information literacy. Using the macro, meso and micro framework presented here, public libraries could develop plans and implement programmes to develop information literacy. Information literacy is a key priority for UNESCO and CILIP, and it should be a priority at a strategic level for all libraries worldwide. At the macro level, by establishing strategies and partnerships with other educational institutions to address information literacy, public libraries could further advance their capacity to develop skills and ameliorate social exclusion. This multiagency approach at the strategic and community levels, where each is interdependent on the other, could be the most effective way of addressing information literacy and information poverty. Hence, at the meso level, tailored programmes could be designed and delivered within communities to develop information literacy, perhaps through partnerships with community organisations or by trained library staff.

6.5.1 Information Literacy: Perspectives From Macro-Level Interviewees

Four of the 15 macro-level interviewees cited information literacy as a factor leading to information poverty. This indicates that not all staff at the macro level were able to give examples of how library services were addressing information literacy. This also provides evidence that Libraries NI does not currently have an information literacy policy. Throughout the interviews I sensed that the actual terms 'information literacy' and 'information poverty' were not well used within Libraries NI, although the concepts were understood by the interviewees. Furthermore, Libraries NI does not have a specific policy detailing how it intends to address either of these concepts. Two interviewees from Libraries NI, however, specifically stated that information poverty was being addressed through a strategic priority called 'Access to Information' (LNI6 and LNI11). One of these interviewees explained that Libraries NI does not 'call it information poverty[,] we call it access to information. It permeates so much of what we do' (LNI6). Information poverty and information literacy were seemingly understood, but the terminology used by Libraries NI is different, acknowledging that it is being addressed through 'Access to Information'.

When asked about addressing information literacy, interviewees typically mentioned partnerships with Health in Mind and government departments such as the Department of Employment and Learning (DEL) and the Department of Agriculture and Rural Development. Information literacy was also being addressed by programmes such as Go ON and Got IT, which 'are about evaluating information' as well as ICT skills (LNI8). Similarly, Libraries NI presents workshops that deliver access to, for example, genealogy ('Ancestry Library Edition') to develop information and digital literacy skills in using particular resources (LNI8). Three interviewees mentioned the class visit programmes which involve both primary school children visiting the library to learn about library resources and where library staff go out to schools to promote library services and encourage a love of reading, as addressing information literacy.

To reduce information poverty, public libraries can share best practices and learn from other information literacy training initiatives. Eve et al. (2007) found that public libraries had a role to play in supporting ICT and information literacy skills of disadvantaged adults. They detailed two Danish projects: first, the 'Barefoot Librarian' in Vejle, which delivers information literacy skills training for ethnic minorities, and second, the learning centre in the Arhus library, where the emphasis was 'less on fostering ICT skills, and more on providing training in information literacy skills' (398). Similarly, Platt (2012) explained that public libraries in New York play a role in information literacy, especially during difficult economic times, for example, helping those who speak English as a second language and in creating curricula vitae. Shen (2013: 6) also observed that public libraries in New York deliver English-language literacy programmes and work in partnership with health organisations to deliver 'coping skills' workshops for immigrants. Shen (2013: 9) argues that:

> ...public libraries as an educational, cultural, and social institution must shape and reshape their priorities to address the policies and services in reducing information poverty for urban immigrants and other marginalized groups...to maximize the equality in people's opportunities and abilities to retrieve information for a better life and future.

Shrem (2012) also detailed the positive impact New York public libraries were having to address information poverty among students and lifelong learners. New York libraries developed a range of initiatives, including information and digital literacy support; for example, their *Broadbandexpress@yourlibrary* provides access to those lacking a broadband Internet connection by increasing opening hours, increasing the number of computer workstations and creating mobile labs to bring broadband to remote areas.

Information literacy skills are a prerequisite to digital literacy skills, which are discussed in the following section.

6.6 DIGITAL LITERACY

This section focuses on the digital literacy skills needed to succeed in modern society and the role of public libraries in developing these. To succeed in modern society, information and digital literacy skills are arguably as important as basic reading, writing and numeracy skills. Jaeger et al. (2012: 3) explain that digital literacy encompasses:

- the skills and abilities to access the digital infrastructure
- an understanding of the language and component hardware and software required to navigate the technology
- an individual's ability to locate, evaluate and use digital information – both technologies (computers) and services (e-mail)

In the seminal book *Digital Literacy*, Paul Gilster (1997) describes digital literacy as 'the ability to understand and use information in multiple formats from a wide range of sources when it is presented via a computer'. Gilster suggests that in modern society 'the skills of the digitally literate are becoming as necessary as a driver's license', and that surviving in the increasingly digital environment requires digital literacy skills. Importantly, Gilster (1997) comments that when 'acquiring digital literacy for Internet use' the most 'essential' competency 'is the ability to make informed judgments about what you find on-line'. This point was reflected in the following comment by an interviewee about the lack of digital and information literacy skills among young people:

> *...even though we say all the young people nowadays can or do have digital literacy, they really don't[; many] of them don't or they can use text speak on their phone but they maybe aren't very good at searching for information or knowing what information they have[,] whether it is actually accredited information.*
>
> *LNI4*

Evidently, information literacy skills are part of the skills required to be considered digitally literate. Digital literacy is now recognised as 'a keystone for civic engagement, educational success, and economic growth and innovation' (Clark and Visser, 2011: 39). The term 'digital literacy' gained popularity in the 1990s and evolved from the concept of the digital divide (Jaeger et al., 2012: 5). Improving the digital literacy skills of citizens can help develop the wider economy because they can contribute as a member of a skilled workforce. In modern society, those lacking in digital literacy skills are at a disadvantage when seeking employment in many areas that require the ability to use a computer. A 2015 survey by the digital skills charity Go ON UK highlighted a serious problem in modern society, whereby 23% of UK adults do not have the 'basic digital skills' needed to complete online tasks such as safely carrying out transactions or avoiding malicious websites. Go ON UK's chief executive officer, Rachel Neaman, referred to a 'digital skills crisis', and that the 'lack of basic digital skills' among UK residents would 'continue to hold back economic growth, productivity and social mobility'. In addition, the Internet entrepreneur Baroness Martha Lane-Fox (2015) argued that the lack of digital literacy skills was 'hurting the country'. Helsper (2015) described the lack of basic digital literacy skills and access in already disadvantaged areas as likely to increase inequality of opportunity around the United Kingdom.[9] The importance of developing the digital infrastructure of countries and the digital skills of citizens is fundamental for wider social and economic growth. Thompson et al. (2014: 75) observe that digital literacy skills are needed for inclusion, and they recognise the important role public libraries play in supporting digital literacy skills and digital inclusion (Thompson et al., 2014: xiv). Thompson et al. (2014: 1) note that the 'term *public policy* is used to indicate decisions and activities by the government to address public problem'. Moreover, digital literacy and digital inclusion have become 'central issues for public policy' in contemporary society (Thompson et al., 2014: 1).

Public libraries play a key role in building a digitally inclusive and information literate society. By providing assistance in the use of technologies and the Internet, public libraries alleviate the potential constraints facing those lacking digital literacy skills and the undereducated, thus enabling digital citizenship. Ferguson (2010: 2) asserts that information literacy and digital inclusion are now central components of the public library's lifelong learning strategy and can contribute to the development of social capital. Digital inclusion is critical for participation in modern society, and public libraries now have a role to play in developing digital literacy skills of citizens and encouraging them to avail of the benefits of being online. Digital literacy is being recognised as 'a keystone for civic engagement, educational success, and economic growth and innovation' (Clark and Visser, 2011: 39). Indeed, it is often those people who are not online or do not have the skills for access who are missing out on the benefits and opportunities that digital access can bring.

6.6.1 Developing Digital Literacy Skills

Delivering training on digital and information literacy skills should be a key priority for public libraries. Libraries should consider a joint approach to

---

[9] See ITV Report (19 October 2015), Nearly quarter of UK adults *'lack basic digital skills', says charity*. Available from: http://www.itv.com/news/2015-10-19/nearly-quarter-of-uk-adults-lack-basic-digital-skills-says-charity/ (accessed 12.11.15).

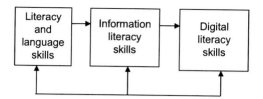

Figure 6.2 Skills continuum.

develop information and digital literacy skills to promote learning. Literacy skills are a prerequisite for ICT skills: people need to be able to interpret the language before being able to utilize the technology. Fig. 6.2 presents a continuum of skills needed for access. As Fig. 6.2 demonstrates, these skills are interlinked, and when public libraries are delivering digital literacy skills training, they should be simultaneously developing literacy and information literacy skills. So, when public library staff are assisting library users on computers, they can simultaneously be supporting the development of basic literacy skills; for instance, if helping someone to print out a curriculum vitae, they can also assist with spelling and grammar. In doing so library staff can have an impact in supporting ICT, literacy and information literacy skills. While I believe that literacy skills are a prerequisite for information literacy and digital literacy skills, these skills complement each other – they are interdependent – and a combination of these skills are necessary in the digital age.

There are, however, implications for libraries when developing the digital literacy skills of citizens. For example, Thompson et al. (2014: 75) explain the challenges of the supporting role of public libraries in developing citizen's digital literacy skills, and they question whether it should be the responsibility of librarians to support digital access. They assert that:

The shift in library service to providing and supporting digital access, literacy, and inclusion has raised concerns for the practice of librarianship. For some…the proper roles of libraries in supporting digital access, literacy, and inclusion remain insufficiently examined questions, including whether libraries should be the institutions with the responsibility of supporting digital literacy, whether digital literacy gaps still exist, and the ways in which literacy can be defined in a digital age.

I believe that public libraries, along with other organisations such as schools and community-based learning providers, have a role to play in developing citizens' digital literacy skills. Libraries can fulfill this role with combined literacy, information and digital skills development programmes, which would be an effective way of developing multiple literacy skills of citizens. To do this, library staff need to have knowledge of the technologies and the skills to support access and the time to design and deliver programmes.

6.6.2 Developing Digital Literacy Skills: Examples From Northern Ireland

This section outlines Libraries NI's approaches to developing digital and information literacy skills. As indicated previously, adult information literacy and ICT skills are being addressed with Libraries NI's strategic priority called 'Support for Learners'. To develop ICT skills, Libraries NI has strategic partnerships with the Department of Finance and Personnel, through their Digital Inclusion Unit (DIU), and the DEL. In Northern Ireland, library Job Clubs, in partnership with DEL, are about developing the participants' digital literacy skills. Job Clubs, which take place in one-third of libraries (Libraries NI Annual Report and Accounts, 2012-13) are a useful initiative to address information poverty and are explored in detail in Chapter 10.

Business in the Community is a partnership with the DIU in which volunteers deliver ICT/Internet 'taster' sessions to senior citizens, on Silver Surfers days.[10] In addition, the DIU runs the Go ON initiative, an introductory ICT course. DCAL's 2013/14 Business Plan (DCAL, 2014: 21) claims that with the improved ICT services provided by e2, a £25 million investment in ICT infrastructure, there will be 'a continued focus on the delivery of Got IT sessions to address digital exclusion issues for those in disadvantaged communities'. Got IT sessions are beginner computer sessions, usually lasting between 45 min and an hour, which are delivered by library staff to all members of the public. Got IT provides informal, one-on-one situations, which suit adults with low literacy/ICT skills who may find the formal setting of a further education college 'very daunting' (LNI9). These sessions are designed to offer basic ICT support and include:

- computer basics (mouse, keyboard, open/close programme)
- basic Internet skills (finding way around a website, using the address bar, performing simple searches)
- e-mail (set up account and send/receive e-mails)

The Go ON sessions are more advanced than Got IT and takes learners one step further. Additional skills learned are social networking, job seeking, searching for travel information and online shopping. Some libraries also offer Go ON iPad introduction sessions. While Got IT and Go ON are evidences of the work to address ICT skills, the Continuous Household Survey 2012/2013 stated that 'Less than one in four (23%)' were aware of 'computer classes/one-to-one sessions'. One interviewee commented that

---

[10] Libraries have also held an ITea and Biscuits Week, delivering information technology awareness sessions in partnership with Age UK (Libraries NI, 2013).

'the Got IT sessions and the Go ON sessions and those sorts of things' are popular within socially deprived areas (TSE1). Evidently, more initiatives should be developed that are carefully tailored to community needs for literacy and ICT, and the library services that can have an impact in those in socially deprived areas need to be promoted more.

An interviewee commented that the basic ICT courses in libraries, such as Got IT and Go ON, are 'specifically targeted' to people with 'no formal qualifications', who prefer informal learning settings and who view libraries as 'non-threatening' and non-stigmatising places (LNI4). Public libraries provide a neutral environment where people from socially deprived areas who perhaps have not succeeded in school can learn and increase their skills. One interviewee suggested that the informal library setting provides an alternative learning environment for people 'who have under achieved at school or have found school very threatening' (LNI9). Libraries offer a 'more subtle approach', encouraging learning that is 'enjoyable', and the people they 'are targeting' are those 'who don't want anything to do with FE [further education] colleges' (LNI6). Furthermore, the library provides a place where 'people from socially deprived areas may feel more comfortable' to learn (LNI11).

The role of libraries in developing ICT skills was confirmed in the survey responses. Library managers working in the 10% most deprived areas in Northern Ireland indicated that targeting individuals with limited literacy and ICT skills was what they believed to be the most effective way for public libraries to reduce information poverty. Survey respondents were asked to select the 5 library services/activities, from a list of 15, which could be most effective at reducing information poverty in socially deprived areas:

1. ICT skills training (77.3%)
2. Social activities/events (73.7%)
3. Access to PCs/technologies (54.5%)
4. Basic literacy support and related initiatives (50%)
5. Tailored information and stock; access to and support for e-government information (45.5%)

Fig. 6.3 presents a complete list of these services/activities.

First, 'ICT skills training' was cited by 77.3% ($n=17$) as the most important library service/activity to reduce information poverty. While positive steps to provide ICT skills training, such as Got IT/Go ON, have been made, I believe that libraries could do more to fulfil potential in this area through promoting and raising awareness of the availability of such courses. Second, 'social events/activities' were cited by 73.7% ($n=16$), which supports the

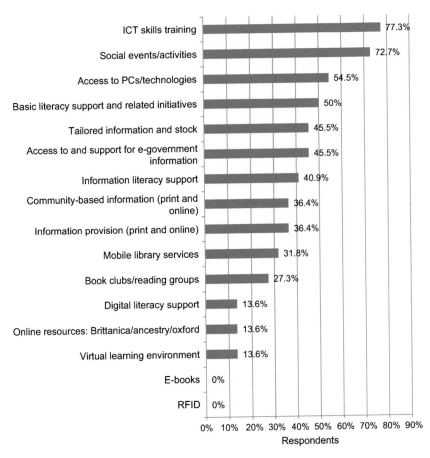

Figure 6.3 Library activities/services able to best reduce information poverty. Values are based on surveys completed by 22 respondents. *ICT,* Information and communication technology; *PC,* personal computer; *RFID,* radiofrequency identification.

argument that is discussed in Chapter 8: that libraries are 'third places' (social spaces: not home, not work) that encourage information sharing and social participation, potentially creating social capital within communities. Third, 'access to PCs/technologies' was cited by 54.5% ($n = 12$). This confirms that providing access to PCs in socioeconomically deprived areas stills remains important. Thus the statistics on lower ICT ownership in deprived areas, discussed previously, confer a supporting role for libraries to provide ICT access in these areas for people without the financial means to buy a computer or pay for a broadband connection. Fourth, 'basic literacy support and related initiatives' were cited by half the respondents ($n = 11$). Initiatives such as the Six Book Challenge address basic literacy, but there needs to be greater

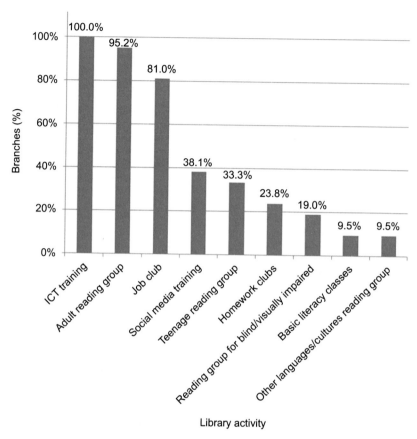

Figure 6.4 Activities in libraries in Northern Ireland. Values are based on surveys completed by 21 respondents. *ICT*, Information and communication technology.

uptake of these, and similar programmes should be developed and actively promoted. Fifth, 'tailored information and stock' and 'access to and support for e-government information' were cited by 45.5% (*n* = 10). 'Tailored information and stock' indicates that more targeted approaches to providing information to different groups is needed. 'Access to and support for e-government information' highlights the role that public libraries can play in supporting access to online government services. Providing 'information literacy support' was cited by 40.9% (*n* = 9). As noted by Buckley-Owen (2011), public libraries could do more to develop the information literacy skills of citizens to allow them to access e-government information.

Fig. 6.4 presents some of the activities in libraries in the 10% most deprived areas in Northern Ireland. With only 2 of 21 respondents stating that their branch had basic literacy classes, there is scope to develop this, possibly in partnership with other skills providers. This is supported by Pateman and Williment (2013: 99), who assert that 'Learning centres, literacy centres and other lifelong learning activities should be developed by public libraries on a much wider scale than at present'. Because support for learners is a key priority for Libraries NI, it could surely do more to support literacy skills as well as ICT skills. As evidenced earlier, doing more to improve literacy skills was ranked by branch library managers as the number 1 area that could be improved. As Fig. 6.4 reveals, all respondents ($n = 21$) indicated that their library provides ICT training. While initiatives such as the Six Book Challenge target those with low literacy levels, more initiatives could be designed and developed to support basic literacy (see Appendix 6, 'Summary and Explanation of Libraries NI's Core Activities and Programmes').

6.7 MAPPING THE INFORMATION POVERTY INDICATORS FRAMEWORK TO LIBRARIES NI'S INFORMATION PROVISION AND SERVICES

The process of mapping information poverty indicators to library activities – which is presented in this book – is original, and is an effective way of measuring how public libraries are addressing information poverty at the macro, meso and micro levels. I developed the process of matching the information poverty indicators to Libraries NI's existing services (see (Table 6.2) below) without assistance from Libraries NI. I believe that other library services could use the indicators in a similar way, mapping these to their interventions to overcome information poverty.

6.8 SUMMARY AND CONCLUSIONS

This chapter discussed how wider European initiatives and strategies for lifelong learning and social and digital inclusion influence public library policy. The chapter considered the lack of digital skills across the United Kingdom and the effect this could have on the wider economy and already disadvantaged areas. The role public libraries play in developing the digital literacy skills of citizens was discussed. By providing free access to ICTs and the Internet, public libraries bridge the digital gap and facilitate lifelong learning. The statistics on Internet usage and computer ownership, literacy levels and poverty in Northern Ireland highlight the need for information poverty indicators. The figures confirm that at 79%, Northern Ireland had the lowest level of Internet users in the United Kingdom. Statistics indicate that people in lower-income households in Northern Ireland are less likely

Table 6.2 Applying the information poverty indicators framework

Macro-level indicators of information poverty	Application of indicator to measure library intervention (evidence)
Physical access to information • Lack of access to information infrastructure • Lack of access to ICTs/PCs, Internet/broadband, information resources and services • Lack of accessible information in different media formats (physical/electronic) • No access to quality-assured information	• Libraries NI infrastructure of 96 libraries, 2 specialist libraries, 26 mobile libraries • ICT infrastructure (e2 providing equipment, Wi-Fi, support) • Strategic priorities of information, learning, culture and heritage • Quality information provided by libraries (eg, online resources such as Britannica, ancestry) • Books, newspapers
Digital inclusion (e-government, digital by default) • No strategy for digital inclusion • No ICT/broadband infrastructure for digital inclusion • No human support to assist with digital inclusion	• Strategic level partnerships to deliver digital inclusion • Free Internet and computers • Support from library staff • Wi-Fi
Educational attainment (Literacy, information literacy and ICT skills) Poverty and social exclusion • High levels of poverty • Sections of marginalised and hard-to-reach groups within communities	• Strategic priorities to support learning and access to information • TSE strategy for community engagement addressing areas of social need in 28 libraries in the 10% most deprived areas

Meso-level indicators of information poverty	Application of indicator to measure library intervention (evidence)
Access to information services in areas of social deprivation • No local libraries • No community centres with information services available • Limited ICT and basic skills support within communities	• Libraries situated within socially deprived areas • Community level partnerships • Community outreach • Targeting hard-to-reach groups

Continued

Table 6.2 Applying the information poverty indicators framework—cont'd

Macro-level indicators of information poverty	Application of indicator to measure library intervention (evidence)
Social participation • Lack of empowerment and knowledge to participate • Limited participation in local library • Little participation in community activities • Limited weak ties needed for participation politically and socially • Limited social networks • Small-world mind-set, not valuing use of libraries, not valuing education or learning for advancement	• Libraries within communities • Developing social networks/encouraging social participation (library activities such as Knit and Natter, reading groups, events) • Targeted interventions to increase usage, marketing services and image • Libraries promoting value of education and reading to socially disadvantaged communities
Community information access • No or limited availability of community information • Low levels of home PCs in area/Internet, ICT resources in communities • No or limited community ICT/skills and basic literacy training and support • No people in social networks to assist with PC/Internet • No access to information that is relevant to communities	• Community information provision • Access to library computers, iPads, free Internet • Access to e-government (support to access online government services) • ICT support
Educational attainment • Qualification levels within an area • ICT qualifications • Basic adult literacy/numeracy/ICT skills within area • Limited participation in part-time higher education courses within areas	• Supporting lifelong learning/informal learning • Partnership with other organisations • Courses such as Got IT/Go ON/Silver Surfers day • Basic literacy support (eg, Six book challenge, Summer reading challenge, Rhythm and Rhyme, class visits)
Ethnic groups/minorities in area • Poor language skills (not speaking English or the language where information is available in) • Limited communication barriers • Cultural barriers	• Library information provision to minority groups • Free Internet access, books, information • Cultural inclusion (multi-cultural events in libraries) • Reading groups for multi-cultural groups

Skills and knowledge deficits	
• Poor literacy • Unable to read • Limited information literacy • Limited digital literacy (computer/ICT skills) • Poor communication skills	• Library's role in addressing literacy, digital literacy and information literacy skills
Information literacy deficits	
• Limited ability to evaluate and use information to improve one's situation • Limited ability to interpret the quality of information • Limited ability to use information appropriately to benefit from it to improve one's life	• Assistance in public libraries • Library delivering courses such as Got IT/Go ON help users evaluate information as well as develop ICT skills
Technical skills	
• Limited ability to use mouse/keyboard • Limited ability to use computer • Limited ability to use Internet • Lacking awareness of and the skills required to use social media	• One-to-one support • ICT training • Free ICT and Internet access • Social media training
Disabilities	
• Physical • Visually impaired/blind • Hearing impaired/deaf • Intellectual (cognitive abilities, learning disabilities) • Autism	• Adherence to Section 75 legislation • Partnership with Action on Hearing Loss, adapt NI, RNIB • Reading groups for hearing and sight impaired • Trained staff • Libraries promote equality of access • Information available in accessible formats • Outreach to groups • Partnerships with organisations (Cedar Foundation)
Information affordability	
• Lack the capacity to buy books, magazines, newspapers • Unable to get library or information service providers because of financial constraints • Unable to afford home PC/laptop/broadband connection • Does not own a mobile phone with Internet access	• Library's role in lending free books, newspapers, magazines • Libraries within communities, in town centres • Free access to PCs and computers

Continued

Table 6.2 Applying the information poverty indicators framework—cont'd

Macro-level indicators of information poverty	Application of indicator to measure library intervention (evidence)
Information behaviour • Lacking the information-seeking skills to find the information you need • No value placed on access to information • No value placed on access to libraries and using libraries • Fear of the technology, using PCs • No interest/desire to get the Internet at home • Choosing not to learn or use information • No interest in reading • Limited/low aspirations, expectations, ambitions	• Developing information literacy skills • Libraries promoting the value of learning within communities through outreach • Libraries providing opportunities for access • Promoting the positives of libraries and information access
Information awareness • Not knowing where to find information • Not knowing why and how to access online government services • Limited awareness of library services • Limited awareness and understanding of health information (health literacy) • Limited awareness and understanding of financial information (financial literacy and benefit information; ability to manage personal finances)	• Libraries promoting awareness of services • Library staff's role in facilitating access ('sign-posting') • Health in Mind partnership (activities and information awareness sessions) • Financial information services (Money Advice Service and Check It Out roadshows, in partnership with Access to benefits)
Institutional barriers • Not wanting to approach information providers; fear of bureaucratic institutions/negative perceptions of libraries/librarians • Lack of trust in information channels (in information providers) • Not using libraries • Language being presented in a bureaucratic way which prevents access	• Library's role as trusted information provider • Promoting the use of libraries • Changing perceptions of libraries and staff

ICT, information and communication technology; *PC*, personal computer; *RNIB*, Royal National Institute of Blind People; *TSE*, Targeting Social Exclusion.

to have broadband than those in higher income households. At an international level, Northern Ireland's literacy levels were below the OECD (2013) average and were particularly low for younger adults.

Having discussed how information poverty can be addressed at the wider, macro level, the next chapter considers how information poverty theories can be used by community engagement staff as a means of understanding the information behaviours within small-world environments in disadvantaged areas.

CHAPTER 7

Investigating Information Poverty at the Meso Level: Part 1

7.1 INTRODUCTION

As well as considering macro-level perspectives, we need to understand information poverty from the sociocultural, meso-level perspective. The conceptualisation of information poverty at the social level illustrates how the cultural norms and information behaviours that exist within communities can constrain information access and use. Information poverty theories from the cultural and social sphere could be adapted and implemented by library and information professionals to develop a deeper understanding of information behaviours and the information needs within communities. Conceptualising information poverty at the meso level is important to understand how groups interact with information, how they value learning and the social factors that may prevent some people from using libraries. Sociocultural approaches to information access and information poverty can be useful from an information profession perspective by allowing an understanding of the communities libraries serve and how to improve services to them; in determining why some groups may not use libraries; and targeting services to meet the information needs of the various small-world groups that surround libraries. Library and information providers must understand the information needs and behaviours within small worlds so that they can deliver the right information to satisfy a community's needs. In doing this, library services can be more effective in lifting people out of poverty. This chapter considers how library and information professionals can use information poverty theories to improve how libraries engage with their communities, users and potential users.

7.2 LOCALISED INFORMATION ENVIRONMENTS

Information poverty from the sociocultural perspective helps us to understand how our information and communication behaviours are determined by the community in which we live, our interpersonal contacts and how the local environment can affect how people value information access and

Overcoming Information Poverty
ISBN 978-0-08-101110-2

learning. Social constructivist approaches at the sociocultural level have examined information poverty within communities (Childers and Post, 1975; Chatman, 1991, 1992, 1996, 1999; Sligo and Williams, 2002; Hersberger, 2003; Hayter, 2005). These meso-level studies consider social norms and information behaviours, and how lifestyles within social groups contribute to information poverty. Burnett et al. (2008: 56) aver that 'Information access is central to library and information science'; however, 'explorations of its conceptual nature have been limited'. Library and Information Science thus far has mainly focused on physical and intellectual access. For a study of information access and poverty to be 'realistic and inclusive' it must also account for 'the array of social issues that significantly influence access' (Burnett et al., 2008: 56). The social aspects of information influence 'how individuals in specific social settings conceive of and use information' and 'how decision makers and information professionals conceptualise information and access' (Burnett et al., 2008: 64–65).

The data gathered from the community engagement staff in this study confirm previous information poverty theories of individuals within localised environments not being aware of the outside world. While the point was made in Chapter 1 that information poverty is a concept constructed to justify the existence of library services, the data gathered indicate that information poverty exists within communities and that there is a role for libraries to play to promoting learning and providing access to information and support for those in socioeconomically disadvantaged communities. The community engagement staff who are directly involved within communities have first-hand experience of the information environments and the personal and social circumstances of people in very deprived communities. For instance, one interviewee noted that the inability to cope with personal circumstances can lead to information poverty. Similarly, health issues were cited as an important factor; people consequently have 'too much going on for them to care about the rest of the world' (TSE2):

there is too much going on in people's lives. Quite a lot of these people suffer from depression ... Looking after themselves and their families is as much as they can cope with. If you give them the responsibility of borrowing books and taking books out it is another thing that they have to do and have to cope with.

TSE2

As this comment demonstrates, the closeness of library staff to socially deprived communities enables them to elucidate further the factors that contribute to information poverty and nonuse of libraries.

When considering the factors that exacerbate information poverty, there is often a vicious circle of materialistic poverty, having no computer and no Internet connection and living in a community that does not encourage learning, which can result in no or restricted economic or social improvement. The following quote highlights how economic, environmental and personal factors exacerbate information poverty:

> ... no Internet access ... leads to information poverty ... poverty is a big factor ... These people ... aren't aware of what's going on in the world because they maybe don't buy newspapers or don't listen to the news. It is so hard to live that they don't care about anything else ... and manage on a daily basis ... If you ... were talking about a world event they haven't a clue what you are talking about or who the Prime Minister is, because they are just wrapped up in whatever is going on in their own life. I think that leads to information poverty ... because they can't cope with their own life, never mind what is going on in the world.
>
> *TSE2*

This quote is important because it illustrates how the social context where individuals reside can lead to information poverty. First, the quote confirms the arguments made by Childers and Post (1975), mentioned in Chapter 3, that some communities live in 'information ghettoes', which are rich in internally generated information yet may not be aware of outside information from the wider society. Second, it is reflective of Chatman's small-world theories (discussed below), whereby people in marginalised communities sometimes live in impoverished information environments. Third, it is reminiscent of earlier information poverty writings by Feather (2013: 131), who made the distinction between information poverty arising from a lack of interest and information poverty arising from lack of access to information:

> In Britain and the USA, ignorance of current affairs is widespread. Public opinion polls reveal that even such basic facts as the name of their own Prime Minister or President are unknown to a significant percentage of the adult population ... Celebrities from the worlds of pop music, the media and sport are, on the whole, more generally recognised than political leaders. Ignorance of public affairs is not a consequence of lack of opportunity, but a lack of interest ...

Interestingly, the point is made that certain sections of society are deliberately choosing not to take an interest in wider society (politics, current affairs) and are content to live in a world of popular culture and celebrity. Arguably, in contemporary society reality, television shows such as 'I'm a Celebrity' and 'Big Brother' constitute a form of information poverty, which can be called *media poverty*. An individual whose life is lived solely within a narrow band of information, for example, celebrity television or celebrity magazine culture, may not see themselves as impoverished; like the early study by Childers and Post (1975), these individuals live in an 'information void' or 'information ghetto'. The information world of some people living in socially deprived areas may be limited, whereby meaningful information that can improve and add purpose to their lives is not entering their world. Meaningful information can be defined as information that:

- enables individuals to understand the world around them
- can be used to improve an individual's career or educational aspirations
- enables individuals to understand their place within their community and the world
- improves an individual's capacity to participate socially
- can contribute to personal fulfillment

It is important to stress that while some sections of the population may live in communities where awareness of the wider society is limited, not everyone living within these communities may have this restricted worldview. Indeed, it is important to remember that within localised environments there are varying levels of information poverty, and we should not apply labels to communities or marginalised groups. Moreover, there is a role for public libraries to promote the value of meaningful information and the value of education and learning to improve life opportunities, enrich lives and escape poverty. By providing access to resources that can improve lives – for example, health, employability, and community information – libraries can provide resources that can add value to people's lives.

The next section looks at people's information-seeking behaviours within socially disadvantaged communities and the role that public libraries can play in supporting information access.

7.3 INFORMATION SEEKING WITHIN DISADVANTAGED COMMUNITIES

As well as developing an understanding of the culture of poverty that can exist in localised information environments, the study by Childers and Post (1975) also enhanced our understanding of the limited information-seeking behaviours of disadvantaged communities. They noted two types of information channels: formal (mass media, social agents and agencies) and informal (interpersonal sources, eg, friends, neighbours, relatives) (Childers and Post,

1975: 38). Similarly, Spink and Cole (2001: 48) distinguish between formal and informal information channels:

- Formal: different tools to access information (journal indexes and abstracts, online public access catalogues and librarians)
- Informal: conversations with colleagues or friends

Both formal and informal information channels are available and used by 'everyone in society'; however, Childers and Post (1975: 38) argue that 'the disadvantaged adult prefers to tap the informal network when he needs a specific piece of information'. However, it is possible that we all prefer informal sources of information in the first instance, and go to formal sources when the information need is not met within our own personal network. Bates (2008: 3) observes there is often a 'hierarchy of information sources beginning with an individual's personal information collection, and moving on to informal interpersonal sources, and then formal sources and channels.' While 'informal, interpersonal sources are valuable and help resolve an information need or problem', Bates posits that 'there are weaknesses associated with a heavy reliance on such information': it may 'not be accurate, factual, complete, up-to-date, or unbiased'. It can be argued that individuals seek information first from people they know; however, people with better access to information sources and networks are more likely to be able to explore avenues outside their immediate environment. As discussed in the next section, those who rely solely on interpersonal sources are more likely to experience information poverty.

Fig. 7.1 is my original information-seeking and information access model; this illustrates how information is accessed in modern society. In developing my own model, I used the macro, meso and micro framework to demonstrate how information can be accessed at each of the three levels. In essence, the model highlights the interconnectedness of each level and how individuals interact with their community and the wider society when accessing information. It also shows how the wider society and community can determine what information is available and the factors that influence an individual's information-seeking behaviours.

As Fig. 7.1 illustrates, the arrows in blue show how individuals first seek information from their own immediate information sources (micro level). When these sources do not fulfill their information needs, they seek information from interpersonal sources within their social network (meso level). When the personal and social information sources do not satisfy information needs, individuals then approach formal sources, such as government agencies and libraries (macro level). The diagram is linked to the three-level

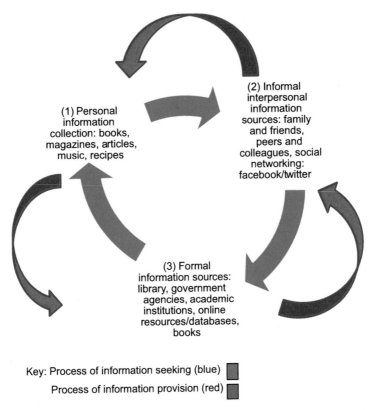

Key: Process of information seeking (blue) ▮
Process of information provision (red) ▮

Figure 7.1 The interdependent levels of accessing and providing information. The process of information seeking is noted by the *blue arrows*, whereas the process of information provision is noted by the *red arrows*.

information poverty framework. For instance, formal information sources can be viewed at a macro level and are designed to meet the information needs at a micro (personal) level. The informal interpersonal information channels are those at the meso level, which are easily accessible within our own social networks (small worlds). The red arrows demonstrate the process of information provision from the macro level, into communities at the meso level, and then to individuals at the micro level. Information provision is interconnected at each level; for example, the micro-level need for information feeds into macro-level strategies and policies. As noted in Section 1.5 of Chapter 1, when access is blocked at each level, information poverty occurs. The diagram in Fig. 7.1 is a way of understanding the cyclical nature of information access and how information is provided at various levels. This innovative model provides Library and Information Science scholars with a new way of understanding information access. The interlinked macro (strategic) and meso (community) levels of information access, as discussed and presented in Fig. 7.1, have an impact on information access at the micro (personal) level. All three levels are interlinked, interdependent and necessary for information access.

7.4 CHATMAN'S INFORMATION POVERTY THEORIES

Similar to the study by Childers and Post (1975), Elfreda Chatman's information poverty theories can be used to enhance our understanding of information-seeking behaviours and information access within disadvantaged communities. In the 1990s, when the digital divide and infrastructural approaches led the information poverty debate, Chatman's ethnographic studies of mainly socioeconomically disadvantaged groups revisited the cultural and behavioural aspects of information poverty (Thompson, 2011: 138). The main strength of Chatman's work is that she developed information behaviour research from a broader sociological perspective, creating what Thompson (2006: 65) describes as a 'new lens' through which to look at and understand information poverty. Chatman found that the context or localised environment in which an individual resides determined their 'perspective on information' and 'shaped an individual's use or non-use of information' (Fulton, 2006: 79). Thus, for Chatman (1996: 205), information poverty is a 'complex social and cultural phenomenon' determined by the constraining information behaviours that exist in small-world environments. Chatman determined that information poverty 'was more closely linked' to 'socially determined attitudes and norms' that prevent information seeking within communities and groups, rather than 'economic poverty' (Thompson, 2006: 50).

Central to Chatman's work is her small-world theories (Thompson, 2006: 61):

- Theory of information poverty (1996): information poverty is linked to small-world behaviour
- Theory of life in the round (1999): extends our understanding of what factors lead to information searching outside of the small-world context
- Theory of normative behaviour (2000): the behaviours within social contexts that determine information seeking and use.

In 1991, Chatman applied gratification theory to poor people and suggested that individuals from socioeconomically disadvantaged backgrounds would be less likely to motivate themselves to access information from outside their own social environment and were reliant on first-hand information from people like themselves. This restricted worldview, reliant on internally generated information from first-hand sources, exacerbates information poverty. Chatman (1991: 440) concluded that because poor people rely on information from people like themselves and personal experiences, 'they live in an impoverished information world' (Chatman, 1991: 440). Echoing the findings of Childers and Post (1975), Chatman also suggested that those from lower socioeconomic groups are more likely to rely on mass media/television for information (Chatman, 1991: 442).

Concepts such as insiders/outsiders, from the field of sociology, were developed from the seminal article 'Insiders and Outsiders: A Chapter in the Sociology of Knowledge' by Merton (1972) and are drawn upon throughout Chatman's research. Chatman's studies into insiders/outsiders and small worlds highlighted the 'importance of social networks in information seeking' and also the constraining factors that might exist within small groups, such as secrecy and mistrust (Caidi and Allard, 2005: 305). Insider/outsider concepts can be applied in all spheres of life since we all live in small worlds, though some are more connected to multiple small worlds than others. As Jaeger and Thompson (2004: 100) suggest, 'All individuals, information rich or information poor, inhabit their own small worlds. It is when one relies only on the small world for information that information poverty ensues'.

Chatman realised that information poverty was not solely the result of personal, individual characteristics, but was also a product of people's small-world lives, the inability or refusal to go beyond their social sphere when seeking information because of suspicion and distrust of outside sources, which subsequently contributes to their use (or nonuse) of information. In Chatman's 'A Theory of Life in the Round' (1999), she explained how 'life in a small world' is 'routine and predictable' (209), where information seeking is limited, thereby creating information poverty. When designing library services for different groups, life in the round is particularly useful, offering 'information service providers insight into the information worlds of their clientele', and can support the 'planning of effective information services' to communities (Fulton, 2006: 81–82). By developing deeper insight into the information behaviours and needs of local communities, public libraries can improve their capacity to design and deliver effective library services to specific groups.

Chatman (1999: 213) describes a small world as a 'community of like-minded individuals who share co-ownership of social reality', where 'mutual opinions and concerns are reflected by its members' (Chatman, 1999: 213). Hence a community can also be perceived as a small world. Community can be defined as those with common bonds: it could be in an area (locale), or it could be numerous groups that share similar interests, culture or information needs (ethnic minority groups, the elderly, the unemployed). Small-world concepts can develop our understanding of how individuals within communities may have connections 'to the larger world through only a very few personal acquaintances' (Thompson, 2006: 51). Within small worlds, people see their world as local and familiar; their primary source of information is family and friends; information is acquired based on local experiences and situations; and people outside familiar surroundings are viewed with suspicion and mistrust (Hayter, 2005: 41). The restrictive boundaries of small worlds create barriers to information access and sharing, and create information poverty. Moreover, the small-world community itself can determine the information behaviours of individuals and create a barrier to accessing certain information (Pla, 2011: 48).

Information access within and between small worlds can be both negative and positive. In their study of information poverty and normative behaviour in relation to e-government, Jaeger and Thompson (2004: 100) noted that the insider/outsider worldview concepts developed by Chatman can illustrate a sense of 'disconnection from larger society' as a result of information poverty, where people seek information only from their own small worlds, 'ignoring what they see as outsider information, actively choosing a state of information poverty'. The feelings of isolation and alienation created by information poverty are highlighted by Jaeger and Thompson (2004: 100). They found that a cause of information poverty was a 'lack of connection to the greater information community' when 'individuals minimise contact with society at large by creating social groups within a particular social status' and then choose to seek information 'mostly from within that social small world'.

Central to the information poverty and small-world theories developed by Chatman is the concept of trust: trusted information and trusted information sources. In 2005 Hayter explored the information worlds of a socio-economically deprived estate in Northeast England. Hayter (2005: 201) revealed two main types of barrier that impeded information access: first, small-world barriers (lack of confidence and trust in outsiders), and second, institutional barriers (formal language and bureaucracy). This study by Hayter found that insularity and a lack of trust impeded access to information, and often this was a lack of trust in institutions that provide information, such as libraries. Hayter (2005: 100) explains that information providers must gain the trust of potential users in order to encourage them to use libraries. There is, then, a role for libraries to provide reliable, trustworthy access to information to the marginalised within society. It is essential for libraries to get to know the communities in which they serve so they can improve information services and position themselves as trusted information providers within their communities.

The following section considers more closely how Chatman's small-world theories can be used by library and information professionals.

7.5 CHATMAN'S SMALL-WORLD THEORIES AND PUBLIC LIBRARIES

Chatman's theories and her personalised approach advanced our understanding of information poverty. Chatman often emphasised how her theories could be interpreted and applied to the library and the information profession to improve their understanding of the information worlds of marginalised groups. Her small-world theories are valuable to understanding how groups interact with information and how library and information professionals can deliver library services to socially deprived areas. Small-world concepts can help library and information professionals to understand how the social environment in which groups exist affects how they interact with information and information providers. The sociocultural aspects of information access enable library and information professionals to develop an understanding of their communities and how they deliver library services in socially deprived areas.

Pollock (2002) asserts that the 'conception of people's small world is a powerful one' and has the potential to provide a theoretical framework that 'can inform public library approaches' to outreach 'programs to specific non-user groups.' Library and information professionals need to know the information environments of users and nonusers. They need to find new, innovative ways of communicating with nonusers/potential users by going into the community and encouraging library usage. By developing an understanding of the small worlds that surround libraries and the information needs of the multiple social types living within them, public libraries can be more effective at identifying the groups that exist within their areas, determining those that could benefit most from library interventions and put them on their radar as potential users. Furthermore, the small-world concepts are useful for public library staff who are targeting hard-to-reach groups and socially excluded individuals within communities. An article by Pendleton and Chatman (1998), which aimed specifically at librarians and information professionals, outlined the potential for applying small-world theories to library provision. Pendleton and Chatman (1998: 738–739) note that 'Many of the pockets of populations that surround a public library can be viewed as small worlds' that exhibit similar characteristics, such as 'cultural norms, common language, [and a] sense of location in the larger social order' (Pendleton and Chatman, 1998: 747). Within these small-world environments, wider society may have no impact, value or relevance to people's lives or communities.

Pendleton and Chatman (1998: 749) make the point that if libraries are 'to remain the "common man's university,"' they 'need to look a little closer at where that common man resides in the information landscape called the Knowledge Society'. Pendleton and Chatman (1998: 750–751) argue that libraries should make information more relevant to small-world lives and seek to understand small worlds in order to improve their capacity to satisfy their information needs. By identifying and targeting outreach to the socially excluded individuals who live in the small worlds surrounding libraries – those who could potentially benefit most from library services – libraries can offer the opportunity for inclusion. In addition, Chatman's small-world theories are useful for information providers to understand diverse communities and improve how they deliver information services to communities who may not see the value of information, libraries or learning. In doing this, public libraries can be more effective in taking people out of the confines of the small world and lift them out of poverty.

The restricted worldview in Chatman's earlier studies was found in the current study in discussion with the community engagement staff. One interviewee referred to information poverty as 'a community where they don't realise the value of learning and information to build their own personal and self-development' (TSE3). Moreover, in the literature there is often a distinct link made between an information-poor lifestyle and not accessing books or formal sources, such as printed material, for information. The important thing for library staff is to be proactively engaged with disadvantaged communities and to work to promote the value of learning and using libraries. One source stressed the importance of 'getting the message across about the benefits of reading and learning … and passing that down … so the next generation comes up with a better understanding' of the value of libraries (TSE3). Community engagement staff are required to promote libraries and reading. They observed that groups with which they work closely have now started reading and taking children to the library because of library outreach:

... it may be the first time in their life they have read a book ... and they would say, "We are actually going to the library now because he loves his books or she loves her books" ... maybe the parents weren't interested in reading or didn't see the importance of it and now because someone took the time to show them that they are realising ... and it is now getting handed down to their children whereas it never got handed down to them.

TSE2

This quote suggests that information poverty and nonuse of libraries is often intergenerational and that there is a challenge for libraries to try to change lifetime habits and attitudes towards libraries. It demonstrates that addressing cyclical issues of poverty and social exclusion can be addressed by library outreach. Community engagement staff stressed that they were trying to show people that taking their children to the library was 'a good outlet for them', 'a therapeutic thing ... in a calm environment' (TSE2). Promoting the benefits of library use can increase the usage of libraries and address information poverty in communities; arguably, it can also contribute to citizens' health and well-being. With library interventions and outreach, public libraries can contribute to tackling cyclical issues of poverty and low educational attainment within deprived areas. Libraries can lay the foundations of education, develop a passion for reading/learning and introduce children to the necessary skills to access information. Libraries should diversify their outreach to small-world communities and focus on specific interventions to groups that are at risk of social exclusion.

A Department of Culture, Arts and Leisure (DCAL) respondent also argued that libraries needed to 'market' and 'tell' people in deprived areas about library services (DCAL1), adding that,

... a far more engaged and proactive approach is required because what we are looking at is cycles within families quite often in communities where they have low expectation, low horizon and ... don't really understand necessarily their potential or what they could achieve.

DCAL1

The comments above echo those of the small-world studies by Chatman (1991, 1999), whereby 'small worlds' or families within communities may not understand the value of education or the benefits of using libraries. The quotation stresses the need for 'engaged and proactive' approaches to address information poverty within socially deprived areas. It suggests that library staff need to be more involved within communities in order to have an impact. This is reiterated by a comment made by a survey respondent that information poverty and non-use of libraries is

> *... a generation thing where their parents aren't working and they don't, and the children aren't pushed or enthused about going to work and ... they haven't been brought to the library to get used to books or gathering information.*
>
> *TSE3*

Similarly, another branch library manager compared information poverty to the nonuse of libraries:

> *there has always been unintentional information poverty that has come through generations ... For some, if their parents didn't use or bring the children to the library.*
>
> *BLM2*

This point confirms that poverty can be cyclical and that combating poverty involves addressing intergenerational issues. Information poverty, too, can be intergenerational, posing a challenge to libraries trying to encourage families to make use of their services. These comments are important because they highlight how 'community' influences how people value 'learning and information' – and, indeed, public libraries – for personal development. It also demonstrates the library's role in promoting awareness of the value of reading and learning. Furthermore, it echoes earlier literature by Goulding (2001) and Britz (2007), who stated that information poverty resulted from people's inability to see the value of information to improve their lives. Thus it suggests that through external intervention, information poverty indicators, such as not valuing information, can be addressed by communicating the importance of learning. So, because information poverty is connected to the nonuse of libraries, library staff need to do more to promote reading and learning within disadvantaged communities, proactively engage with communities and get more people to use library services.

The environment in which individuals reside, where they are so immersed in getting by that the benefits of reading become irrelevant to their lives, was a factor in creating information poverty, as evident in this interview comment:

> *I think there is a huge problem with information poverty in that ... a lot of people ... just [live] day in and day out and don't realise what there is ... like the benefits of reading, we talk to so many groups and parents don't realise the importance of talking to a child or reading to a child.*
>
> *TSE2*

This quote also highlights the need for libraries to promote the value of information, reading and learning, as well as the benefits of using libraries.

The meso-level interviews emphasised that health issues and coping with everyday life can be factors leading to information poverty and nonuse of libraries. Having poor literacy, information literacy or ICT skills can prevent people from accessing the information they need that could improve their health and well-being. Shen (2013: 1) asserts that by 'reducing information poverty', public libraries play a role in 'promoting community well-being'. The role of libraries in promoting the value of education, information access and learning, and supporting skills development within socially disadvantaged communities, is crucial to improving community life. The examples provided here highlight how the application of small-world theories can be used by public libraries to promote the value of libraries, learning and information.

7.6 SOCIAL PARTICIPATION

This section considers how public libraries can offer a social space for inclusion. It discusses how information poverty can be reduced by providing social spaces to facilitate social participation and information sharing. It considers the strong ties/weak ties theory as a means of understanding information seeking and information poverty. In addition, it considers the potential for public libraries to create environments that support information access and social participation, which is fundamental to addressing social exclusion. Public libraries can reduce information poverty by being a facilitator of social networks, a community hub – a third space that facilitates information access.

Libraries can encourage social participation through activities such as author talks, creative writing classes, literacy and ICT classes, family activities, reading groups and events. The role of libraries as a social place for people to meet with friends and meet new people is fundamental to reducing information poverty and encouraging social engagement. Through social activities, libraries can provide an opportunity for people to become involved in their local community and develop networks beyond their usual social sphere. In doing so, libraries can contribute to reducing information poverty by providing a social hub that brings people together and establishes 'bridging networks', which develop social capital.

The free events organised in libraries are often subtle approaches to increase library usage by getting people in, promoting services and encouraging them to join. One interviewee argued that by providing free leisure activities and events to those who cannot 'afford' other avenues such as the 'theatre, cinema or art exhibitions', libraries provide a space for social inclusion (LNI6). The historical role of libraries as a 'meeting place' that has unique social value was highlighted by one interviewee (LNI5). Regarding libraries as a social space, it was recognised that 'older people value libraries as a place of social interaction' (LNI5), places 'where older people come to feel comfortable, to keep warm, to meet other people' (LNI6). Mayes (2010: 3) asserted that older people view 'their local library not only as a source for the services they offer but also as a focal point for social interaction and community involvement.' Increased social interaction can give individuals the confidence to play a part in their communities and thus gain social capital.

Typically, the interviewees stated that libraries were creating social networks to reduce social exclusion: for example, Knit and Natter, a social venue for women that addresses 'their information poverty within their community' (LNI4). One interviewee commented that Knit and Natter was good for making friends, 'social engagement and for people who are depressed or socially isolated' (LNI11). Children's activities such as Rhythm and Rhyme and story time provide the opportunity for young families and single parents to make new friends and expand their social networks. In addition, public libraries provide free opportunities to learn, to 'socialise', to spend 'leisure time' – especially in times of economic downturn as 'not everyone can afford' to go to the theatre, the cinema or art exhibitions (LNI6). For some people, the public library can be a place to be alone, to relax or meet up with friends or even to meet new friends. As well as providing access to information, public libraries can facilitate social engagement, creating spaces where people can extend their weak ties and subsequently develop human, cultural and social capital. Libraries can, on the one hand, create weak ties, which introduce people to new avenues of knowledge. On the other hand, they can arguably reinforce the 'small worlds' that Chatman highlighted (1991, 1999); for example, individuals may only be interacting with similar people from their own community in groups such as Knit and Natter. In developing weak ties, public libraries have the potential to build social capital, which is discussed in the following section.

7.7 STRONG TIES/WEAK TIES THEORY AND PUBLIC LIBRARIES

Similar to Chatman's small-world concepts is Granovetter's (1973, cited in Thompson, 2006: 42–43) strong ties/weak ties theory:

- Strong ties: family members, close friends, others with similar backgrounds, tastes, lifestyles
- Weak ties: individuals who reside outside of one's subculture or social network

Thompson (2006: 40) explains that this reliance on strong ties and interpersonal networks, such as friends and family, 'can lead to difficulty in solving problems that extend beyond the experience of the immediate network'. Consequently, relying on strong ties within the small world constrains information access, resulting in closed information networks and information poverty. This prevents individuals from accessing the information needed for social, educational and financial advancement. Weak ties – with neighbours, work colleagues or in the library context through participation in activities/events – create bridging social capital, involving broader membership of groups in the area, whereas strong ties, with friends and family, create bonding social capital, leading to strong, personal relationships (Power and Willmott, 2007: iii). Weak ties and strong ties create social capital by binding communities and society together.

According to Granovetter (1973), people who have a large number of weak ties in their social networks have an advantage in obtaining job information because strong ties tend to possess highly homogeneous information' (Granovetter, 1973, cited by Yu, 2011: 666). Johnson (2007: 884) cited the theory of social capital, as posited by Lin (2001), and highlighted the importance of developing weak ties. Johnson (2007: 884) explains that, according to Lin's theory,

> social capital resides mainly in the weak ties that allow individuals to reach upwards in the social hierarchy or tap into other networks to gain access to resources not available from their close social network.

Hence, it is by developing social contacts with a higher social status that people gain access to better-quality sources of information 'related to health matters, finances, and education' (Johnson, 2007: 884). Developing weak ties enables individuals to broaden their information environment and information choices, encouraging participation in cultural and political life. Furthermore, weak ties enable them to reach beyond their small-world environment and develop more useful information resource bases.

Public libraries have an important role to play in building social capital, by offering free community space, in a neutral environment, where socially excluded members of society have access to information and support they need to enable participation. Yu (2011: 667) comments that there is a 'connection between people's socio-economic status' and their 'social networks'. The networks of the disadvantaged social group are 'characterised by small size, strong ties and physical proximity' and 'utilise very few other information channels, particularly formal information channels' (Yu 2011: 667). Because people from socioeconomically disadvantaged communities may have limited information reach and be reliant on insular, interpersonal information sources, the role of libraries as an information intermediary is fundamental. As Hayter (2005: 6) observes, 'People in affluent communities tend to have the connections needed to ensure access to information; those in the least integrated neighbourhoods, however, may not.' In essence, public libraries, as formal information providers, can potentially bridge the gap for the socioeconomically disadvantaged when seeking necessary information about jobs, education and health – information that is not available in localised, small-world environments. The strong ties/weak ties model is important when targeting social exclusion and developing social capital; this is re-visited when discussing the micro-level findings in Chapter 10. The next section continues the discussion of how libraries support social participation by creating 'third places'.

7.8 PUBLIC LIBRARIES AS THIRD PLACES SUPPORTING INFORMATION SHARING

Public libraries provide neutral, shared social spaces that can benefit all sections of the population. They can be places that facilitate social interaction, where people can develop social connections and a link to the community and wider society. Libraries provide spaces that bring people together by establishing 'bridging networks', which are crucial to the development of social capital. As well, a library can be viewed as an 'information ground', a place where information is shared and communicated, facilitating social participation. Based on fieldwork by Pettigrew (1998, 1999, 2000) at community foot clinics, information grounds generate a social context and location for people to gather and 'engage in social interaction' and encourage both 'formal and informal sharing of information' (Fisher, 2006: 185–186). Information grounds are smaller than the small worlds in which individual's live and can include libraries, dentists' waiting rooms and coffee shops (Spink, 2010: 65). As a meeting place, public libraries are often comfortable spaces for socialisation. Information grounds are similar to the concept of third places (not home, not work), informal social spaces that create a sense of place and community (Fisher and Naumer, 2006: 94–95). As information grounds, public libraries can facilitate informal social interaction and contribute to social capital.

In his 1990 book *The Great Good Place*, Oldenberg coined the phrase the 'third place' and stated that 'society desperately needs third places that are neither home nor work' (Oldenburg, 1990, quoted in Secker and Price, 2008). Third places are informal gathering places and are important because they promote friendship, encourage sociability and create a sense of place and community. Arguably, public libraries can fulfil this idea of a third place – not home, not work – where people can escape, relax and unwind. Secker and Price (2008: 66) suggest that 'These spaces allow people from different parts of a community to come together and engage with one another. Many public libraries in the USA and more recently in the UK are recognising that they play an important role as a "third place."' The next section considers how the library space, both physical and online, is changing to meet the needs of library users, and small-world environments, in both the physical library and the virtual library.

Third places exist in the digital/virtual environment, where online library communities can communicate and interact with their local library via Facebook and Twitter, blogs and Flickr (photo sharing). The online space is becoming increasingly important in modern society with access to information now available 24/7 and library resources becoming more digitalised. Further, the online environment offers opportunities for libraries to deliver services for users who cannot access resources within the physical library location. Public libraries are adapting to the changing ways people access information, and they now apply a multiplatform approach to providing information, with books, online, ebooks, iPads, the virtual library environment and Wi-Fi. In doing so, public libraries can provide a platform in which excluded sections of society can have a voice through the use of ICTs and its shared space. The library as a social space and third place, both physically and online, will continue to evolve in the future. Public libraries as physical spaces, with a significant part to play in the communities they serve, shall undoubtedly remain fundamental to community development, promoting lifelong learning and tackling digital and social exclusion.

7.9 SUMMARY AND CONCLUSIONS

This chapter further illuminated an understanding of information poverty and the potential for libraries in addressing it. Viewing information poverty from a sociocultural perspective highlights the importance of engaging with the small worlds that exist around public libraries and developing library services tailored to their needs. This chapter examined the sociocultural approaches to information poverty and showed that the social aspects of information access must be considered as well as the macro-level aspects. In doing so, it highlighted how the theories could be applied by libraries to:

- understand the communities they serve and improve services to them
- understand information sharing and seeking among groups
- improve their capacity to target social exclusion
- target services to meet the information needs of various small-world groups that surround libraries

The chapter illustrated how information poverty theories can be used by public library staff to enhance their capacity to understand the information behaviours within marginalised communities. The findings articulated the role of libraries in promoting learning and raising awareness of library services within socioeconomically disadvantaged communities. Community engagement staff demonstrated an understanding of socially deprived communities living in 'small-world' environments, where information from outside the local environment was deemed to be irrelevant. Information poverty was linked to community and environment. Moreover, information poverty and nonuse of libraries was often intergenerational, where communities may have limited contact with libraries or place little value on learning.

The chapter also considered the role of libraries as community spaces that can facilitate social interaction and inclusion within the wider community and society. The premise that public libraries facilitate social participation, develop social connections and weak ties, and provide a link to community and wider society was discussed. It could be argued that public libraries have a responsibility to encourage socially excluded sections of society to use their services and are providing an avenue for engagement within socially deprived areas. Public libraries should therefore focus on promoting their social space for information sharing and social engagement, encouraging usage of and increasing participation in their services.

Chapter 8 continues the meso-level investigation into information poverty and looks at the challenges facing branch library managers and community engagement staff within socially deprived areas. The chapter focuses on library interventions to marginalised groups within communities.

Investigating Information Poverty at the Meso Level: Part 2

8.1 INTRODUCTION

Chapter 7 examined how information poverty theories can be used as a means of understanding the information behaviours of groups and their attitudes towards information, learning and public libraries within socially deprived communities. Chapter 8 now considers how strategies to address information poverty can be operationalised within communities. It begins by considering the challenges facing library managers who are attempting to increase library usage in disadvantaged areas. In addition, it highlights the importance of developing community partnerships and provides more specific examples of community engagement with marginalised groups, such as the elderly, the mentally and physically disabled and the homeless. The chapter concludes by discussing how public libraries could improve their approaches to community engagement.

8.2 CHALLENGES FACING LIBRARY MANAGERS IN SOCIALLY DEPRIVED AREAS

To have an impact on information poverty, it is essential for library staff to forge a closer connection with communities; therefore community outreach should be a core priority for libraries. There is often a challenge for some library staff when engaging with excluded groups and overcoming barriers they may experience when engaging with these groups. The small-world concepts (see Chapter 7) are useful for public libraries as they target socially excluded individuals within communities. Understanding the challenges library managers face has important implications for public libraries: it may enable them to more effectively counter these challenges through support and training and by developing skills to target social needs.

Survey respondents explained some of the external and internal challenges they have when addressing information poverty in socioeconomically deprived areas. For instance, one stated that libraries 'should try to

Overcoming Information Poverty
ISBN 978-0-08-101110-2

provide people with the information they want, not the information they think they want' (BLM18). Public libraries need to provide services that are beneficial for people. Clearly, libraries need to create relevant services based on people's needs and expectations. To do this, proactively communicating and engaging with groups, and adapting services based on what communities need so that resources are spent wisely, is essential. It is important that public libraries use their stock budgets effectively to reflect the needs of their communities; money should not be wasted on stock that people do not need or want. To improve library usage in socially deprived areas, public libraries need to prioritise and target specific groups by engaging with them and through proactive marketing, ascertaining their information needs and designing tailored library services based on those identified needs. Another source claimed that while alleviating information poverty should be a priority, there were 'other groups in the area all trying to do the same' (BLM6). Evidently, libraries must either compete with other community-based programs providing similar services, such as information and communication technology (ICT) facilities and support, or else work in partnership with other organisations for the benefit of the whole community. To address information poverty, libraries need to demonstrate the additional services they can bring to disadvantaged communities that other providers do not have. Libraries also need to demonstrate what their purpose is and what makes them a destination of choice. This reveals a need for libraries to be competitive within communities, demonstrate their value and offer a unique selling point – one that differentiates them from other community organisations. This was affirmed by McGettigan (2014) when detailing how public libraries need to reinvent themselves as 'street-corner universities', a phrase used earlier by the macro-level interviewees. Hence, this is a case of reaffirming what public libraries were originally set up to do: play a levelling role to help the educationally and socially disadvantaged within society. Importantly, it is about being prepared to change and adapt to the changing information needs in modern society.

Survey respondents were asked to choose from a list of challenges they faced when targeting socially disadvantaged areas: connecting with people who do not use libraries, convincing people that libraries have something to offer, and promoting library services to individuals with no tradition of library use were the three main challenges. A fourth – 'identifying and developing links with hard-to-reach groups' – was cited by 59.1%. To overcome these challenges, libraries need better marketing, need more outreach to hard-to-reach small worlds, and need to proactively raise people's awareness of library services. It is essential that public library staff go into their communities, target hard-to-reach groups and try to entice them into the library building. There may be barriers – for instance, some may never have been in a library building – but it is essential that library staff try to break down these barriers to library usage through proactive engagement and by basing services on what communities need and want. Fig. 8.1 presents the findings from the survey. Developing local community partnerships was cited as a challenge by 40.9%; this is given further consideration in Section 8.6.

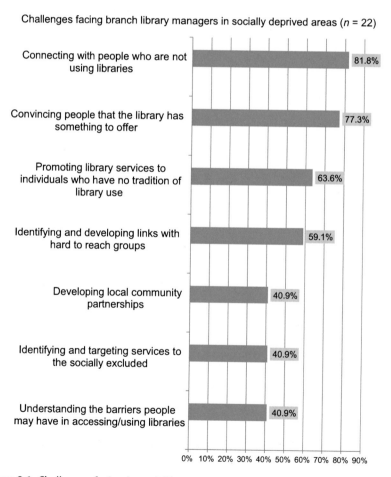

Figure 8.1 Challenges facing branch library managers in socially deprived areas. Data are compiled from surveys completed by 22 respondents.

Targeting hard-to-reach groups can be difficult for some branch library managers because of the low level of interest in the services they offer. Survey respondents commented that when they tried to engage with the local community, there was sometimes little interest in what libraries were offering. For example, one respondent described how they arranged an Information Day 'in partnership with a local community group', but 'only seven turned up' (BLM6). Despite the efforts of some library managers, communities demonstrated a lack of interest in what libraries are offering. While initial engagement may be disheartening, a process of continual reinforcement of the positive impacts of libraries is necessary to build relationships within communities. Furthermore, when library managers attempt to engage with local communities, they often have to find a balance between managing their library, dealing with staffing issues and providing community outreach. Other challenges face library managers in Northern Ireland: Some deprived areas already had established community-based setups to target social and educational disadvantage. Consequently, libraries were sometimes viewed as a threat to the funding and jobs of other community-based agencies that were providing similar services. In these situations, public libraries can compete with other organisations, promote the uniqueness of the library brand and establish libraries as destinations of choice. Alternatively, libraries can take a more integrated approach and develop partnerships with community-based organisations so that libraries can fully integrate within communities.

8.3 COMMUNITY PARTNERSHIPS

Information poverty can be addressed through external intervention and in partnership with community-based organisations. Chapter 6 highlighted the importance of strategic partnerships to address poverty and social and digital exclusion. At the meso level, public libraries need to develop community partnerships so that they become more involved and integrated within communities. Macro-level interviewees asserted that library managers should be networking within communities, promoting a positive image of libraries and highlighting the benefits of participation in library services. With the Targeting Social Exclusion (TSE) strategy, library managers are encouraged to develop partnerships with groups dealing with 'social exclusion' and 'disability and unemployment' (LNI1). Library managers are being freed up from branch duties to engage with communities and develop community partnerships. By communicating more with adult groups and finding out how library services could be tailored to their needs, libraries can develop programmes and activities to cater to a broader range of potential library users.

Libraries could consider working in partnership with other organisations that are addressing similar issues (low educational attainment, poverty, social exclusion), rather than being competitors, so that an integrated approach to targeting information poverty can be implemented. Furthermore, library managers should seek out opportunities to create partnerships with other organisations. Library services should evolve from proactive engagement with local communities, be focused on community needs and develop local skills such as ICT and literacy. As Hayter (2005: 240) suggests, 'libraries must take all opportunities available to work in concert with other information and help providers' and 'be part of all community partnerships working with vulnerable and disadvantaged groups or communities if they truly want to be accessible to all'.

In Northern Ireland, targets have been set for libraries in the most socially disadvantaged areas to develop partnerships and increase participation. Of 22 responses, 86.4% ($n = 19$) had developed community partnerships. Interestingly, 3 of 22 respondents (13.6%) had not developed any community partnerships. One respondent had not developed any community partnerships because they were 'unsure how to' and needed 'guidance and assistance' (BLM17). The data indicate that library managers may need extra support and training in the skills required to develop partnerships.

Partnerships can strengthen the role of libraries within communities and can enhance their outreach. By partnering with other community-based organisations, public libraries can promote the services they provide – such as books, free ICT and the Internet – that can develop the skills base of citizens in socially disadvantaged areas. Moreover, community partnerships enable public libraries to consolidate their position as part of the social fabric of communities. When they do this, libraries can contribute to the educational, cultural, recreational and economic growth of communities and society. An example of working in partnership to deliver basic literacy was provided by community engagement staff who were at the initial stages of setting up an essential skills class for literacy and numeracy through an employability project that offers information, advice and guidance to the unemployed. This involves a partnership with the local further education college, which would deliver the essential skills classes and use library premises and facilities. While these partnerships with community organisations and local colleges are important, public libraries need to have trained staff who can develop these partnerships and engage with local communities.

In addition, developing community partnerships can have a snowball effect. For instance, they can often enable library managers to establish further contacts with other organisations within communities that may be tackling similar issues, such as developing adult literacy and ICT skills or facilitating children's literacy. By taking the initiative, targeting the locations where groups and families meet, such as after-school clubs, adult education providers and elderly residents' homes, library managers can seek out opportunities to extend the library's influence within communities.

Survey respondents provided examples of partnerships with resident groups that enabled library managers to become more involved in the community, promote library services, be more involved in community issues, reinforce their role as information provider and understand the community and thereby ascertain its needs. For instance, one respondent referred to a library partnership with a local resident group campaigning for the local environment: they 'attend meetings representing the library' and 'act as an information centre' for the group (BLM25). Another interesting partnership was working with a community association 'and others on a job creation project' (BLM18). Thus the role that libraries can play in regenerating communities – and thereby make a socioeconomic impact – is evident here. These examples can raise the profile of libraries within communities, and such partnerships should be encouraged.

When building partnerships, it is important that library managers seek to forge links with all age groups and social spectrums within communities (disabled, minorities, homeless) and with various organisations (employment, education, recreation and sport, health). In doing this they will penetrate into the heart of local communities. Pateman and Williment (2013: 88) aver that partnerships are 'useful in shaping initiatives for targeting particular audiences' and 'engaging with hard-to-reach groups'. Libraries can align their services with those of other organisations with similar priorities to develop literacy, as well as information and digital literacy skills, to improve opportunities for social participation.

8.4 GROUPS THAT PUBLIC LIBRARIES COULD TARGET MORE EFFECTIVELY

Public libraries could improve their capacity to address information poverty by more effectively targeting groups and developing programmes tailored specifically to those groups' needs. Public libraries need to engage a wide variety of age groups to have a greater social impact. Once public libraries have identified the small-world groups within their communities, they can begin to more effectively target services towards those local communities

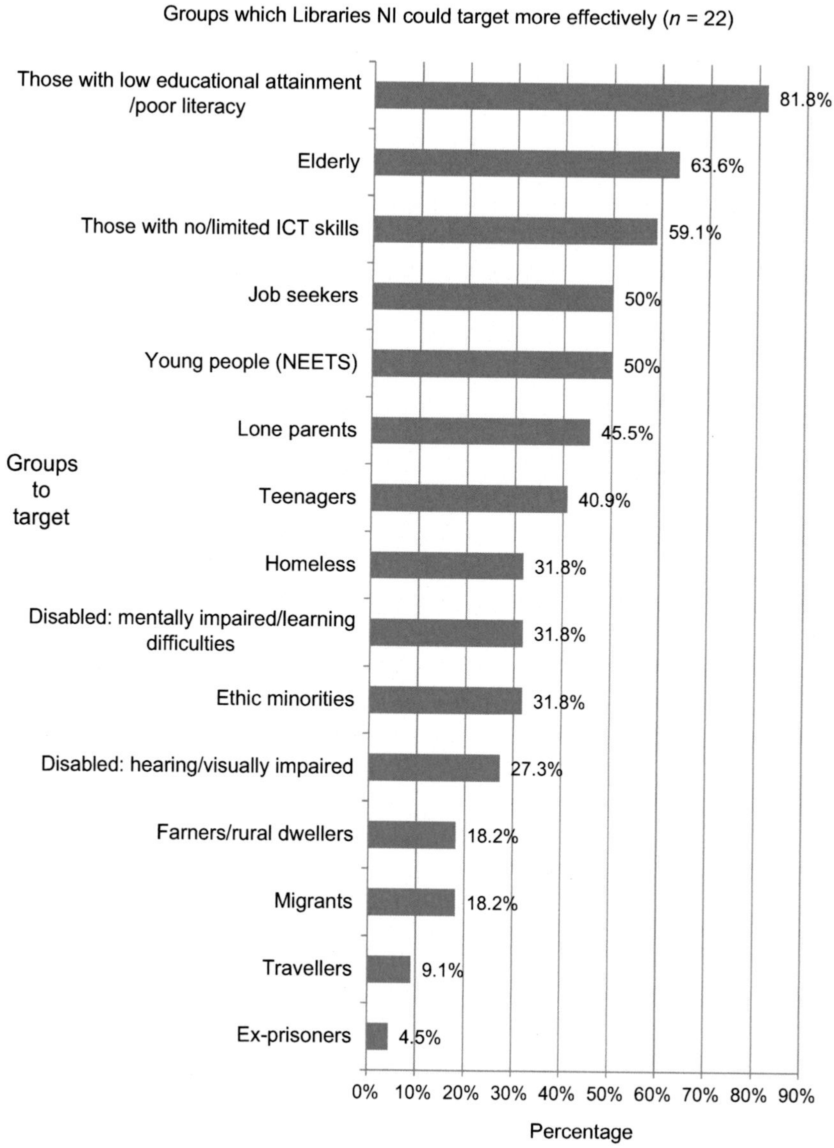

Groups which Libraries NI could target more effectively (*n* = 22)

Figure 8.2 Groups that libraries could target more effectively. Data are compiled from surveys completed by 22 respondents. *ICT*, information and communication technology; *NEET*, not in education, employment or training.

and specific groups. Survey respondents were asked to select five groups that they believed should be targeted in disadvantaged areas (Fig. 8.2):

1. Those with low educational attainment/poor literacy (81.8%)
2. The elderly (63.6%)

3. Those with no/limited ICT skills (59.1%)
4. Jobseekers and young people aged 18–24 years (not in education, employment or training [NEET]) (50%)
5. Lone parents (45.5%)

In addition, half of the respondents cited 'jobseekers' and 'young people 18–24 (NEETs)' as a group that could be targeted more effectively. Library services to these two groups are examined in more detail in Chapter 9, where I present the findings of two focus groups. Lone parents were cited by 45.5% ($n = 10$). Following these, 'teenagers' (40.9%; $n = 9$); 'ethnic minorities', 'disabled (mentally impaired/learning difficulties)' and 'homeless' (31.8%; $n = 7$); 'disabled (hearing impaired, visually impaired)' (27.3%; $n = 6$); and 'farmers/rural dwellers' and 'migrants' (18.2%; $n = 4$) were cited as groups to target more effectively.

Reaching marginalised groups within socially deprived areas is fundamental to alleviating information poverty and social exclusion. Survey respondents gave examples of their outreach to the unemployed; travellers; ethnic communities; the deaf and blind; the homeless; ex-prisoners; people with no ICT skills; adult men; people with literacy difficulties; the elderly and teenagers; young mothers; and adults with learning difficulties. Examples of hard-to-reach groups were wide ranging, reflecting the diversity of groups at which library services are targeted. The sections below provide some examples of how library managers and community engagement staff in Northern Ireland have targeted groups to alleviate information poverty.

8.5 LIBRARY SERVICES AND THE ELDERLY

Library services to those with low educational attainment/poor literacy and those with no/limited ICT skills were detailed in Chapter 6. This section considers how libraries can engage with the elderly, who were cited as the second most important group to target; 63.6% ($n = 14$) of respondents cited this group as being in need of support from libraries. In Northern Ireland, 'the population aged under 65 is projected to increase by 1.5% (24,000 people) from 2012 to 2022', whereas the 'population aged 65 or more will increase by 26% (71,000 people)' (Northern Ireland Statistics and Research Agency, 2012). A growing older population presents challenges and opportunities for public libraries in identifying what this demographic wants from libraries and tailoring services based on their needs. As Mayes (2010: 6) points out, 'public libraries need to be in touch' with what older people 'want from their library service'. This was acknowledged by one interviewee who commented that libraries 'need to keep in step with an aging population' (LNI8). Mayes (2010: 21) concluded that it 'would seem that many libraries today are often preoccupied with developing children's services, than other services, mainly those for older people, are often overlooked' (21). Public libraries 'need to be aware of the needs of older people' and should develop 'their staff to work with older people' (Mayes, 2010: 21–22). Furthermore, libraries should develop strategies to enable older people to be more effective at reducing social exclusion (Mayes, 2010: 21–22). The elderly are a group that public libraries can target more effectively; this is especially important because this is a growing demographic.

As illustrated in Table 5.1, in 2015, older people in the United Kingdom were less likely to use the Internet: 33% of adults aged ≥75 years were recent Internet users, compared with 99% of adults aged 16–24 years. While the number of older adults using the Internet may be slowly increasing, there are still large gaps among older people using the Internet on a regular basis or at all. Evidently, generational factors can create information poverty: the older generation may have difficulties coping with technological advances, and some may not even have basic ICT skills. Fear of accessing technology and the skills to use it is a factor that can prevent older people from participating online and from accessing information that may be of benefit to them. This is certainly an area that public libraries could tap into to introduce older adults to the benefits of being online and to provide support for them to develop the necessary skills to use ICTs and the Internet.

Interviewees typically acknowledged that the difficulties older people have when accessing digital information can lead to information poverty. Furthermore, one explained that a priority for libraries was to address the 'digital divide' that the older generation may face when accessing information 'because things are done so differently now [compared] to the way they have ever had to do [them]' (LNI6). In relation to the digital exclusion that some older people can experience, one interviewee described going to an older residents' group, where a man in his 70s commented that he felt the way his 'mother and father felt when' he 'could read and write and they couldn't' (TSE2). Significantly, this example highlights the information poverty experienced by the elderly, and the 'the kind of gap that is starting to appear between the older people with technology' who feel 'illiterate when it comes to technology' (TSE2). That comment confirms what Haider and Bawden (2007: 547) noted: information poverty 'is portrayed as a novel inequality specific to the twenty-first century' and that the 'inability to use a computer' is the problem, rather than 'the inability to read or write'.

Public libraries can address the barriers and generational factors that can sometimes prevent older people from accessing digital information. By providing the facilities and the one-to-one support with basic ICT 'taster' sessions, such as Got IT, libraries can introduce older people to new technologies and encourage them to get online. ICT training programmes are popular with the elderly and could be encouraged more, but as one interviewee explained, this also requires 'more staff' (TSE2). I also know from experience that there is increasing popularity of iPad courses in public libraries, especially among older people. In light of an increasing older population – people are living longer because of improvements in health – and a need for older people to access government services and communicate online, public libraries need to ensure that adequate financial and staffing resources are provided for programmes directed to this group. It is important that the information needs of the elderly are addressed and that public libraries develop services for this demographic to improve their capacity for social and digital participation. By identifying the types of library services the older population wants and tailoring those services to meet their needs, public libraries will be more able to support this growing demographic in becoming more socially and digitally included. Marketing library services to the elderly is fundamental, as is promoting what libraries can offer them so that they can make the most of those services.

8.6 LIBRARY SERVICES TO THE DISABLED

Being aware of the difficulties in accessing information and seeking innovative ways to address these challenges are important for library and information professionals when delivering inclusive library services. This section considers the difficulties in accessing information faced by people with physical and mental disabilities, such as sensory impairments, limited cognitive and intellectual skills, and library outreach to excluded individuals.

The ability to physically access information can determine 'information wealth or poverty' (Thompson, 2007: 91). Physical disabilities, hearing and visual impairment and cognitive disabilities can impede information access. Other disabilities preventing information access include 'information processing skills such as short term memory, verbal and numerical reasoning or comprehension, or spatial visualisation' (Thompson, 2006: 31). Thus the ability to take full advantage of available information is impeded by physical impairments that prevent access, rather than economic or intellectual factors. Furthermore, the physically disabled can face barriers when accessing information, such as the inability to get to information providers such as libraries or being unable to access information because of visual, hearing or other sensory impairments. Disabilities such as hearing and vision impairments and mental health concerns can be barriers to accessing information and can create information poverty.

Library and information professionals should be aware of the physical barriers which impede information access and design information in multiple formats (Thompson, 2007: 93). For example, in libraries, ICTs need to be specifically designed to accommodate those with limited information-processing skills, such as redesigning a computer keyboard to a touch-screen format to facilitate access. Similarly, delivering library services to housebound patrons who cannot physically get to libraries is important. Hence it is essential for an inclusive library service to be aware of the physical barriers that impede information access, and to design and deliver information services in accessible formats. In addition, it is important to develop appropriate partnerships at the strategic and community levels to support information access by those with physical disabilities. In Northern Ireland, strategic partnerships with Action on Hearing Loss, Adapt NI, the Royal National Institute for Blind People and Action on Hearing Loss enable public libraries to work in partnership with other organisations to facilitate equality of access for disabled users. One interviewee noted a 'sensory engagement project' delivered to library staff 'in how to approach and how to work with' a '[visual- or hearing-]impaired customer' can make library staff aware of the needs of people with sensory impairments and assist in developing the skills to support disabled library users (LNI11). In addition, to deliver an inclusive service, some libraries offer reading groups for the visually impaired/blind and hearing impaired/deaf (LNI11).

As evidenced in *Lifetime Opportunities* (Office of the First Minister and Deputy First Minister, 2006: 69), the government's Anti-Poverty and Social Inclusion Strategy for Northern Ireland, adults with 'disabilities and special education needs' are a vulnerable demographic and often at risk of poverty and social exclusion. Those who are disabled, or who have learning difficulties or an impairment, were cited by almost one-third of survey respondents (31.8%; $n = 7$) as a group of people who could be targeted more effectively.

Interviewees evidenced engagement with adults who have learning difficulties to encourage reading to demonstrate how library outreach can contribute to the government's social inclusion agenda. In partnership with the Down Syndrome Trust, community engagement staff introduced a variety of library programmes, such as taking them to a museum and doing 'a six week course using publisher'to design 'a leaflet on staying safe'; they also are planning to do a 6-week local history course with the adults with Down syndrome (TSE2). One interviewee explained that an important feature of working with adults with learning difficulties is ensuring they integrate with other people who are unlike themselves, and 'learn how to mix in the real world' (TSE2).Thus, being in a library fulfils the social inclusion agenda for adults with learning difficulties because they are able to participate in a diverse environment (TSE2). An essential aspect of library outreach is 'slowly breaking' down the barriers to accessing libraries and changing people's perceptions of libraries (TSE2). Similarly, Shrem (2012) noted how public libraries in New York developed programmes to support socioeconomically disadvantaged students and disabled students, for example, Child's Place for Children with Special Needs in Brooklyn, New York.

As the evidence shows, by implementing an effective community engagement strategy, public libraries can target disadvantaged adults (and children) who can benefit from library services. Importantly, when libraries develop links with hard-to-reach groups and organisations such as the Down Syndrome Trust, they need to be ongoing. Furthermore, when public libraries have more staff in community engagement roles, they can develop more partnerships and thus be more effective at reducing information poverty and social exclusion.

8.7 OUTREACH TO THE HOMELESS

Homeless people were cited by almost one-third of survey respondents (31.8%; $n = 7$) as a demographic that could be targeted more effectively and are recognised in the *Lifetime Opportunities* document (Office of the First Minister and Deputy First Minister, 2006) as a vulnerable group and at risk of social exclusion. Outreach to a homeless shelter involved bringing a group of adults on a 'tour of the library [and] explaining services, especially free computer use' (BLM25). This outreach to the homeless was further discussed in the interviews with community engagement staff, who detailed how the library set up and delivered a reading group in the hostel housing homeless people hostel and invited them to an employability roadshow and a Job Club in the library (TSE3). Muggleton (2013: 16) asserts that 'wider efforts to improve functional literacy and ICT literacy should also engage with marginalised communities, including the homeless'. The initiative with homeless adults in Northern Ireland provides evidence of libraries developing the skills of a marginalised group and contributing to the government's social inclusion agenda. Such initiatives demonstrate how libraries can contribute to social inclusion by encouraging the most marginalized and vulnerable in society to participate. These are important outreach activities, but they must be sustainable and long term, with financial and staff resources set aside to maintain them.

8.8 ENGAGEMENT WITH LONE PARENTS

Lone parents have been identified in *Lifetime Opportunities* (Office of the First Minister and Deputy First Minister, 2006) as a group at risk of social exclusion. Survey respondents indicated that lone parents were the fifth most important group for libraries to target, with 45.5% ($n = 10$) citing this demographic. Community engagement staff described their engagement with a women's aid organisation that provides emergency accommodation for women and children affected by domestic violence, detailing how they provided storytelling, Rhythm and Rhyme and after-school reading sessions with children, and were promoting basic ICT courses in the library, such as Got IT and Go ON. As part of World Book Night, free books were distributed to the women's aid group. Community engagement staff demonstrated how their outreach was influential in encouraging greater participation in library activities such as Rhythm and Rhyme. Similarly, outreach to a family centre involved promoting the 'therapeutic' benefits of reading and the importance of reading to children (TSE2). The community engagement staff completed the Six Book Reading Challenge with a group at the family centre and 'read to lead' activities, which 'is where you pick a short story or a piece of literacy out of [a] novel [or] a poem and you read it to people and you instigate a discussion' (TSE2). These initiatives demonstrate how libraries can develop literacy skills and encourage a love of reading, and they highlight the benefits of community engagement. The link with the family centre came about from having a presence at a local conference involving professionals from organisations such as Youth Justice, Sure Start and local health centres (TSE2). As evidenced here, it is important for library staff to take advantage of networking opportunities and promote their services to organisations that develop learning, inclusion and well-being.

Libraries could consider engaging with lone parent groups within communities to ascertain how library services could be tailored for their needs. This engagement could lead to the development of a library service policy for lone parents based on needs identified within specific areas. Since 45.5% of survey respondents indicated that lone parents should be targeted more effectively in socially deprived areas, it is imperative that libraries communicate and engage with this group and ascertain what they can do for them. This would allow libraries to design relevant services that would support lone parents in developing the skills to obtain employment and to guide their children through learning. Hence it is fundamental that public libraries consider the statistics relating to lone parents within deprived communities, develop appropriate services tailored to their needs, raise awareness of these services and show lone parents that libraries have something that can improve their lives.

8.9 IMPROVING COMMUNITY OUTREACH

Based on the survey findings and the data from interviews with community engagement staff, I gained many useful insights that can be used to improve the capacity of public libraries to address information poverty within socioeconomically deprived areas. The evidence from the survey and the interview data indicated that public libraries are in a prime position to address information poverty, but based on the findings from the Northern Ireland study, more community engagement, marketing and provision of the services that communities need are needed. Interviewees and survey respondents at the meso level believed that libraries could do more to encourage library usage by marketing library services and changing the image of libraries and library staff within socially deprived areas. Importantly, public libraries need to focus on addressing barriers to library use. By being less bureaucratic, being more flexible in their approaches to marginalised individuals and removing some of the prevalent rules, public libraries could become more welcoming to the most disadvantaged in society. Improving the usage of libraries, especially within socially deprived areas, would further advance the public library service's ability to reduce information poverty.

Targeted marketing, aimed at increasing awareness of library services and usage within socially disadvantaged areas, is an area that public libraries need to focus on. One interviewee explained that the 'big thing that is stopping libraries [from] being bigger than they are, is that people don't know about them', and they need to be promoted more (TSE2). This interviewee suggested that libraries could have a 'big advertising campaign on the TV' as well as more 'localised marketing' (TSE2). Clearly, promoting what libraries have to offer and adapting services to satisfy what groups and communities want are fundamental, as evident in this response:

> ... [libraries] need to do more about looking at what communities want in terms of information[,] so making sure we have got the right kind of mix of resources there and making sure that those resources are available to the community where they want them to be available' (LNI1).

Libraries need to know what communities want them to provide and what literacy, information and ICT support they can give. Outreach, communication and acting on what groups are asking libraries to provide are paramount. This outreach requires more staff in and resources allocated to community engagement roles; those in these roles can make links with local communities, ascertain community needs and raise awareness of library services. Furthermore, public libraries need to have a balanced approach to targeting services across all age spectrums and social groups. They need to identify which groups are at risk of social exclusion and those who are not using libraries and target services towards them. In doing this they can have a greater impact in addressing social and digital exclusion and be more effective at encouraging library usage and promoting the value of information access and learning.

In addition, the meso-level interviewees stressed that there needed to be sustainable, long-term approaches to community engagement and tackling social exclusion. One interviewee asserted that since TSE was one of the Department of Culture, Arts and Leisure's 'main targets', and with the government focus on creating 'jobs and building up the economy', it would be good if the current approach to community engagement lasted because it 'is not going to be quick fixes. You are talking about changing traditions and lifetime habits for some people' (TSE3). This quote is reminiscent of comments from one of the participants at the macro level, who noted that long term, sustainable solutions to address poverty and social exclusion are needed. Ensuring the sustainability of library interventions to target social need is fundamental. As Pateman and Williment (2013: 163) observed, 'one of the major problems with social exclusion initiatives is that they nearly always tend to rely on extended funding and short-term timescales', which subsequently prevent 'the work from being embedded within the strategy, structures, systems and organisational culture of the organisation'. They further argue that 'Social exclusion is a long-term problem which requires long-term solutions and not short-term fixes' (Pateman and Williment, 2013: 164). While public libraries are facing budgetary constraints and increasingly having to demonstrate the impact of their services, I believe that long-term commitments and strategies need to be developed to maintain the capacity of services to target social need.

While public libraries are restrained by their budget and staff, they should focus on channelling resources in areas where libraries can have the most impact. Public libraries need to have staff in roles that are able to engage effectively with local communities. They need to encourage library usage and design library services which can improve the literacy, information and digital literacy skills of communities. Public library services should evolve from proactive engagement with local communities, focus on community needs, develop the skills of citizens (such as ICT and literacy) and encourage social and digital participation. As described in Chapter 7, library leaders should not lose touch with the small-world lives of those living in socially deprived areas and the issues facing them: educational underachievement, poverty and social deprivation. If those involved in developing policy and setting strategy are to develop strategies to alleviate information poverty, they need to understand what information poverty is and be aware of the needs of those in socially deprived areas and the circumstances of the socially and digitally excluded. Public libraries will then be able to get into the heart of society and communities and return libraries to their original ethos of meeting the needs of the most disadvantaged.

8.10 CONCLUSIONS

This chapter has highlighted how important targeting groups and community outreach are to addressing information poverty. An integrated approach using a combination of survey and semi-structured interviews provided a comprehensive account of how libraries are addressing information poverty within communities. The evidence indicates that public libraries need to develop strategies targeted towards specific groups, especially those with low educational attainment/poor literacy and those with no/limited ICT skills. The data show that libraries need to better identify and target interventions to marginalised groups that are at risk of social and digital exclusion. More initiatives – carefully tailored to support the development of literacy and information and digital literacy skills – should be developed within socially deprived areas. Libraries should also emphasise delivering services that are most beneficial to communities and should buy the stock that local communities want.

The interview data also indicated that it may be necessary to develop a more embracing community engagement strategy that involves outreach to groups across society, not just specifically to deprived areas. In addition, the data highlighted the challenges of targeting these areas and the need for long term, sustainable approaches if libraries are to have a lasting impact. As with the macro-level interviews, meso-level interviewees also commented that libraries need to be better at marketing and increasing awareness of library services, especially in socially deprived areas where library usage is low and where negative attitudes towards libraries and learning are evident. Another important comment heard often during the meso-level interviews that, as well as engaging with socially deprived urban areas, public libraries need to engage with isolated rural areas, since poverty and social exclusion can happen anywhere. Outreach into rural areas is needed so that those in the most remote areas can get support from library services.

The next chapter analyses findings from two focus groups to investigate information poverty at the micro level.

CHAPTER 9

Investigating Information Poverty at the Micro Level

9.1 INTRODUCTION

This penultimate chapter presents the micro-level findings from two focus groups. The micro-level investigation, using unemployed people in both library and non-library settings, was shaped by the data presented in the previous chapters. As mentioned in Chapter 3, unemployed people have been identified in the literature as likely to be prone to information poverty (Childers and Post, 1975; Chatman, 1986; Haider and Bawden, 2007). Chapter 2 pointed out that Northern Ireland has the highest consistent unemployment of all regions in the United Kingdom, and revealed that adults who had never worked were less likely to use a library. In addition, in Chapter 8, half of the survey respondents cited jobseekers – and, likewise, half of the respondents cited young people aged 18–24 years (not in education, employment or training [NEET]) – as a group to target more effectively in deprived areas. Thus the micro-level investigation provided the opportunity to explore library services from both a user and non-user perspective, and to explore information poverty within the context of unemployed people.

Focus group 1 was conducted with non-library users in a job club in a community centre in a socially deprived area; this job club had no connection to public libraries. Focus group 2 was conducted with library users participating in a job club in partnership with the Department of Employment and Learning (DEL) in a public library situated within the 10% most deprived areas in Northern Ireland. On the basis of data from these focus groups, this chapter examines the information poverty indicators presented in Chapter 4 (Table 4.2), and the impact that public library strategic policies can have on individuals. Thus the focus groups were useful in seeking out evidence of information poverty and in measuring the impact of library interventions. The analysis of the focus groups involved extracting information poverty indicators from the data, for example, 'being able to afford a home computer' or 'having limited ICT [information and communication technology] skills'. Fig. 9.1 shows how the study evolved and how a process

Overcoming Information Poverty
ISBN 978-0-08-101110-2
185

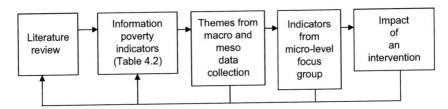

Figure 9.1 Process used to measure information poverty.

was developed – from the literature review to the three-stage data collection – which enabled me to measure indicators of information poverty.

While Chapters 5–8 looked at the macro- and meso-level findings, this chapter investigates how the macro-level strategies are translated into meso-level programmes in branch libraries. Importantly, the chapter examines the impact of library interventions and suggests ways libraries could improve their services to the unemployed and to young people.

9.2 PUBLIC LIBRARIES AND THE UNEMPLOYED

Public libraries have a role to play in developing employment opportunities, by giving people the skills needed to succeed in the workforce. In doing so libraries have the potential to contribute to the wider economy and build a skilled workforce by, for example, providing the support to develop skills needed for work and the facilities to complete and print application forms and curricula vitae (CVs). Indeed, public libraries also can be involved in developing the economy during an economic downturn or recession. Public libraries provide a social space, facilities and knowledgeable staff to support information access for the unemployed. Interviewees typically observed that, for the unemployed, libraries play an important role in developing literacy and information and digital literacy skills by providing resources and support to the economically disadvantaged. In addition, they provide a warm social space, free access to the Internet, job-seeking information and books, facilities and assistance to type CVs and complete job application forms and printing services. Moreover, the interviewees stressed that, in an economic downturn, the library space was important for mental health and provided a non-stigmatising space for the unemployed.

Public libraries could enhance their ability to receive financial support from government by providing evidence of what they can do to assist people into employment – for example, developing ICT and literacy skills. Public libraries can work in partnership with other agencies in supporting the economically inactive, as evidenced in this investigation, where a partnership with the DEL led to the creation of over 30 job clubs in libraries across Northern Ireland. As well as supporting individuals while searching for jobs, job clubs are also influential in addressing information poverty by developing the ICT skills of participants and encouraging usage of their local library. The DEL job clubs track the progress of participants in finding work, which can be used to demonstrate the 'impact that the library service is making' through partnership (DCAL1). It was acknowledged, however, that a difficulty for public libraries is proving their contribution to someone becoming employed:

The difficulty is proving what interventions…When you try to tackle poverty how do you know what you are actually doing is going to make a difference to somebody on the ground. Are you actually going to lift somebody out of poverty, are you going to get somebody into employment? Is it as a result of the library service being provided person getting a job? It is difficult to prove that unless somebody stood up and said "I got a job because of the libraries"

(DCAL2)

The above quotation is important because, first, it highlights the challenges of being able to demonstrate how an intervention can 'lift somebody out of poverty' or 'get somebody into employment', and second, it emphasises the need to obtain evidence of the impact of library services.

As previously mentioned, being unemployed can lead to information poverty in that someone who is unemployed may not be able to afford information (print or online); for example, one may not be able to afford a computer or a broadband Internet connection at home, or may not be able to afford newspapers, which may contain information about jobs. This limited capacity to access information, resulting from reduced financial resources, affects an individual's ability to improve his or her life situation. While being unemployed may exacerbate information poverty as a result of the inability to afford the information one needs, unemployment can also be a result of information poverty (eg, not having access to the right information, not having the ability to apply for jobs or the qualifications and skills needed to gain employment). The vicious circle of being unemployed and its associated effects, which can exacerbate information poverty, can arguably be alleviated by the 'virtuous circle' in the form of help from public libraries. Unemployed people are a group that is in need of library services, such a free access to ICTs, the Internet, books and newspapers and support from library staff (see Fig. 9.2).

The next section analyses the first focus group with a group of young people aged 18–24 years (NEET).

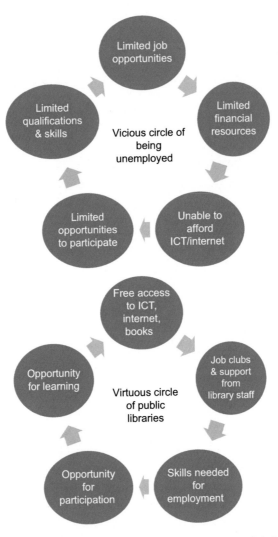

Figure 9.2 The vicious circle of unemployment, the 'virtuous circle' of public libraries and their associations with information poverty. *ICT*, information and communication technology.

9.3 FOCUS GROUP 1: YOUNG PEOPLE AGED 18–24 YEARS (NEET)

Significantly, the DEL's (2012b) strategy for young people, titled 'Pathways to Success: Preventing Exclusion and Promoting Participation of Young People', states that, 'there are currently 46,000 16–24 year olds who are not in education, employment or training in Northern Ireland'. This figure has risen by 59% from 29,000 in 2000 (DEL, 2012b). Moreover, with the 16- to

19-year-old category, the figure has risen by 56% to 14,000, 'up from 9000 in 2000' (DEL, 2012b). As identified in the survey, young people aged 18–24 (NEET) are an important demographic to target and a group on which public libraries could have a greater impact.

It was also important to ascertain insight into non-library use by young people in deprived areas. Because focus group 1 consisted of young people who lived near and knew each other, I felt that some participants seemed reluctant to participate in the discussion. The reason for some participants saying more than others, however, could be because of communication skills: some of these young people were more confident at speaking within a group setting than others. Barbour and Kitzinger (1999: 48) acknowledge that 'questions of sensitivity may arise when using focus groups'. Hence, a challenge during the focus group discussion was managing sensitive issues, for example, when asking questions about skills, ICT ownership and Internet access. Although addressing sensitive topics can be challenging, focus groups are 'one of the few' research techniques 'which permit investigation of groups whose writing skills are limited' (Gorman and Clayton, 2008: 148). Focus groups, therefore, were deemed to be appropriate when investigating information poverty, wherein the participants may not be able to express themselves online or through writing. Because sensitive issues were being discussed during the focus groups – such as skills and education, ownership of technologies and being unemployed – it was essential to develop a rapport with the participants and provide assurance that the data were confidential and would remain anonymous. Participants in focus group 1 were much younger group than those in focus group 2, and each noted different indicators and different perceptions of libraries.

Focus group 1, comprising young people aged 18–24 (NEET) in a community centre in a socially deprived area, consisted of eight participants, two of whom were young youth leaders, one male and one female, who worked in the centre. The contribution of the youth leaders was vital: first, they had a stronger grasp of the questions being asked; second, they offered useful insights into what the centre does to assist the young unemployed; third, they encouraged the six unemployed young people to talk and fourth, they helped to manage the discussion. Participants were asked to fill in consent forms, and it was explained that data would be recorded and would remain anonymous. Participants were asked why they joined the job club at the community centre, what assistance they receive to complete job applications and what, if any, other support they receive within the community. They were asked whether they used the local library for job-seeking support, to read or to avail of other library services. Participants were also asked

Table 9.1 Focus group 1: Community centre job club respondent labels

Respondent category	Abbreviation
Youth leader(s)	YL1,YL2
Unemployed male(s)	UM1, UM2, UM3
Unemployed female(s)	UF1, UF2, UF3

questions relating to support they need with computers, their ICT skills, information sharing and their use of the local library for job-related information. As well, they provided useful perceptions of the local library. Specifically, their non-use of the library, lack of interest in what it offers and lack of awareness were evident. They also suggested how the library could do more for them and were also asked to suggest ways they believed libraries could improve services to jobseekers and to young people. Table 9.1 shows how the participants were labelled; the following section discusses their responses.

9.3.1 Resources and Support at the Community Centre

The community centre was providing employability support in an environment in which the young people felt comfortable. A youth leader pointed out that, in the centre, the secretary would attach the latest job vacancies from the job centre Website and post these on Facebook. The community centre runs courses on, for example, ICT skills, and another reason for joining was the chance to get 'qualifications to get a job' (UM1). One youth leader explained to the participants who had just started attending the job club that the community centre could help them find jobs through such methods as offering training, arranging work placements and providing voluntary opportunities to gain experience within the community (YL1). The youth leader helps them apply online for the courses and explains the layout of both the printed and the online prospectus and takes them to the local Further Education College on Open Days (YL1).

The data collected illustrate how the centre is involved in guiding young people within the community to obtain employment, fill in application forms and gain access to further education. The data suggest that guidance for seeking employment, advice on further education and support to complete job applications are services that public libraries could provide. Public libraries could develop services that are more tailored to younger adults who are not specifically in the NEET category, and provide more employability skills support. Furthermore, a possible avenue for public libraries could be to develop community partnerships and share resources with other groups that provide skills support within communities. These partnerships could be developed through engagement with community organisations, as described in the previous chapter. An integrated approach within communities would enhance the capacity for public libraries and other organisations to reduce information poverty.

9.3.2 ICT/Internet Access and Skills and Qualifications

Interestingly, five of the six unemployed people said they had a home computer or laptop. The participant who did not have a home computer said he would use those at the centre and he had Internet access on his phone. The centre is equipped with ICT facilities, and it is also partnered with a nearby educational resource centre that has access to laptops. On the whole, the participants said they were comfortable with ICT, although one added that there were people in the centre who could help them if they needed assistance. The participants all had basic ICT skills; one explained that they were taught basic ICT in the first three years of secondary school. Most of the young people NEET in focus group 1 were interested in returning to further education and pursuing courses. One respondent said that he was also 'going to Further Education College', and he preferred to do a practical ICT course where he would be 'building computers' rather than learning word processing (UM2). One young man also suggested that he wanted to leave Belfast: 'I'm getting out of here, I don't like Belfast…the weather and everything and the people…I want to move out of the whole country', probably to America (UM1). While this young man was hoping to study engineering at college, he indicated that his longer-term plan was to move elsewhere. I questioned whether this was the same sense of fatalism echoed in earlier research studies of deprived communities, such as those by Childers and Post (1975) and Hayter (2005), or whether it was evident that this young man could see outside the insular, small-world environment and recognised that, for him, life opportunities may be better pursued elsewhere.

The next section considers the participants' use of, and attitudes towards, the local library.

9.3.3 Use of the Local Library

Of the six young unemployed participants, all had been to the local library with their primary school. Although they said that they had used the library in primary school, the participants were asked whether they still used the library for books. They all replied that they did not. One participant commented that they 'used to go down' to the library 'all the time…to get chased' (UM3). He explained that he was 'barred' from the library for 'messing about'

(UM3). I questioned whether this was typical of other public libraries across the United Kingdom and farther afield, where some children and teenagers see the library as a source of amusement, 'to get chased' and subsequently 'barred' for misbehaviour. The data highlight the challenges faced by library staff, as well as the question of how to prevent these from happening and – more important – how to ensure that children and teenagers respect their library and do not have negative experiences. It suggests that when children are engaged by public libraries during primary school, the libraries emphasise that a library is a place to be respected and valued within the community and is to support them and to enhance their learning and development.

One source said that she stopped using the library in 'First Year' because 'it is boring' (UF3). The data suggest that for some children in socially deprived areas, contact with the library stopped at secondary school and that at a certain age children lose interest in what libraries offer. The challenge for public libraries is to continue to make their services and learning interesting and relevant for all age groups, and to ensure their services are not targeted towards certain groups. It also highlights the need for marketing and promoting the value of library services and learning within deprived areas. However, these focus group participants acknowledged they used the school library in secondary school. The data suggest that more communication and outreach with secondary schools are needed to maintain the contact and the library usage that was evident in primary school. The data also indicate that closer links could be made with school libraries and public libraries.

The participants were asked whether they would think of going to the library during the summer. One replied:

> Definitely not...It would be the last place you would want to go to over the summer...It would be like going to school having to read and all
>
> **(UM1)**

This comment validates previous comments made by the macro-level interviewees and found in the survey responses: that in socially deprived areas, libraries reminded people of school and formal learning. Consequently, this association with school and formal education became a barrier to using libraries. Changing this perception of libraries and of reading is a fundamental challenge public libraries must overcome if they are to be more successful at improving literacy across society.

One of the youth leaders explained that a reason young people were not using the local library was because they already have access to up-to-date technologies:

People can get books on their iPads and all now so there is no need and you have all those Kindles and all coming out so I think that is the reason why people are going to the library less...Everything is technology now. People have e-Books on their phones so there is no need for the library

(YL1)

What is interesting about this comment and the data above, which show that most of these young people had computer access at home, is that public libraries need to have another avenue to engage young people. The youth leader was very aware of the changes in technology and how people currently access information. At this point in the discussion, I explained that the library has eBooks now, but the youth leader replied that 'People don't know' (YL1). This important comment highlights the necessity for library staff to promote services and resources more successfully to groups that are not using libraries. The lack of awareness of library resources was evident in a survey conducted by Ipsos MORI (2014), which confirmed that there was less usage of eBooks among people in lower social grades. There is the potential to increase the usage of eBooks in socially disadvantaged areas by promoting them more. For instance, just under one-fifth (18%) of all adults surveyed were aware that libraries provided a free downloadable eBook service (Ipsos MORI, 2014). Of the 18% who were aware of eBooks, those in social group ABC1 were more likely to be aware of eBooks (25%) compared with 12% in the C2DE social group. Research by Mann (2013: 81) also found that 'those with lower incomes were more likely to have never used an eBook' and that awareness of eBooks among those group was lower. Mann (2013: 87) also observed that the reasons for 'never using eBooks' were 'not owning a device', 'too complicated and financial restraints'. eBooks may cater to some library users, but when addressing information poverty, eBooks may exclude people living in socially deprived areas, who may have low educational attainment, poor literacy and lack the financial means to purchase a device.

While none of the six unemployed participants had been to the library to get help with jobs, a youth leader said that before getting the job in the community centre, he would have gone to the library 'to fill in job application forms' and use the library space and printing facilities (YL1). The other youth leader, however, pointed out that she had not 'been inside' the library and did not 'know what the library has' (YL2). When asked whether anyone from the library ever came out to speak to the people in the community centre, the youth leader replied 'No' (YL2). The community centre where the focus group took place is the type of centre that public libraries should be making and maintaining a connection with, but the data evidenced not library outreach into this centre, or area. Apparently, the focus group participants' awareness of library resources was low; this should be addressed through outreach and promotion. Furthermore, it indicates that there are gaps in engagement with socially deprived communities, which also need to be addressed; accurate means to measure this engagement are required to ensure that all groups have been contacted by libraries and are aware of library services.

9.3.4 Reading

When asked whether they read books, there was an emphatic 'no' from the participants. Two participants stated they read the local community newspaper because it was 'local and interesting' (UM1). Another participant said that she read the local community newspaper 'because it has the up-to-date stuff on it', she might see someone she knew in it and she liked to find out about the community (UF3). When asked whether she thought that the library had anything in it to make her visit it, she said no (UF3). It was evident that the young participants had an interest in their local community and issues affecting their area. The data indicate that participants were only interested in the information that affects their own small worlds. Evidently, libraries have a role in promoting community information to young people and must increase their awareness of library resources that would be of interest to them, which could then open up access to other information. The disconnection of the library from these young people's lives was clearly evident and should be addressed by public libraries through community outreach.

9.3.5 Making Public Libraries More Appealing to Young People

While not everyone is interested in books and reading, public libraries need to consider other ways that could make them appealing to younger adults; key to this is outreach, communication and designing library services based on identified needs. The participants were asked whether anything would entice them to use the library. One respondent suggested that 'If they had good stuff like if they had games and all' (UM2). Gaming in libraries has been explored by McAdams (2010). McAdams (2010: 2) commented that 'computer gaming is part of popular culture and is currently being used in educational environments'. She adds that gaming 'has been linked to informal learning and is run successfully in libraries in the U.S., Europe and more recently, the UK', and 'it is slowly being acknowledged that computer gaming can have a positive impact on children's education' (McAdams, 2010: 12). This study by McAdams recognised the potential for gaming in libraries, not only to enhance literacy, ICT and social skills but also to be used as a 'marketing tool, to raise the profile of libraries' (McAdams, 2010: 58). Thus gaming could be used 'to attract unrepresentative groups in to the library' (McAdams, 2010: 60). McAdams noted that 'Libraries NI are planning to introduce some pilot gaming programmes into selected libraries in the next few years' (McAdams, 2010: 23), although I found no evidence that these have been introduced yet. Imaginative approaches to libraries are needed to encourage library usage across society and specifically among young, disaffected adults. Importantly, public libraries should be prepared to try new, innovative ways to engage with young people; in this they can learn from initiatives in other countries.

A youth leader suggested that the library could 'have a book club to help single parents' (YL1). A book club specifically for single parents could be considered as a means of targeting this demographic, and it could encourage information sharing and social participation. What is also important is that the youth leader was reflecting the circumstances of the community in which he lives, which arguably has a large proportion of single parents in comparison with more affluent areas. Moreover, as mentioned in Chapter 8, lone parents were identified by 45.5% survey respondents as a demographic that could be targeted more effectively in socially deprived areas. In addition, the youth leader suggested that the library could 'run workshops' similar to the ones they have at the community centre and things like that, the way we 'run courses' (YL1). This is an important comment and indicates that public libraries could learn from activities being run by community centres and offer more courses to develop ICT and employability skills. Such courses could be developed in libraries through partnerships with other community-based organisations and training providers; however, this could present challenges for public libraries in terms of financial resources. The other youth leader suggested that the library could 'have study groups and advertise food', commenting that a café and food would attract her (YL2). Because this youth leader had earlier confirmed that she had never been in the library, she was unaware that the local library already has a café. Exploring the possibility of having 'study groups' for adults could be an interesting and worthwhile activity in libraries. On a social note, she suggested that the library could also have 'speed-dating' (YL2). Imagination on the part of library strategists and managers is necessary to explore possible ventures that could improve the public library's capacity to reduce information poverty. The data indicated that public libraries need to be more flexible, innovative, imaginative and creative when designing services and activities that would appeal to those who do not use libraries. The need to base library services around what communities want and their information needs was noted by the community engagement staff, who suggested that whenever libraries are developing programmes, they,

> ...need to look and see what the communities are actually looking for. What sort of things they want in terms of IT, in terms of literacy, in terms of support for their children...Finding out what they want and not telling them what we can give them
> **(TSE1)**

The important thing for public libraries is to engage with communities, listen to what they want and act on this by creating relevant library services.

To improve library services for jobseekers, one of the youth leaders suggested a partnership with the job centre and possibly running English General Certificate of Education (GCSE) classes (YL1). As discussed in Chapter 6, public libraries have a role to play in developing literacy and ICT skills either in partnerships or by library staff themselves. The other youth leader added that library usage could be increased by 'advertising it' (YL2). This shows that marketing must improve. She added that they could help people 'do CVs' and provide courses 'to help people find jobs' and 'apply for jobs... because not everyone is interested, well I am not interested in the books' (YL2). Study skills support could be offered in public libraries; so too could programmes on financial literacy, career planning and creating CVs. As mentioned earlier and highlighted in the preceding quote, not everyone is interested in reading; this indicates that while reading is at the core of library services, libraries should be prepared to adapt to meet individuals' other needs.

9.3.6 Extracting Information Poverty Indicators From the Community Centre Focus Group 1

The participants acknowledged the social benefits of coming to the job club, enabling them to develop job-seeking skills and share information about jobs. Basically, the job club provided an opportunity for information sharing and social participation with people like themselves and from the same area. They explained that they were all friends outside the centre because they all live 'beside each other' (UF1). While there are many benefits to having the job club in the centre, the findings indicate that it is also an insular environment, reliant on informal strong ties with the local community and the small world. The data indicated that their information reach was limited, being confined to the community centre and local area; they relied on localised social networks to satisfy their information needs. This echoed Chatman's (1991) gratification theory, where she suggested that individuals from socioeconomically disadvantaged backgrounds would be less likely to seek information from outside their own social environment. The main information poverty indicators in focus group 1 were:

- social participation;
- the small-world environment (living close by each other with limited weak ties and insular social networks);
- reliance on trusted information sources such as friends/family;
- reliance on intimate sources rather than expert sources;
- limited awareness of library services;
- not using or valuing access to libraries and
- no interest in reading.

The data gathered from this focus group suggest that libraries need to change the perceptions of young people – to show they have something to offer them and to improve their services aimed at the younger generation. Fig. 9.3 presents the key indicators harvested from focus group 1.

Figure 9.3 Focus group 1: information poverty indicators.

9.3.7 Focus Group 1: Key Findings

There were seven main findings from focus group 1, comprising young people participating in a job club at a community centre in a socially deprived area:

- There was evidence of information poverty indicators, such as reliance on strong ties.
- Participants were reliant on intimate sources rather than expert sources and did not value access to library services.
- Evidence of a disconnection from the library; that is, these young people did not see the library as *their* library.
- The participants had computer and Internet access at home or within the community centre.
- There was evidence of an insular, 'small-world' information environment with a limited capacity to develop weak ties. The participants' information reach was within their local environment. This could be improved through collaboration with the library, the job centre and further education colleges.
- The library service was not having any impact on these young people; therefore libraries need to engage more with community-based organisations to develop community members' skills and address issues such as unemployment.
- The data suggest that public libraries need to address the disconnection with the younger generation and develop policy to target (1) young people NEET and (2) young people across the social spectrum.

The following section discusses the second focus group.

9.4 JOB CLUBS IN LIBRARIES

Since public libraries can support information access and provide a social space to the unemployed, it is important that they develop policies and strategies to target this demographic. In Northern Ireland, job clubs, in partnership with DEL, are taking place in 30 libraries (almost one-third) and demonstrate the benefits of working in partnership with other organisations to tackle information poverty. Through this partnership, DEL is responsible for delivering the sessions that focus on job-seeking strategies, interview skills and enhancing ICT skills (eg, learning how to create e-mail accounts and to use social media). As part of this partnership, libraries are responsible for providing the facilities and staff to support the unemployed when using computers and accessing information.

9.5 FOCUS GROUP 2: THE LIBRARY JOB CLUB

Focus group 2 was conducted with eight individuals participating in a job club, in partnership with DEL, in one of the libraries situated within the 10% most deprived areas in Northern Ireland.

Two job club leaders from DEL led the library job club sessions, which take place in the library 2 days/week over 4 weeks. Two participants were aged 18 to 24 years, and the others were of various ages. Participants in focus group 2 were asked whether they used the library before coming to the job club and for their opinions of library services, of the benefits of having the job club in the library, and, importantly, of how libraries could improve services to jobseekers. To supplement the focus group data, interviews were conducted with two job club leaders from DEL. The leaders were asked about the barriers to unemployment and the support that job club participants receive from library staff, as well as how DEL's partnership with Libraries NI was benefitting job club participants. The DEL job club leaders who were interviewed were labelled as DEL1 and DEL2. Table 9.2 shows how the focus group participants were labelled.

The job club helps participants to develop digital literacy skills, write CVs, create e-mail accounts, complete job applications and, at times, set up LinkedIn profiles. Similar to the job club in the community centre used in focus group 1, this job club introduces participants to social media (eg, Facebook and Twitter) as a 'means of job searching' (DEL2). Access to computers and the Internet in a neutral environment makes the library an ideal setting. Unlike focus group 1, within the community centre, the participants in the library job club did not know each other and were from diverse backgrounds and of various ages. Thus, this group potentially provides an environment where weak ties could be developed. It was a diverse group, and two of the participants were 18–24 years old.

One participant explained that being unemployed creates a sense of isolation, and a benefit of being at the job club was 'Realising you are not alone. There are so many different people here with their own problems about getting work' (JCUM1). This shows how participation in activities such as the job club can contribute to reducing social exclusion, and

Table 9.2 Focus group 2: Library job club respondent labels

Respondent category	Abbreviation
Unemployed males	JCUM1–4
Unemployed females	JCUF1–4

highlights how, through partnerships, public libraries can bring people together to develop skills, share information and build relationships.

Seven of the eight participants had GCSEs, half had A-levels, and one had a degree. The participant without a GCSE explained that he/she had completed 'ICT' and 'number skills courses' (JCUM1). Only one participant confirmed he/she had an ICT qualification. The data revealed that the participants had a varied range of ICT skills and qualifications. All but one stated they would use the Internet to look for jobs. Interesting findings emerged from the data, which provided evidence of information poverty and how it can be addressed by libraries. For instance, one participant stated that:

> I would be pretty reliant on the library computers. I would occasionally get onto a family member's computer once and a while…not since my last one basically gave up and just died. I haven't been able to afford a new one since
>
> (JCUM3)

This important quotation highlights the problems associated with being unemployed, such as not being able to afford a computer, which can exacerbate information poverty. It also emphasises the role of libraries in supporting access for those without the appropriate financial resources. Similarly, a participant who said that he does not seek job information online stated that:

> I don't have a computer at home. I have access to one, but I am only getting on to it through Job Club how to go about checking for jobs…I am old fashioned…I look at the paper and from word of mouth, but I am getting onto the computer now
>
> (JCUM1)

The importance of access to a 'computer at home' and being online is evidenced here. The quote also demonstrates how the library job club was encouraging him to access computers to search for jobs and to enhance his ICT skills.

9.5.1 Library Usage

The job club helped increase usage of the library: all participants are required to become members of the library to access library computers, although seven of the eight participants said they had used the library before coming to the job club. One participant explained that he had 'only joined the library in the last five weeks' since joining the job club (JCUM1). This respondent described how an older couple he knew were 'amazed to see' him 'come into the library' (JCUM1). This point highlights the perceptions people may have of who is a typical (or atypical) library user. Moreover, it indicates that public libraries can be welcoming places for everyone, and that partnerships, such as the DEL job club collaboration, can bring into libraries people who may never have used them before. Another participant noted that he 'used to' use the library but recently 'signed up just to get access to the computers' (JCUM3). He further explained that he would use the library:

Mainly just for job searching on the computer and printing out CVs, but I also joined because I wanted to be able to access books that would give me more information...

(JCUM3)

Likewise, another respondent described how he had used the library before coming to the job club, 'for printing out application forms' (JCUM2). These comments illustrate the vital role that libraries play in facilitating information access for those without a home computer, as well as access to relevant books. In doing this, libraries can assist in reducing information poverty.

One participant asserted that the library was 'good for children's books' and that he would bring his 2- and 4-year-old children, who 'love being read stories' by library staff and taking books home (JCUM4). Another participant highlighted the benefits of the library service, explaining that when she was at university she was able to 'get some real obscure texts' from the library that would have been too expensive to 'buy on the Internet' (JCUF1). This respondent thought that the library was 'a fabulous institution' and that she 'would have been stuck without it, from the basics of printing out your CV and applications...to really specialised things' (JCUF1). As the responses reveal, the local library can often be a place to obtain access to printed and online information, and resources and support are needed for those without the financial means to afford books, computers or printers.

The following section discusses the benefits of having the job club in the library, then outlines how the participants felt library services for jobseekers could be improved.

9.5.2 Benefits of the Library Job Club

The participants typically indicated that the library provided an easily accessible location and was less formal than the sometimes intimidating environment of the job centre; the public library can provide a more appealing and relaxing environment for jobseekers. Again, the welcoming library space was important to the job club participants. In addition, the library computers and the helpful library staff made the library an ideal location to facilitate this partnership. Another benefit of having this partnership in the library is that it provides an opportunity to promote the library's facilities (newspapers, books, ICT/Internet, free Wi-Fi), the support from library staff and the services to improve ICT skills, such as Got IT/Go ON. The library job club partnership is a good example of a collaborative working to help people become employed by developing the skills they need. By being imaginative and exploring new avenues for partnerships, public libraries can work with other organisations in tandem and in a mutually beneficial way that can enable both to tackle information poverty.

The next section investigates the information poverty indicators derived from focus group 2. Following this, the interviews with two job club leaders, added to supplement the focus group data, are discussed.

9.5.3 Extracting Information Poverty Indicators From the Library Job Club Focus Group

When the job club leaders outlined the main barriers for people seeking employment – financial, educational (literacy, ICT and numeracy skills), language – I could see similarities with the factors creating information poverty. The information poverty indicators that were harvested from the second focus group were different than those from the first. Members of the second focus group were more appreciative of the role that libraries could play compared with those in the first group, who were alienated from the local library. This could be because those in the second focus group were benefitting from participation in library services through the job club partnership. Where focus group 1 highlighted the insular environment of participants and the social indicators of information poverty, focus group 2 demonstrated contributing financial factors, such as lack of access to the Internet/personal computer and being unable to afford a home computer/Internet or books, and illustrated their limited ability to use a computer/Internet. These examples reflect information poverty indicators within the literature and the role of libraries in addressing these through library facilities and support. Fig. 9.4 summarises the indicators from focus group 2.

9.5.4 Focus Group 2: Key Findings

There were six main findings from focus group 2, comprising participants in a job club at a library situated within the 10% most socioeconomically deprived areas:

- The library job club was creating social capital by helping the participants to develop contacts outside their own community. Weak ties are possibly more likely to enhance their ability to obtain information about jobs.
- Information poverty indicators, such as limited access to computers/the Internet and being unable to afford a computer/the Internet, were being addressed.

Figure 9.4 Focus group 2: information poverty indicators. *PC,* personal computer.

- More positive opinions of library services were expressed, and the library services that benefit them were acknowledged.
- The group's responses highlighted how partnerships can be effective in delivering collaborative approaches to reduce information poverty.
- Job clubs bring people into libraries and encourage usage. Although they may not have previously been library users, these job club participants could now see value of library services.
- The group's responses indicate that developing services to the unemployed, for example, help with writing CVs, is an area that public libraries could provide more of.

The next section considers how public libraries could learn from other locations when developing services for the unemployed.

9.6 LEARNING FROM OTHER LOCATIONS

When public libraries develop initiatives, such as the job club partnership with DEL, they can be more effective at tackling information poverty and reducing social exclusion. The evidence in this chapter can be used to demonstrate, first, how information poverty can be addressed at the micro level, and second, how the data can be used to share best practices of joined-up approaches to library services to alleviate information poverty. By sharing best practices from other locations, public libraries can improve their capacity to overcome information poverty. An example of a public library strategy to assist the unemployed comes from the Republic of Ireland, where money has been provided to develop library staff to work with this group. For instance, Monaghan County Library has been involved in a number of partnership projects, such as the EU Leonardo Programme, which focuses on vocational training of library staff. In partnership with Bulgaria, Slovenia, Romania, Austria, Finland and Serbia, Monaghan County Library Services have been granted €18,000 to develop a model for the education of library staff to work with jobseekers and the long-term unemployed (Committee for the Development of the Public Libraries Strategy Ireland 2013–2017, 2013: 18). Similarly, Child and Goulding (2012: 644) provide the following examples of innovative outreach to the unemployed that are being implemented in libraries in England:

- The Thurrock Council (2010), held 'Bite Back at the Credit Crunch' workshops to help people through the recession and provided free sessions to assist local jobseekers update their CVs and search online for employment opportunities.
- Northumberland's library service hosted benefit and debt information sessions in partnership with the Citizens' Advice Bureau, Northumberland Care Trust, Jobcentre Plus and Northumberland Credit Union Ltd.
- Rotherham Libraries offered a Credit Crunch Roadshow, providing demonstrations of how to write job applications and apply for jobs online.

These are useful examples of how public libraries are 'targeting marketing to people on low-income' (Child and Goulding, 2012: 645). In New York, public libraries are playing a significant role in helping people into employment. Shrem (2012: 21) pointed out that, 'According to New York Mayor Michael Bloomberg, public libraries throughout the city helped place people in 35,000 jobs in 2011'. This evidence demonstrates the impact public libraries can have when they develop services to support the unemployed. Clearly, public libraries can learn from initiatives in other countries and develop a strategy to improve their services to the unemployed. Importantly, other locations could learn from the partnership that Libraries NI has with DEL and develop similar job clubs in their libraries.

9.7 SUMMARY AND CONCLUSIONS

This final section sums up how the focus groups were used successfully to investigate information poverty at the micro level. The framework presented in Chapter 4 (Table 4.2) was used to extract information poverty indicators from the focus group data. The micro-level findings highlighted various indicators, such as social participation, not having access to a computer/the Internet, being unable to afford a computer/the Internet and not valuing access to libraries. Attitudes towards libraries were very different in each of the focus groups. The first one, including participants of a job club in a community centre, expressed more negative attitudes. These young people were unaware of the library's offerings and assumed that it did not have anything to interest them.

The community centre job club and the library job club could learn from each other. Both focus groups had their own strengths. For instance, the job club in the community centre was in a familiar environment in which participants felt comfortable. While this had its advantages, it can also be an insular and restricting environment in terms of sharing information, accessing resources, and providing opportunities to build new relationships outside the local environment. This job club could also benefit from collaboration with the library, the local job centre and further education colleges. The first focus group validated some of the reasons why people in disadvantaged areas were not using libraries, which were also noted by interviewees at the macro and meso levels. Perhaps most important, focus group 1 highlighted the need for greater engagement with socially deprived communities to raise awareness of library services, develop closer links and design and deliver services based on community needs.

The library job club was an example of a partnership working effectively to the benefit of participants, a government department (DEL) and the library service. Furthermore, the DEL job club partnership provides evidence that strategy at the macro level can have an impact on individuals at the micro level. While the data do not show evidence of people getting jobs by using library services, it clearly demonstrates the contribution of libraries in reducing information poverty and developing skills for employment. The findings show that, by gathering evidence of participants' attitudes towards libraries and the ICT skills and information resources available within the social networks of individuals in deprived areas, the focus groups were an effective way of investigating information poverty at the micro level.

I believe that the information poverty indicators could be used in other library settings to measure the impact of library services. For instance, they could be used to assess how well macro-level strategies to support learning and develop skills are being implemented and delivered by public libraries through ICT programmes. In addition, the indicators could be used to measure the effectiveness of services to other groups, such as the elderly, and how library services can alleviate information poverty among rural dwellers.

Chapter 10 concludes the book, summing up some of the main points raised and providing final recommendations for public libraries.

CHAPTER 10

Concluding Thoughts and Recommendations

10.1 INTRODUCTION

The premise of this book has been to examine what information poverty is and how it can be addressed by public libraries. This concluding chapter synthesises the main findings of the book and provides recommendations for policies and practices that could be applied to public libraries in any setting to improve their capacity to address information poverty. Moreover, it considers the wider implications of the book, both within the library and the non-library context, and suggests that the macro, meso and micro information poverty framework could be applied in other settings.

10.2 SUMMING UP

In essence, this book articulates and promotes the purpose, role and ethos of the public library in the early 21st century and the potential impact libraries can have on society, communities and individuals. The preceding chapters illustrate the changing educational and social role of public libraries. Importantly, they investigate what public libraries can do to develop learning and tackle social exclusion; together, the chapters consider libraries' potential impact on society when services are targeted in the appropriate direction. *Overcoming Information Poverty* adds to the literature on the strategic direction of public libraries and the challenges they face in terms of funding, remaining relevant, adhering to government policies and being prepared to adapt and change to meet future information and communication needs.

This text further develops an academic understanding of information poverty and how it can be addressed by public libraries. It is based on a significant piece of research conducted at a time when information poverty is an area of concern in modern society. The three-level approach used here is effective in reflecting the interrelationships of the various levels of information poverty and how they can be addressed by public libraries. The evidence articulates what information poverty is, what the causes and

Overcoming Information Poverty
ISBN 978-0-08-101110-2

impacts are and how public libraries can play a leading role in alleviating it. This book further demonstrates that whilst public libraries have a significant role in combating information poverty, they also have a valuable part in tackling poverty in general. In doing this public libraries can contribute to a more information-rich society, tackle poverty and low educational attainment and enhance social, cultural and digital inclusion.

Overcoming Information Poverty is important at three levels. First, at an academic level, it contributes to the existing literature on information poverty, social exclusion and the role of libraries. Second, the research is important for public libraries in that the recommendations arising from it can be used to inform future library policies. Third, this research is of value to policymakers at the government level who may be attempting to reduce information poverty and educational underachievement and to alleviate social deprivation. Thus, this book examines information poverty from theoretical and practical perspectives and can be a useful tool for academics and researchers, library strategists, branch library managers, policymakers and practitioners, as well as education specialists and government departments responsible for tackling poverty, education and lifelong learning and social and digital exclusion.

Using the Northern Ireland context to investigate information poverty, *Overcoming Information Poverty* identifies the areas where public libraries are making an impact, but also the areas in which library services could be improved to increase library usage. Evidently, more people need to use library services and avail themselves of the facilities and support that library staff can provide. When completing my PhD thesis (upon which this book is based), I concluded that for Libraries NI to be more effective at addressing information poverty, its service priorities should be reflected in its staffing structures. Importantly, because targeting poverty and social exclusion is the main focus of the Department of Culture, Arts and Leisure, I concluded that Libraries NI needs to channel its resources more effectively and commit more fully to this by having more staff in community engagement roles. This study highlights the important work of community engagement staff. It is imperative that community engagement positions be permanent and sustainable, since temporary solutions to developing library usage within socially deprived areas will not work. I believe that public libraries should place a stronger focus on community outreach so that they can effectively address information poverty in both urban and rural locations.

While the Northern Ireland context was used throughout this text, the macro-, meso- and micro-level framework of indicators can be adapted and applied to any public library setting and within other educational and social contexts to address information poverty. Furthermore, because information poverty is widespread within modern society, it needs to be addressed not just by public libraries and librarians, but at a national and even global level by government departments. While this book focuses specifically on information poverty and libraries, the findings may also be applicable for policymakers involved in addressing information poverty, social exclusion and skills development. Other library sectors, governments or community organisations could apply the framework to their own individual setting. Consequently, *Overcoming Information Poverty* advances the understanding of information poverty on an international, national and local scale.

10.3 FUTURE CHALLENGES FOR PUBLIC LIBRARIES

In the future public libraries will face many challenges. First, they need to be able to demonstrate clearly their impact on society, communities and individuals in order to secure government funding. Second, remaining socially and technologically relevant and adapting to meet changing information and communication technologies (ICTs) is fundamental. Third, library marketing and image need to improve, with a focus on changing people's perceptions of library staff and libraries. They also need to be able to raise awareness, promote the uniqueness of library services and address the issue of non-usage. Fourth, public libraries need to be more proactive in their outreach to socioeconomically deprived communities, communicating with small-world groups and developing information and library services that can assist marginalised groups to become socially and digitally included. Finally, libraries need to work collaboratively with other government departments to overcome social and digital exclusion, and they require effective leadership who can communicate a vision for libraries. These issues are given further consideration below.

If public libraries are to improve low educational attainment and limited skills, they need to identify areas of need, target outreach to these communities and develop more services based on these needs. Importantly, libraries need to connect with socially deprived areas and communicate with those who have never used a library and those who are not using libraries anymore; libraries must show that they are worthwhile places. While library outreach is key to addressing information poverty and encouraging participation in library services, this requires additional resources such as staff and financing. The challenge for public libraries is identifying where they can have the most impact and can target resources most effectively, then making this engagement sustainable.

In addition, to improve the capacity of public libraries to overcome information poverty, better marketing and promotion are needed so that more people are made aware of and encouraged to use the resources and support that public libraries provide. The importance of marketing and promoting library services was noted throughout the interviews and is clearly a major issue that libraries need to improve on if they are to increase usage by those who could benefit most from their services. Public libraries need to be more creative and innovative in their bid to keep customers and attract new users – to market and promote what they are good at, which is enriching the lives of citizens, and that they are free to all, a place to learn and a communal space where people of all ages, social backgrounds and nationalities are welcome. Changing people's perceptions of public libraries and enhancing their awareness of what libraries can do to enrich their lives is paramount to libraries' future success. An area that needs attention is targeted marketing, aimed at increasing awareness of library services and usage within socially disadvantaged areas. A key challenge for public libraries is that they must meet the changing and growing expectations of 21st century users. The public library service needs to be more proactive in its approach to attracting non-library users by more effectively promoting its services, being more flexible, and being willing to develop services based on identified needs.

Library leaders and managers face many challenges in relation to how libraries will maintain the relevance of their services and improve and sustain library usage. There needs to be a vision of how the library service can remain influential and meet the needs of 21st century users. Library leaders need to be able to communicate their purpose and develop a vision that can promote the ethos of public libraries as they exist in modern society. As public library services change and evolve to meet the information and communication needs of their users, a culture change will be required of staff, whose roles will adapt to incorporate new technologies and new ways to access information. Libraries need to take advantage of the opportunities provided by new technologies, particularly more sophisticated ICTs, and target these resources to those with the greatest need. Consequently, remaining relevant in the digital age is fundamental for the survival of public libraries.

My recommendations, emanating from my research findings, are listed below. These recommendations provide a comprehensive framework to improve the capacity of public libraries to overcome information poverty at strategic and community levels, and they can influence public library strategies and the future vision for public libraries within the United Kingdom and farther afield.

10.4 RECOMMENDATIONS FOR POLICY AND PRACTICE

The research presented here demonstrates that the macro-, meso- and micro-level indicators are an effective way of measuring the impact of library services on reducing information poverty. The recommendations presented in this section are based on the key themes that emerged from the data and reflect the broad range of discussion in the previous chapters.

10.4.1 Recommendation 1: Develop an Information Poverty Strategy

Public library authorities should develop an information poverty strategy that is aligned to their government priorities to tackle poverty, address skill deficits and low educational attainment, and alleviate social and digital exclusion. I make the following related recommendations:

• Library policymakers and staff at all levels should understand what information poverty is and the part public libraries play in addressing it.

• Public libraries should develop policies to address information poverty that are aligned to government responsibilities to create more socially, culturally and digitally inclusive societies.

• Addressing information poverty requires multilevel solutions; therefore public libraries should develop strategic and community-level partnerships with government departments and educational organisations that are attempting to reduce information poverty and reduce social and digital exclusion.

• Public libraries need improved collaboration with educators at government levels to develop literacy, information literacy and digital literacy skills.

• Public libraries should develop close links with the academic research community in their areas to conduct research and share knowledge regarding social, political and technological issues, poverty, libraries and information access.

• Public libraries should have a digital strategy to promote access to and support for online government, social and educational information.

• Wi-Fi should be freely available in all public libraries to both library members and non-members.

- Strategies should be developed to tackle information poverty in both rural and urban locations.
- Public libraries should strategically focus on how ICTs can be used to improve digital access by the socially and digitally excluded within society.

10.4.2 Recommendation 2: Develop and Implement a Community Engagement Strategy

Developing and implementing an effective community engagement strategy is key to promoting library services and to targeting those groups who could benefit most from libraries. Public libraries need to develop long-term, sustainable community engagement strategies and plans. This involves having more community engagement staff (at the grade above branch library manager) with a specific remit to support branch managers and to develop links with hard-to-reach groups and raise awareness of library services. I make the following recommendations:

- Long-term approaches to community engagement are needed. Therefore collaboration with community groups should be continuous and resources – financial and human – should be provided for this.
- Libraries should be at the heart of communities, fully integrated into community life and built around the community hub concept.
- Library staff working within communities should understand what information poverty is and their role in reducing it.
- Branch library managers should network within their communities, focusing on local information and educational needs and establishing community partnerships.
- There needs to be more proactive engagement with local communities and more partnerships with voluntary agencies and educational groups to promote public libraries and ensure they reach out to all members of society.
- Community-level partnerships should be developed with organisations so that an integrated approach to addressing information poverty is implemented within socially deprived areas.
- Outreach to isolated rural communities is needed.
- There should be greater community involvement in the design and delivery of library services. Hence local communities should have more influence on the services provided in libraries; these services should be based on communication with these communities and ascertaining what local groups want their library to provide.

10.4.3 Recommendation 3: Further Develop the Educational Role of Public Libraries

Public libraries need to tackle educational and social disadvantage. For public libraries to be more successful at reducing information poverty, their educational role has to be at their core. I make the following recommendations:

- Public libraries should work at a strategic level with other organisations, educational bodies and government bodies to develop partnerships to improve literacy standards.

- There needs to be greater collaboration with the adult education sector, and the role of libraries in informal learning in the digital age needs to be promoted.

- Libraries should build links with adult learners and community-based education providers. Learning programmes for literacy and ICT should be based on the needs of communities and groups.

- Libraries need to be innovative and develop a skills strategy to improve their capacity to promote reading, literacy and ICT skills development.

- A skills strategy should be developed to target those with low educational attainment/poor literacy and poor information and digital literacy skills.

- An information literacy skills strategy should be developed and implemented within communities to focus on empowering communities and individuals with the knowledge of where to obtain information and the skills to access essential information.

- Libraries should promote their educational role to adult learners, especially in socially deprived areas. The role of libraries as 'street-corner universities' should be promoted.

- Libraries need to develop closer links with local schools: primary and secondary, school librarians, further education colleges and universities.

- Where possible, libraries should deliver both ICT and adult literacy classes, in partnership with other organisations and further education colleges, or by trained library staff.

- Where possible, introduce adult literacy and language classes in areas where there is an identified need, for example, areas with low educational attainment or targeted at minorities who need support.

- Libraries need to more effectively promote reader development, especially among those with basic literacy skills.

10.4.4 Recommendation 4: Further Develop the Social Role of Public Libraries

Overcoming Information Poverty demonstrates the social value of public libraries as places where information can be shared in neutral, non-stigmatising environments. Libraries as community hubs can be places where any member of society is welcome. I make the following recommendations:

- Public libraries should promote their role as an information hub, a community hub and a social hub.
- Promote the role of libraries in facilitating social interaction and bringing together people from diverse backgrounds.
- The social value of libraries (both the physical and online space) should be developed and promoted more to encourage social participation.
- Libraries should promote their capacity to develop weak ties and provide spaces where people can develop and extend their social networks.
- Libraries should further develop online communities for reading and learning and should encourage participation.
- Where possible, libraries should develop social spaces that encourage specific groups such as teenagers, young adults and minority populations.

10.4.5 Recommendation 5: Raising Awareness and Marketing

Improving the usage of public libraries will further advance their ability to tackle information poverty: marketing and raising awareness are fundamental to this. I make the following recommendations:

- Public libraries need proactive marketing strategies aimed at increasing library usage and participation, specifically in socioeconomically deprived areas where people could benefit most from using libraries.
- Libraries should identify which demographics within specific areas are not using library services, for example, young people, the elderly, the disabled and minorities.
- Library leaders should work to raise the profile of libraries within government and educational organisations in order to promote and raise awareness of library resources.
- National marketing campaigns to raise awareness of library services and reading should be implemented to promote library services and create a positive image of libraries. This will cost money but would be a worthwhile promotional tool.
- The role of libraries in developing informal learning should be promoted more effectively.

- The enhanced role of libraries in supporting digital access to government information should be promoted at the national level to politicians, government advisers and ministers.
- Public libraries need to promote a more positive image of libraries and library staff than the one which currently prevails. They need to change the stereotypical perception about libraries and library staff.
- Change the young people's perceptions of libraries by showing that they have something to offer them, and develop library services aimed at the younger generation.

10.4.6 Recommendation 6: Identifying and Targeting Groups

Specific groups could be identified and targeted more successfully. Outreach and dialogue with groups are needed to ascertain their information needs. I make the following recommendations:

- Public libraries should develop partnerships with government departments and agencies that are addressing the needs of groups such as the disabled, minorities, lone parents, the elderly, the unemployed, those with limited qualifications/skills and young people not in education, employment or training.
- Libraries need to develop policies that specify how certain groups will be targeted.
- Libraries should identify and target those with no qualifications and limited ICT and literacy skills who are most at risk for information poverty.
- Libraries need to make a connection with the younger generation and make younger people feel that the library is their place. Teenagers could be targeted through outreach to schools. Young people aged 18–24 years who are not in education, employment or training should also be targeted.
- Libraries need to develop a process of continual communication and outreach to schools, colleges and community organisations.
- Services for an increasing older population should be improved. Initiatives for ICT/Internet/email training, iPad training, reading groups and social activities should be targeted to this demographic.
- Adult men should be targeted more effectively. Encouraging adult men to read more and to see reading as a family activity is important. More partnerships with local organisations that target men – for example, through sport, hobbies (arts, crafts, gardening), ICT skills training – could attract this demographic.
- Libraries need to focus on marginalised/hard-to-reach groups, communicating with them and identifying their needs.

10.4.7 Recommendation 7: Developing Services for the Unemployed

Public libraries have a key role in developing skills needed for the workforce. Libraries can potentially contribute to wider government initiatives to create a better qualified and more skilled workforce. I believe that the role of libraries in preparing people for the job market could be promoted and developed more. I make the following recommendations:

- Public libraries should develop strategies to encourage use of libraries by unemployed people.
- Libraries should promote their value and provide support to develop workforce skills, marketing the library as a social space for unemployed people.
- Libraries should be promoting their role in contributing to government agendas to create a more skilled workforce.
- Library leaders should seek to develop innovative partnerships with government departments and agencies to improve the employability skills of those trying to find work and support their access to information.
- Libraries should share best practices about how public libraries have assisted people back to work in other locations.
- Develop training in libraries for unemployed people, either in partnership with other organisations or by library staff themselves: for example, sessions on writing curricula vitae, using social media, enhancing employability skills and job searching.
- Within local communities libraries should develop programmes to improve ICT skills, literacy skills and the information skills of unemployed people.
- Libraries need to develop partnerships with community-based organisations that work with the unemployed, for example, local job clubs, job clinics, drop-in centres and employment agencies.
- Libraries need to provide appropriate stock and information for jobseekers, on curriculum vitae building, attending interviews.
- Promote access to information and support to assist people to set up a business.

10.4.8 Recommendation 8: Improving Stock

Appropriate stock, tailored to meet the needs of specific groups, is fundamental. I make the following recommendations:

- Library stock should be based on what people want so that resources are not wasted on books that are not read.
- Partnerships should be developed with government departments and the education sector to promote library stock.

- Stock policy should consider adults with basic or limited literacy skills.
- Stock should be based on engagement with groups, reflecting the specific needs of communities and groups.
- Stock and resources should be tailored for specific groups, for example, ethnic minorities, the disabled (visually impaired) or touch-screen technologies for those who are illiterate.
- Provision of local community information should be developed and promoted in libraries.
- Library stock should reflect practical needs (eg, the driving theory test).
- Libraries should provide improved stock for parents who are trying to support their children in mathematics, English, science.
- Libraries should have stock for children and adults who are trying to learn English.

10.4.9 Recommendation 9: Library Staff

Staff are key to the success of public libraries. If public libraries are to be effective at addressing information poverty, they need to have staff with expert skills and knowledge who are able to support the public. I make the following recommendations:

- Library leaders need to manage and communicate changing priorities for library services.
- Library leaders need to promote a vision for libraries and demonstrate their impact.
- Public library leaders should identify appropriately qualified and skilled staff for leadership positions, mentor them and encourage their professional development.
- Where possible, public libraries should create positions, such as cultural inclusion officers or cultural engagement officers, to develop strategy and focus on improving services and information access by ethnic minorities and migrants.
- Library staff need awareness training to enhance their understanding of the needs of those with low educational attainment and those at risk of social exclusion.
- Library staff at various levels should develop marketing skills to promote and raise awareness of library services.
- Library staff need to keep up to date with new technologies. Continual training on new technologies and social media is important.
- Staff should develop teaching/training skills to support library users with language, literacy, and information and digital literacy skills.

- Libraries should deliver awareness sessions on what information poverty is, its impacts and the role of libraries in addressing it.
- Staff should be aware of learning within communities and be able to direct adult learners to formal and informal learning providers.
- Staff development should be continuous and encouraged, with a focus on keeping up to date with technologies, and providing superior customer care and being aware of social exclusion.
- Staff should maintain awareness of recent developments and services provided elsewhere.
- Library staff should be encouraged to gain Library and Information Management qualifications.

I now offer some concluding thoughts.

10.5 CONCLUDING THOUGHTS

As this book reveals, information poverty affects many elements of society and can affect an individual's capacity to participate in wider society. *Overcoming Information Poverty* highlights the important role of public libraries in addressing information poverty and the need for library strategists and policymakers to see it as a priority within their strategic plans. It is imperative that library leaders develop an awareness of poverty and its impacts, be aware of barriers to accessing libraries and adopt strategies to improve library usage. Focusing library services on the digitally and socially excluded may require a change in the organisational culture and an acceptance that public libraries can have the greatest impact when they target the most educationally and socially disadvantaged within society.

The book is based on up-to-date, evidence-based research on an issue in which public libraries play a fundamental part. This text can be used by library managers and leaders, policymakers within the government and educators who are interested in improving their understanding of how people access information. Real-life examples of how information poverty affects society, communities and individuals are provided herein; therefore knowledge of information poverty can be further developed by using this book. Moreover, an in-depth examination of what public libraries were historically, what they are currently and how their role is evolving to satisfy both digital and social inclusion agendas is provided. In addition, examples of practical measures to overcome information poverty are described. The previous literature in the area of information poverty was synthesised with empirical data from a recent study to illustrate how public libraries in the 21st century can reduce information poverty.

While *Overcoming Information Poverty* is based on examples from Northern Ireland, this unique information poverty framework to measure the impact of public libraries is also adaptable and undoubtedly has wider appeal. This book is based on transferable research, and the framework could be modified and applied to evaluate strategies and services in other contexts. The three-level framework is a significant tool for evaluating public library services and can be used in various library settings.

I hope this book stimulates thought and debate on information poverty and how it may be addressed by public libraries, education departments and governments.

APPENDICES

APPENDIX 1: MACRO- AND MESO-LEVEL INTERVIEWEES

Macro-level interviewees
Chair of the Libraries NI board
DCAL Deputy Principal
DCAL Director
Chief Executive of Libraries NI
Director of Library Services, Libraries NI
Director of Business Support
Assistant Director Area A (e2)
Assistant Director Area B (Bibliographic and Stock Services)
Assistant Director Area C (Culture and Heritage)
Assistant Director Area D (Learning and Information)
Head of Themes
Specialist Manager, Heritage and Digitisation
Operations Manager Area A
Operations Manager Area B
Operations Manager Area D
Staff Development Officer
Stock Manager
Meso-level interviewees
TSE Community Project Officer
TSE Community Support Officer 1
TSE Community Support Officer 2

APPENDIX 2: SURVEY QUESTIONS

1. Do you agree to the consent information listed on this form?
2. How long have you held the position of Branch Library Manager? (Please tick)
   Answer options: Under 1 year, 2–5 years, Over 5 years.
3. In which of the following tier groups is your library situated? (Please tick)
   Answer options: Tier 1, Tier 2, Tier 3.
4. As a branch library manager, do you have experience targeting library services to socially deprived areas? (Please tick)
   Answer options: Yes/No, Please explain your answer.

5. What are the main challenges facing branch library managers in socially deprived areas? (Tick the five main challenges from the list.)
   - Connecting with people who are not using libraries
   - Providing relevant information resources and services
   - Promoting library services to individuals who have no tradition of library use
   - Understanding community information needs
   - Understanding the barriers people may have in accessing/using libraries
   - Developing local community partnerships
   - Addressing low levels of library use/participation
   - Convincing people that the library has something to offer
   - Identifying and targeting services to the socially excluded
   - Identifying and developing links with hard-to-reach groups
   - Learning about the community's social and cultural norms
6. In the space below give one example of a 'hard-to-reach group' in your area.
7. In the space below give one example of how you have targeted 'hard-to-reach' groups in your area.
8. Is information poverty a new concept to you?
   Answer options: Yes/No, Please explain your answer.
9. Do you think that addressing information poverty should be a priority for Libraries NI?
   Answer options: Yes/No, Please explain your answer.
10. In your view, which of the following library activities/services can best reduce information poverty? (Tick the five that you feel are the most important.)
    - Access to personal computers/technologies
    - Tailored information and stock
    - Radiofrequency identification frequency
    - Mobile library services
    - Community-based information (print and online)
    - Information and communication technology (ICT) skills training
    - Virtual learning environment
    - Information literacy support
    - Ebooks
    - Online resources (eg, Britannica, Oxford, Ancestry)
    - Basic literacy support and related initiatives
    - Book clubs/reading groups

* Social activities/events
* Digital literacy support
* Information provision (online and print)
* Access and support to e-government information

11. Please rank, from 1 to 7, with 1 being the most important, the areas that Libraries NI should be developing more to target social need.
    * Access to information relevant to community needs
    * Promote and support online access to government services
    * Improve numeracy skills
    * Improve access to personal computers/technologies
    * Improve adult literacy skills
    * Improve information and communication technology skills
    * Improve information literacy skills

12. In the libraries situated within the 10% most socially deprived areas, to which of the following groups do you think that Libraries NI could be more effectively targeting information access and services? (Tick the five who could be better targeted.)
    * Homeless
    * Those with low educational attainment/poor literacy
    * Lone parents
    * Jobseekers
    * Ex-prisoners
    * Young people aged 18–24 years (Not in Employment, Education or Training)
    * Disabled (mentally impaired/learning difficulties)
    * Travellers
    * Disabled (hearing impaired, visually impaired)
    * Farmers/rural dwellers
    * Elderly
    * Ethnic minorities
    * Those with no/limited ICT skills
    * Teenagers
    * Migrants

13. For jobseekers, does your library provide the following? (Please select all that apply.)
    * Job clubs
    * Assistance for curricula vitae/applications
    * Appropriate information/stock for jobseekers
    * Employability roadshows

- Career events
- One-on-one support to develop digital and information literacy skills
- Targeted support for younger adults aged 18–25 years

14. Select which of the following targets for TSN apply to your branch. (Tick all that apply.)
   - Storytime
   - Deliver ICT skills training (one-on-one or group)
   - Reading groups
   - Develop partnerships
   - Increasing usage of e-books and online resources
   - Rhythm & Rhyme
   - Increase usage/membership/participation
   - Increase Public Access Terminals (PAT)/WiFi use
   - Basic literacy initiatives
   - Setting up or developing an existing job club
   - Class visits
   - Cultural activities/events
   - Health in Mind activities
   - Deliver programmes outside the library

15. Which of the following activities/programmes do you have in your library? (Please tick all that apply.)
   - Adult reading group
   - Teenage reading group
   - Junior reading group
   - Reading group for blind/visually impaired
   - Other languages/cultures reading group
   - Homework clubs
   - Basic literacy classes
   - Job clubs
   - Social media training
   - ICT training

16. In the space below, give one example of community outreach where you have delivered a library activity/programme outside the library building?

17. Have you developed any community partnerships within socially deprived areas?
   Answer options: Yes/No, Please explain your answer.

18. In socially disadvantaged areas people may not use libraries because they…
   - use the Internet for their information needs.

- have poor literacy and limited education.
- have low self-esteem and lack self-confidence to come in to the library.
- are not interested in education or see the value of lifelong learning to improve their life chances.
- do not think libraries provide information that is relevant to their needs.
- see libraries as being like formal education/school.
- get the information they need from within their own social networks such as friends, family and neighbours.
- find the library layout/signage confusing and not accessible to them.
- have negative images of library staff, they feel that staff are patronising and elitist.
- see libraries as dusty and silent places.
- are not aware of the range of resources and services available in libraries.
- feel that libraries are only for educated, middle-class people.

Answer options: Strongly disagree, Disagree, Unsure, Agree, Strongly agree.

19. Thank you for taking the time to fill in this questionnaire.

If you wish to add any further comments please do so in the space below.

APPENDIX 3: INFORMATION POVERTY INDICATORS FROM THE MACRO-LEVEL DATA

The indicators derived from the macro-level interviews with the Department of Culture, Arts and Leisure and Libraries NI are presented in the table below. These indicators are mainly consistent with the indicators detailed in the literature review and presented in Table 4.2.

Information Poverty Indicators (IPIs) From Macro-Level Interviews

Information Poverty Indicators (IPIs)
IPI 1: Access to Information
- Lack of access to infrastructure and the knowledge to use it
- Lack of access to information in different media format (physical/electronic)
- Limited access to quality forms of information
- Not having access to relevant information
- Information not being presented in an accessible way.

IPI 2: Literacy
- Low literacy skills
- Poor literacy among parents, including young/single mothers
- Low literacy levels in areas of social need.

IPI 3: Educational Attainment
- Limited education (poor literacy, basic skills, no/few qualifications).

IPI 4: Information and Communication Technology (ICT) Skills
- Lack of computer/ICT skills
- Inability to access online government services
- Pace of change in ICT.

IPI 5: Information Literacy
- Inability to use information appropriately and apply information to one's own situation
- Inability to evaluate and interpret the quality of information
- Limited awareness and understanding of financial information; limited financial literacy skills and benefit information
- Limited awareness and understanding of health information (limited health literacy skills).

IPI 6: Information Affordability
- Unable to afford information technology infrastructure and equipment
- Unable to afford a home computer and/or laptop
- Unable to afford a broadband/Internet connection
- Does not have a mobile phone with Internet access
- Unable to afford access to printed information (books, newspapers, magazines).

IPI 7: Information Behaviour
- Does not value access to information
- Chooses not to use libraries or access information (personal choice).

IPI 8: Information Opportunity
- Limited ability/opportunity to be part of the information society
- Limited ability/opportunities to access information to improve one's life
- Limited/few aspirations, expectations, ambitions.

IPI 9: Social Participation
- Limited social networks; social barriers (small world)
- Unable to access information that is available to communities through social media
- Lack of empowerment and knowledge to participate.

IPI 10: Institutional Barriers Preventing Access
- Language is presented in a bureaucratic way, which prevents access
- Lack of confidence and trust
- Has a poor experience of formal education.

IPI 11: Information Awareness
- Does not knowing the range of information available.

APPENDIX 4: THE 20 MOST CITED INDICATORS OF INFORMATION POVERTY IN THE LITERATURE

1. Literacy (34)
2. Language (32)
3. Lack of access to information and communication technology (ICT)/ personal computers (PCs) (28)
4. Being online/Internet access (28)
5. Lack of ICT skills competency/capabilities, digital skills, ability to use ICT, use software (20)
6. Lack of education, unequal education, poor education (20)
7. Lack of an information infrastructure (20)
8. Lack of access to information (19)
9. Information literacy (16)
10. Being economically poor, socioeconomic status (15)
11. Technical skills/competency to access and use information (14)
12. Cognitive disability (13)
13. Telephones at home/telephone access (13)
14. Reliance on informal information networks (13)
15. Information overload, information burden, 'infobesity' (12)
16. Inability to physically access information as the result of a physical disability such as blindness, deafness, physical handicap (11)
17. PC ownership (13)
18. Ethnicity/cultural diversity/immigrants/cultural barriers and limitations (9)
19. Mobile phone ownership/iPhone/mobile phone access (8) + television at home/no access to television (8)
20. Information value (inability to ascertain the value and usability of information) (8)

APPENDIX 5: INFORMATION POVERTY INDICATORS FRAMEWORK

Macro-level indicators of information poverty
1. Physical access to information
2. Digital inclusion (e-government, Digital by Default)
3. Educational attainment (literacy and information and communication technology skills)
4. Poverty and social exclusion

Meso-level indicators of information poverty

5. Access to information services in areas of social deprivation

6. Social participation

7. Community information access

8. Educational attainment

9. Ethnic groups/minorities in area

Micro-level indicators of information poverty

10. Skills and knowledge deficits

11. Information literacy deficits

12. Technical skills

13. Disabilities

14. Information affordability

15. Information behaviour

16. Information awareness

17. Institutional barriers

APPENDIX 6: SUMMARY AND EXPLANATION OF LIBRARIES NI'S CORE ACTIVITIES AND PROGRAMMES

Rhythm & Rhyme	Rhythm & Rhyme is for pre-school children. In most libraries sessions run on a weekly, fortnightly or monthly basis and last for around 30 min. Each session incorporates a mixture of songs, rhymes and stories suitable for this age group.
Got IT	One-on-one or small-group computer sessions are delivered by library staff to any member of the public. Sessions last between 45 min and 1 h, and participants can attend up to five sessions. The session includes computer basics (mouse, keyboard, open/close programmes); basic Internet skills (finding way around a Website, using the address bar, simple searches) and email (set up account, send/receive emails).
Go ON	These information and communication technology sessions are more advanced than Got IT and takes learners one step further. Additional skills learned are social networking, job-seeking, searching for travel information and shopping online. Some libraries offer Go ON iPad introduction sessions.
Six Book Challenge	The Six Book Challenge is a tool developed by the Reading Agency to encourage reluctant readers to engage with books. This programme is for adults with basic literacy skills. It encourages less confident or motivated readers to read any six books over an agreed-upon period and to record their reading in a diary.

Story time	Story times are held in most libraries on a weekly, fortnightly or monthly basis. They are suitable for children between 5 and 8 years old. Sessions usually lasted for around 30 min and consist of stories read by members of library staff.
Class visits programme	Schools are invited to their local library for a programme consisting of three visits for primary 4 (7–8 years) and primary 6 (9–10 years) children. These sessions provide children with an introduction to the library, a tour of the library, an activity related to library stock and an introduction to the use of the computers in the library. School children are encouraged to join the library.
Reading group	Reading groups meet in many of the libraries, usually on a monthly basis. Some libraries provide a mixture of adult, children's and teenage reading groups. Some reading groups cater specifically to disabled users, for example, visually or hearing impaired readers. In addition, some libraries host reading groups in other languages, such as Irish. Reading groups are sometimes tailored to specific reading tastes, for example, classic literature.
Homework club	Some libraries offer help with homework for Primary school children. These are sometimes themed homework support to coincide with celebrations within the library, such as Shakespeare week.
Summer Reading Challenge	This project is organised by the Reading Agency and offers children the opportunity to continue in the reading habit during the summer. It encourages independent reading for pleasure and for children to read at least six books over the summer holidays. Incentives are offered, and children who complete the challenge are presented with a certificate upon completion. This activity is aimed at children aged 4–12 years across Northern Ireland, with all libraries and mobile libraries participating.
Knit and Natter	A group for people who enjoy knitting, crocheting, cross-stitching and other crafts. It provides the opportunity to share tips, swap patterns, meet new friends and develop new skills.
Job club	Job clubs are a partnership with the Department of Employment and learning (DEL). They are led by staff from DEL and use library facilities, such as computers and Internet access. They run for 4 weeks and enable participants to develop information-seeking skills, write curricula vitae and develop social media skills. Participants are required to become members of the library so they can access library computers and the Internet.

Reminscence sessions	These involve library outreach to residential homes for the elderly. Library staff bring photographs and newspaper articles from the library service's heritage collection. The sessions encourage discussion about the photographs and articles so the elderly participants can reflect on their youth and a bygone era. These sessions can be therapeutic and beneficial for the mental well-being of the elderly residents.
Online resources: Ancestry Library Edition	Ancestry Library Edition enables users to search census records to retrieve information about their ancestors. It is only available on Libraries NI computers and cannot be accessed from home.

REFERENCES

Anderson, B., 2005. The value of mixed-method longitudinal panel studies in ICT research: transitions in and out of "ICT poverty" as a case in point. Information, Communication and Society 8 (3), 343–367.

Barbour, R.S., Kitzinger, J., 1999. Developing Focus Group Research: Politics, Theory and Practice. Sage, London.

Barja, G., Gigler, B.S., 2007. The concept of information poverty and how to measure it in the Latin American context. In: Galperin, H., Mariscal, J. (Eds.), Digital Poverty: Perspectives from Latin America and the Caribbean. International Development Research Centre, Ottawa, pp. 11–28.

Bates, J., 2008. The Information Needs and Information Seeking Behaviour of Adults Living in a Working-Class Neighbourhood in Dublin (Unpublished Ph.D. thesis). University College, Dublin.

Bawden, D., Robinson, L., 2009. The dark side of information: overload, anxiety and other paradoxes and pathologies. Journal of Information Science 35 (2), 180–191.

Bawden, D., Robinson, L., 2012. Introduction to Information Science. Facet, London.

Bell, D., 1960. The End of Ideology: On the Exhaustion of Political Ideas in the Fifties. Free Press, Glencoe, IL.

Big Lottery Fund, 2004. The People's Network Evaluation Summary [online]. Big Lottery Fund, London. Available from: www.biglotteryfund.org.uk/assets/peoples_network_eva luation_summary.pdf (accessed 21.10.13.).

Birdi, B., Wilson, K., Cocker, J., 2008. The public library, exclusion and empathy: a literature review. Library Review 57 (8), 576–592.

Boekhorst, A.K., 2003. Becoming information literate in The Netherlands. Library Review 52 (7), 298–309.

Bradshaw, Y., Britz, J., Bothma, T., Bester, C., 2007. Using information technology to create global classrooms: benefits and ethical dilemmas. International Review of Information Ethics 7.

Britz, J.J., Blignaut, J.N., 2001. Information poverty and social justice. South Africa Journal of Library and Information Science 67 (2), 63–70.

Britz, J.J., 2004. To know or not to know: a moral reflection on information poverty. Journal of Information Science 30 (3), 192–204.

Britz, J.J., 2007. A Critical Analysis of Information Poverty From a Social Justice Perspective (Unpublished Ph.D. thesis). University of Pretoria.

Britz, J.J., Lor, P., 2010. The right to be information literate: the core foundation of the knowledge society. Innovation: Appropriate Librarianship and Information Work in Southern Africa 41, 8–24.

Brophy, P., 2005. The development of a model for assessing the level of impact of information and library services. Library and Information Research 29 (93), 43–49.

Brophy, P., 2004. The People's Network: Moving Forward. Available from: http://timbookt oo.files.wordpress.com/2009/10/pn_moving_forward_2004.pdf (accessed 11.08.14.).

Brophy, P., 2006. Measuring Library Performance: Principles and Techniques. Facet, London.

Buckland, M., 1991. Information as thing. Journal of the American Society for Information Science 42 (5), 351–360.

Buckley-Owen, B., 2011. The Development of UK Government Policy on Citizens' Access to Public Sector Information (Unpublished Ph.D. thesis). Loughborough University.

Burkett, I., 2000. Beyond the 'information rich and poor': future understandings of inequality in globalising informational economies. Futures 32 (7), 679–694.

Burnett, G., Jaeger, P.T., Thompson, K.M., 2008. Normative behaviour and information: the social aspects of information access. Library and Information Science Research 31, 56–66.

Caidi, N., Allard, D., 2005. Social inclusion of newcomers to Canada: an information problem? Library and Information Science Research 27 (3), 302–324.

Cameron, D., 2010. Quoted in Key Principles of the Coalition Government: Implications for the revolving doors group. Available from: http://www.revolving-doors.org.uk/documents/key-principles/.

Cameron, D., 2011. Conference, Tuesday 22nd March 2011, Strand Palace, London. Tackling Social Exclusion in the Big Society: The Next Steps, Available from: http://www.inside government.co.uk/other/exclusion-social/ (accessed 01.03.13.).

Capurro, R., Hjørland, B., 2003. The Concept of Information. Annual review of information science and technology Information Today, Medford, NJ, pp. 343–411. Available from: htt p://www.capurro.de/infoconcept.html (accessed 29.03.15.).

Carnegie Trust, 2012. A New Chapter – Public Library Services in the 21st Century: Data from Northern Ireland about Attitudes to and Use of Public Libraries. Available from: http://w ww.carnegieuktrust.org.uk/getattachment/500da962-3024-4240-8abe-c8cc455a5dc2/A-New-Chapter–Northern-Ireland-Factsheet.aspx (accessed 15.02.14.).

Casselden, B., Pickard, A., McLeod, J., 2014. The challenges facing public libraries in the Big Society: the role of volunteers, and the issues that surround their use in England. Journal of Librarianship and Information Science 1–17.

Catts, R., Lau, J., 2008. Towards Information Literacy Indicators. UNESCO, Information for All Programme (IFAP), Paris. Available from: http://www.ifla.org/files/information-literacy/publications/towards-information-literacy_2008-en.pdf (accessed 01.11.12.).

Chatman, E.A., 1986. Diffusion theory: A review and test of a conceptual model in information diffusion. Journal of the American Society for Information Science 37 (6), 377–386. HYPERLINK http://onlinelibrary.wiley.com/doi/10.1002/(SICI)1097-4571(198611) 37:6%3c%3e1.0.CO;2-R/issuetoc.

Chatman, E.A., 1991. Life in a small world: applicability of gratification theory to information-seeking behaviour. Journal of the American Society for Information Science 42, 438–449.

Chatman, E.A., 1992. The Information World of Retired Women. Greenwood, Westport, CT.

Chatman, E., 1996. The improvised life-world of outsiders. Journal of the American Society for Information Science 47 (3), 193–206.

Chatman, E., 1999. A theory of life in the round. Journal of the American Society for Information Science 50 (3), 207–217.

Chatman, E.A., 2000. Framing social life in theory and research. The New Review of Information Behaviour Research 1, 3–17.

Child, R., Goulding, A., 2012. Public libraries in the recession: the librarian's axiom. Library Review 61 (8/9), 641–663.

Childers, T., Post, J.A., 1975. The Information Poor in America. Scarecrow Press, Metuchen, New Jersey.

Clark, L., Visser, M., 2011. Digital literacy takes centre stage. In: Freeman, D. (Ed.), The Transforming Public Library Technology Infrastructure, Library Technology ReportsAmerican Library Association 47 (6), 38–42.

Clarke, C., Yu, L., Yu, C., Fu, L., 2011. How far can we go in ensuring equality of access to public library services? the re-visitation of a core professional value in the context of regional and urban-rural inequalities in China. Libri 61 (1), 23–56.

Committee for the Development of the Public Libraries Strategy Ireland 2013–2017, 2013. A Strategy for Public Libraries, 2013–2017. Available from: http://www.environ. ie/en/Publications/LocalGovernment/PublicLibraries/FileDownLoad, 33998,en.pdf (accessed 26.08.14.).

Continuous Household Survey, 2013. Experience of the Public Library Service by Adults in Northern Ireland. Available from: http://www.dcalni.gov.uk/libraries_bulletin_ chs_2012-13.pdf (accessed 15.02.14.).

Continuous Household Survey, 2015. Experience of the Public Library Service by Adults in Northern Ireland. Available from: https://www.dcalni.gov.uk/sites/default/fi-les/publications/dcal/experience-of-the-public-library-service-by-adults-in-North-ern-Ireland-201415.pdf (accessed 25.11.15.).

Crawford, J., Irving, C., 2012. Information literacy in employability training: the experience of inverclyde libraries. Journal of Librarianship and Information Science 44 (2), 79–89.

Davies, R., Butters, G., 2008. Public libraries, learning and the creative citizen: a European perspective. In: Brophy, P., Craven, J., Markland, M. (Eds.), Libraries Without Walls: Exploring 'anywhere, anytime' delivery of library services. Facet, Cornwall, pp. 137–146.

De Beer, C.S., 2007. Africa in the globalising world: digital divide or human divide? Communicatio 33 (2), 196–207.

Denscombe, M., 2007. The Good Research Guide: for small-scale social research projects, 3rd. McGraw-Hill, Maidenhead.

Department for Culture, Media and Sport, 2014. Independent Library Report for Libraries in England. Available from: https://www.gov.uk/government/uploads/system/uploads /attachment_data/file/388989/Independent_Library_Report-_18_December.pdf (accessed 20.02.15.).

Department of Culture, Arts and Leisure, 2014. Business Plan, 2013–2014. Available from: http://www.dcalni.gov.uk/dcal_business_plan_2013-14_-_final_ version_for_publication.pdf (accessed 18.07.14.).

Department of Culture, Arts and Leisure, 2009. DCAL Learning Strategy. Available from: htt p://www.dcalni.gov.uk/quick_links-dcal_learning_strategy (accessed 10.08.13.).

Department of Culture, Arts and Leisure, 2006. Delivering Tomorrow's Libraries. Available from: http://www.dcalni.gov.uk/final__delivering_tomorrow_s_libraries__document_ -_july_2007_-_1mb_document_for_website.pdf (accessed 01.02.14.).

Department of Culture, Media and Sport, 1999. Libraries for All: Social Inclusion in Public Libraries.

Department of Culture, Arts and Leisure, 2013a. Findings from the Continuous Household Surveys (Northern Ireland), 2012/13. Available from: http://www.dcalni.gov.uk/librar ies_bulletin_chs_2012-13.pdf (accessed 25.10.13.).

Department of Culture, Arts and Leisure, 2013b. Impact of Poverty on Attendance at Libraries in Northern Ireland. Available from: http://www.dcalni.gov.uk/impact_of_poverty _on_atendance_at_libraries_in_northern_ireland_r.pdf (accessed 01.07.14.).

Department of Culture, Arts and Leisure and Libraries NI, 2014. Mapping the Library Service in Northern Ireland 2014: A Collaborative Research Project between Libraries NI and DCAL. Available from: http://www.dcalni.gov.uk/mapping_of_static_and_mobile _libraries_in_northern_ireland.pdf (accessed 11.08.14.).

Department of Culture, Arts and Leisure, 2013c. Review of 'Delivering Tomorrow's Libraries' (Hard Copy, Supplied to the Researcher by the Department of Culture, Arts and Leisure). .

Department of Culture, Media and Sport, 2013a. Framework for the Future Libraries, Learning and Information in the Next Decade. Available from: http://dera.ioe.ac.uk/4709/ 1/Framework_for_the_Future1.pdf (accessed 27.02.14.).

Department of Culture, Media and Sport 1999. Libraries for All: Social Inclusion in Public Libraries.

Department of Culture, Media and Sport, 2013b. Taking Part. Available from: https://www .gov.uk/government/uploads/system/uploads/attachment_data/file/244895/Taking_ Part_2013_14_Quarter_1_Report.doc.pdf (accessed 01.11.13.).

Department of Employment and Learning, 2012a. Graduating to Success: A Higher Education Strategy for Northern Ireland. Available from: http://www.delni.gov.uk/graduat ing-to-success-he-strategy-for-ni.pdf (accessed 15.08.14.).

Department of Employment and Learning, 2012b. Pathways to Success: Preventing Exclusion and Promoting Participation of Young People. Available from: http://www.delni.gov.uk/del-pathways-to-success-v6.pdf (accessed 28.08.14.).

Department of Employment and Learning, 2006. Success through Skills: Skills Strategy for Northern Ireland. Available from: http://www.delni.gov.uk/skills_strategy_2006.pdf (accessed 15.08.14.).

Department of Investment, Trade and Investment, (2014). Northern Ireland Labour Market Report October 2015. Available from: https://www.detini.gov.uk/sites/default/files/publications/deti/Labour-Market-Report-October-2015-Final.pdf.

Dervin, B.L., Greenberg, B.S., 1972. The Communication Environment of the Urban Poor. Michigan State University, Department of Communication, East Lansing, MI. CUP Report No. 15.

Dervin, B., 1977. Useful theory for librarianship: communication, not information. Drexel Library Quarterly 13 (3), 16–32.

Diener, R., 1986. Information poverty. In: Hurd, J., Davis, C. (Eds.), Proceedings of the 49th ASIS Annual Meeting, 23, Learned Information. New Jersey, Medford, pp. 69–74.

European Commission, n.d. Digital Agenda for Europe: A Europe 2020 Initiative. Available from: http://ec.europa.eu/digital-agenda/ (accessed 15.08.14.).

Eve, J., de Groot, M., Schmidt, A.M., 2007. Supporting lifelong learning in public libraries across Europe. Library Review 56, 393–406.

Feather, J., 2008. The Information Society: A Study of Continuity and Change, fifth ed. Facet, London.

Feather, J., 2011. Free and equal access. In: Baker, D., Evans, W. (Eds.), Libraries and Society: Role, Responsibility and Future in an Age of Change. Chandos, Oxford, pp. 67–80.

Feather, J., 2013. The Information Society: A Study of Continuity and Change, sixth ed. Facet, London.

Ferguson, S., 2012. Are public libraries developers of social capital? A review of their contribution and attempts to demonstrate it. Australian Library Journal 61 (1), 22–33.

Ferguson, S., 2010. Social capital, lifelong learning, information literacy and the role of libraries. In: Media, Democracy and Change: Refereed Proceedings of the Australian and New Zealand Communication Association Conference 2010. University of Canberra. Available from: http://www.canberra.edu.au/anzca2010/attachments/pdf/Social-capital,-lifelong-learning,-information-literacy-and-the-role-of-libraries.pdf (accessed 28.08.12.).

Foucault, M., 2000. The subject and power. In: Foucault, M. (Ed.), Power, Essential Works of Foucault 1954–1984, vol. 3. Penguin Books, London, pp. 326–348. Available online at: https://wuecampus2.uni-wuerzburg.de/moodle/pluginfile.php/77615/mod_resource /content/1/Foucault_The_Subject_and_Power.pdf (accessed 03.10.14.).

Fisher, K.E., 2006. Information Grounds. In: Fisher, K.E., Erdelez, S., McKechnie, L. (Eds.), Theories of Information Behaviour, second ed. Information Today, New Jersey, pp. 185–190.

Fisher, K.E., Naumer, C., 2006. Information grounds: theoretical basis and empirical findings in formation flow in social settings. In: Spink, A., Cole, C. (Eds.), New Directions in Human Information Behaviour. Springer, Dordrecht, pp. 93–111.

Flor, A., 2001. ICT and poverty: the indisputable link. In: Paper for Third Asia Development Forum on "Regional Economic Cooperation in Asia and the Pacific" Organised by Asian Development Bank 11–14 June 2001, Bangkok, Thailand Available from: http://citeseerx.ist.psu.edu/viewdoc/download?rep=rep1andtype=pdfand doi=10.1.1.196.8822 (accessed 01.09.13.).

Floridi, L., 2011. The Philosophy of Information. Oxford University Press, Oxford.

Forbes, T., Sibbett, C., Miller, S., Emerson, L., 2012. Exploring the Community Response to Multiple Deaths of Young People by Suicide. Centre for Effective Education, Queen's University Belfast, Belfast. Available from: http://www.contactni.com/cmsfiles/ContactResearchReport/Contact-Main-Report-Exploring-a-Community-Response-to-Multiple-Deaths-of-Young-People-by-Suicide.pdf (accessed 30.09.14.).

Fulton, C., 2006. Chatman's life in the round. In: Fisher, K.E., Erdelez, S., McKechnie, L. (Eds.), Theories of Information Behaviour. Information Today, New Jersey, pp. 79–82.

Garner, S., 2005. High-level Colloquium on Information Literacy and Lifelong Learning. Report of a Meeting Sponsored by the United Nations Education, Scientific and Cultural Organisation (UNESCO), National Forum on Information Literacy (NFIL) and the International Federation of Library Associations and Institutions (IFLA), Available from: http://unesdoc.unesco.org/images/0014/001448/144820e.pdf (accessed 01.08.14.).

Gebremichael, M., Jackson, J., 2006. Bridging the Gap in Sub-Saharan Africa: A Holistic Look at Information Poverty and the Region's Digital Divide. Government Information Quarterly 23 (2), 267–280.

Gehner, J., 2010. Libraries, low-income people, and social exclusion. Public Library Quarterly 29 (1), 39–47.

Gigler, B.S., 2011. Informational Capabilities: The Missing Link for the Impact of ICT on development, E-Transform Knowledge Platform, Working Paper The World Bank. Available from: http://www.appropriatingtechnology.org/sites/default/files/InformationalCapabilitiesWorkingPaper_Gigler%20%282%29.pdf (accessed 02.08.13).

Gilster, P., Rilster, P., 1997. Digital Literacy. John Wiley and Sons, New York.

Gordon, D., 2008. Measuring child poverty and deprivation. In: UNICEF Global Study on Child Poverty and Disparities Workshop Policy Analysis Techniques Related to Child Poverty and Disparities University of Southampton, 18th–28th August 2008 Available from: http://www.southampton.ac.uk/ghp3/docs/unicef/presentation4.1.pdf (accessed 02.08.14.).

Gorman, G.E., Clayton, P., 2008. Qualitative Research for the Information Professional: A Practical Handbook, second ed. Facet, London.

Goulding, A., 2001. Editorial: information poverty or overload? Journal of Librarianship and Information Science 33 (3), 109–111.

Goulding, A., 2006. Public Libraries in the 21st Century: Defining Services and Debating the Future. Ashgate, Hampshire.

Government, 2010. State of the Nation report: Poverty, worklessness and welfare dependency in the UK. Available from: http://www.bristol.ac.uk/poverty/downloads/keyofficialdocuments/CONDEM%20-poverty-report.pdf.

Grabe, M.E., Lang, E., Zhou, S., Bolls, P.D., 2000. Cognitive access to negatively arousing news: an experimental investigation of the knowledge gap. Communication Research 27 (1), 3–26.

Granovetter, M.S., 1973. The strength of weak ties. American Journal of Sociology 78 (6), 1360–1380.

Great Britain, Cabinet Office, 2010. Digital by Default Proposed for Government Services. Available from: https://www.gov.uk/government/news/digital-by-default-proposed-for-government-services (accessed 18.09.14.).

Great Britain, Cabinet Office, 2013. Government Digital Strategy. Available from: https://www.gov.uk/government/publications/government-digital-strategy (accessed 01.02.14.).

Haider, J., Bawden, D., 2006. Pairing information with poverty: traces of development discourse in LIS. New Library World 107 (9), 371–385.

Haider, J., Bawden, D., 2007. Conceptions of "information poverty" in LIS: a discourse analysis. Journal of Documentation 63 (4), 534–557.

Hamelink, C.J., 2003. Moral Challenges in the Information Society. Available from: http://www.waccglobal.org/en/20024-communication-rights-in-the-information-society/668-Moral-challenges-in-the-information-society.html (accessed 12.03.12.).

Harding, J., 2008. Information literacy and the public library. Australasian Public Libraries and Information Services (APLIS) 21 (4), 157–167. Edited version available from: http://www.thefreelibrary.com/Information+literacy+and+the+public+library. -a0190747227 (accessed 25.02.13.).

Harle, J., Tarrant, J., 2011. Tackling inequalities around the globe: the challenge for libraries. In: Baker, D., Evans, W. (Eds.), Libraries and Society: Role, Responsibility and Future in an Age of Change. Chandos, Oxford, pp. 119–140.

Harrington, M., 1962. The Other America: Poverty in the United States. Macmillan, New York.

Hayter, S., 2005. The Information Worlds of a Disadvantaged Community (Unpublished Ph.D. thesis) Northumbria University. Available from: http://nrl.northumbria.ac.uk/34 16/1/hayter.susan_phd.pdf (accessed 09.11.11.).

Hendry, J.D., 2000. Social inclusion and the information poor. Library Review 49 (7), 331–336.

Hernon, P., Matthews, J.R., 2013. Reflecting on the Future of Academic and Public Libraries. Preface xi–xiv. American Library Association, Chicago.

Hersberger, J., 2003. Are the economically poor information poor? Does the digital divide affect the homeless and access to information? Canadian Journal of Information and Library Science 27 (3), 45–63.

Hull, D., 2011. Background Briefing: Northern Ireland Library Authority (Libraries NI) Northern Ireland Assembly Research and Information Service Briefing Paper. Available from: http://www.niassembly.gov.uk/Documents/RaISe/Publications/2011/Culture-Arts-Leisure/8211.pdf (accessed 14.08.14.).

Hyman, H.H., Sheatsley, P.B., 1947. Some reasons why information campaigns fail. Public Opinion Quarterly 11, 412–423.

IFLA, 2006. Information Literacy. Available from: http://www.ifla.org/information-literacy (accessed 06.08.14.).

IFLA, 2014. Beacons of the Information Society: The Alexandria Proclamation on Information Literacy and Lifelong Learning. Available from: http://www.ifla.org/publications/beacons-of-the-information-society-the-alexandria-proclamation-on-information-literacy (accessed 15.09.14.).

Ipsos, M.O.R.I., 2009. The Libraries Omnibus Survey. Available from: http://www.culture.go.uk/images/research/Libraries_omnibus.pdf.

Ipsos MORI, 2013. Envisaging the Library of the Future: Phases 1 and 2 Full Report. Available from: http://www.artscouncil.org.uk/media/uploads/pdf/Envisioning_the_library _of_the_future_phases_1_and_2_full_report.pdf (accessed 10.03.14.).

Ipsos MORI, 2014. Market Research: Reading, Presentation on 28.03.2014. Unpublished, commissioned by Libraries NI.

ITV Report, October 19, 2015. Nearly Quarter of UK Adults 'Lack Basic Digital Skills', Says Charity. Available online at: http://www.itv.com/news/2015-10-19/nearly-quarter-of-uk-adults-lack-basic-digital-skills-says-charity/ (accessed 12.11.15.).

Jaeger, P.T., Thompson, K., 2004. Social information behaviour and the democratic process: information poverty, normative behaviour, and electronic government in the United States. Library and Information Science Research 26 (1), 94–107.

Jaeger, P., Bertot, J., Thompson, K., Katz, S., De Coster, E., 2012. The intersection of public policy and public access: digital divides, digital literacy, digital inclusion, and public libraries. Public Library Quarterly 31 (1), 1–20.

Jaeger, P.T., Burnett, G., 2010. Information Worlds: Social Context, Technology, and Information Behaviour in the Age of the Internet. Routledge, New York.

Jaeger, P.T., Bertot, J.C., Fleischmann, K.R., 2011. Evolving relationships between information technology and public libraries. In: Bertot, J.C., Jaeger, P.T., McClure, C.R. (Eds.), Public Libraries and the Internet: Roles, Perspectives and Implication. Libraries Unlimited, California, pp. 3–14.

Johnson, C.A., 2007. Social capital and the search for information: examining the role of social capital in information seeking behaviour in Mongolia. Journal of the American Society for Information Science and Technology 58 (6), 883–894.

Johnson, C.A., 2012. How do public libraries create social capital? An analysis of interactions between library staff and patrons. Library and Information Science Research 34, 52–62.

Joseph Rowntree Foundation, 2014. Monitoring Poverty and Social Exclusion in Northern Ireland. Available from: http://www.jrf.org.uk/sites/files/jrf/northern-ireland-poverty-summary.pdf.

Kennan, M.A., Lloyd, A., Qayyum, A., Thompson, K., 2011. Settling in: The Relationship between information and social inclusion. Australian Academic and Research Libraries 42 (3), 191–210.

Kim, M.C., Kim, J.K., 2001. Digital divide: conceptual discussions and prospect. In: The Human Society and the Internet-Related Socio-Economic Issues. Springer, Berlin, pp. 78–91.

Komito, L., 2008. Information society policy. In: Hearn, G., Rooney, D. (Eds.), Knowledge Policy: Challenges for the 21st Century. Edward Elgar, Cheltenham, pp. 83–97.

Krueger, R.A., Casey, M.A., 2009. Focus Groups: A Practical Guide for Applied Research, fourth ed. Sage, London.

Lai, H.J., 2011. Information literacy training in public libraries: a case from Canada. Journal of Educational Technology and Society 14 (2), 81–88.

Lane-Fox, M., 2010. Directgov 2010 and beyond. revolution not evolution Available from: https://www.gov.uk/government/uploads/system/uploads/attachment_data/file/60993/Martha_20Lane_20Fox_s_20letter_20to_20Francis_20Maude_2014th_20Oct_202010.pdf.

Lane-Fox, M., 2013. Martha Lane Fox, a "force of Nature" to Get Britons Online. The Observer (Tech Monthly Section, p. 26) 10 November, Available from: http://www.theguardian.com/media/2013/nov/13/martha-lane-fox-britons-online-lastminute-com (accessed 10.11.13.).

Leith, P., 2012. Europe's information society project and digital inclusion: universal service obligations or social solidarity? International Journal of Law and Information Technology 20 (2), 102–123.

Lewis, O., 1959. Five Families: Mexican Case Studies in the Culture of Poverty.

Libraries Act, N.I., 2008. Libraries Act (Northern Ireland). Available from: http://www.legislation.gov.uk/nia/2008/8/pdfs/nia_20080008_en.pdf.

Libraries NI, 2013. Libraries NI Annual Equality Progress Report, 2012–2013. Available from: http://www.librariesni.org.uk/AboutUs/OurOrg/Equality/Annual_Equality_Report_2012-2013.pdf (accessed 13.05.14.).

Libraries NI, 2014a. Health in Mind Homepage. Available from: http://www.yourhealthinmind.org/events/45 (accessed 01.05.14.).

Libraries NI, 2014b. Libraries NI Business Plan, 2014–2015. Available from: http://www.librariesni.org.uk/AboutUs/OurOrg/Business%20Plans/Business_Plan_2014-15_Final_Version.pdf (accessed 01.07.14.).

Lievrouw, L.A., Farb, S., 2003. Information and equity. In: Cronin, B. (Ed.), Annual Review of Information Science and Technology (ARIST). vol. 37. Information Today, Medford, pp. 499–540.

Lin, N., 2001. Social Capital: A Theory of Social Structure and Action. Cambridge University Press, Cambridge.

Lloyd, A., Kennan, M.A., Thompson, K.M., Qayyum, A., 2013. Connecting with new information landscapes: information literacy practices of refugees. Journal of Documentation 69 (1), 121–144.

Lloyd, A., Lipu, S., Kennan, M.A., 2010. On becoming citizens: examining social inclusion from an information perspective. Australian Academic and Research Libraries 41 (1), 42–53.

Llywodraeth Cymru Welsh Government, 2011. Libraries Inspire: The Strategic Development Framework for Welsh Libraries 2012–16. Available from: http://wales.gov.uk/docs/drah/publications/111104librariesinspireen.pdf (accessed 01.06.14.).

Lor, P.J., Britz, J.J., 2007. Is a knowledge society possible without freedom of access to information? Journal of Information Science 33 (4), 387–397.

Machlup, F., 1962. The Production and Distribution of Knowledge in the United States. Princeton University Press, Princeton, NJ.

McAdams, P., 2010. Do Library Staff Consider Computer Gaming to Be a Useful Tool in an Informal Learning Environment? MSc Library and Information Management, Available at the Ulster University Library, Jordanstown.

McGettigan, L., 2014. Reinventing the street corner university: the infinite possibilities for libraries and librarians. In: Keynote Speech at/Library Association Ireland (LAI)/CILIP Ireland Joint Conference and Exhibition Seizing Opportunities, Leading Change, Waterford, Ireland, Friday 11th April, 2014.

McKee, B., 2006. Interviewed by Goulding, A. In: Public Libraries in the 21st Century: Defining Services and Debating the Future, Ashgate, Hampshire.

McKeown, A., Bates, J., 2013. Emotional intelligent leadership: findings from a study of public library branch managers in Northern Ireland. Library Management 34 (6/7), 462–485.

McKeown, A., 2015. How can information poverty indicators be used to demostrate the impact of Libraries NI'S information services. Available in print at the Ulster University library, Jordanstown. accessible online from: http://ethos.bl.uk/OrderDetails.do?uin=uk.bl.ethos.648024?.

McMenemey, D., 2009. The Public Library. Facet, London.

McMillan, K., Weyers, J., 2007. How to Write Dissertations and Project Reports. Pearson Education, Harlow.

MacDonald, L., 2012. A New Chapter: Public Library Services in the 21st Century: Full Report. Carnegie Trust. Available from: http://www.carnegieuktrust.org.uk/getattachment/b04629b2-aa09-4bd0-bc3a-9b9b04b7aba1/A-New-Chapter.aspx (accessed 01.11.12.).

Mann, W., 2013. E-Book Usage, Awareness and Book Consumption Habits of Public Library Users in Northern Ireland. MSc Library and Information Management, Available at the Ulster University Library, Jordanstown.

Markless, S., Streatfield, D., 2006. Evaluating the Impact of Your Library. Facet, London.

Martin, B., 2005. Information society revisited: from vision to reality. Journal of Information Science 31 (4), 4–12.

May, J.D., 2012. Digital and other poverties: exploring the connection in four east African countries. ITID 8 (2), 33–50. Available from: http://itidjournal.org/itid/article/viewFile/896/375 (accessed 12.07.14.).

Mayes, J., 2010. Developing Library Services for Older Adults: An Investigation into the Baby Boomer Generation. MSc Library and Information Management, Available at the Ulster University library, Jordanstown.

Merton, R.K., 1972. Insiders and outsiders: a chapter in the sociology of knowledge. American Journal of Sociology 78, 9–47.

Muddiman, D., Durrani, S., Dutch, M., Linley, R., Pateman, J., Vincent, J., 2000. Open to All? The Public Library and Social Exclusion. Overview and Conclusions. Library and Information Commission Research Report 84, vol. 1., Resource: the Council for Museums, Archives and Libraries, London. Available from: http://eprints.rclis.org/6283/1/lic084.pdf (accessed 01.08.14.).

Muggleton, T.H., 2013. Public libraries and difficulties with targeting the homeless. Library Review 62 (1/2), 7–18.

Northern Ireland Assembly Research, 2012. Poverty and Social Deprivation Mapping Executive and Departmental Strategies, Policies and Programmes in Northern Ireland. Available from: http://www.niassembly.gov.uk/Documents/RaISe/Publications/2012/social_dev/14512.pdf (accessed 01.03.14.).

Northern Ireland Statistics and Research Agency Census, 2011. Key Statistics for Northern Ireland. Available from: http://www.nisra.gov.uk/Census/key_stats_bulletin_2011.pdf (accessed 15.01.13.).

Northern Ireland Executive, 2013. Literacy Levels of Adults Improving in Northern Ireland. Available from: http://www.northernireland.gov.uk/news-del-081013-literacy-levels-in (accessed 13.08.14.).

Northern Ireland Statistics and Research Agency, 2014. Population and Migration Estimates Northern Ireland (2013) Statistics Press Release. Available from: http://www.nisra.gov.uk/archive/demography/population/midyear/MYE13_PR.pdf (accessed 03.09.14.).

Northern Ireland Statistics and Research Agency, 2012. Statistical Report: 2012 Based Report Population Projections. Available from: http://www.nisra.gov.uk/archive/demography/population/projections/Northern%20Ireland%20Population%20Projections%202012%20-%20Statistical%20Report.pdf (accessed 25.09.14.).

O'Beirne, R., 2010. From Lending to Learning: The Development and Extension of Public Libraries. Chandos, Oxford.

O'Loan, S., McMenemy, D., 2005. The role of the twenty-first century public library. In: McMenemy, D., Poulter, A. (Eds.), Delivering Digital Services: A Handbook for Public Libraries and Learning Centres. Facet, London, pp. 3–18.

Office for National Statistics, 2015a. Statistical Bulleting, Internet Users, 2015. Available from: http://www.ons.gov.uk/ons/rel/rdit2/internet-users/2015/stb-ia-2015.html?format=print (accessed 28.09.15.).

Office for National Statistics, 2013. ONS Internet Access Quarterly Update, Q1 2014. Available from: http://www.ons.gov.uk/ons/rel/rdit2/Internet-access-quarterly-update/q1-2014/stb-ia-q1-2014.html (accessed 10.08.14.).

Office for National Statistics, 2015b. Statistical Bulletin: Regional Labour Market, July 2015. Available from: http://www.ons.gov.uk/ons/rel/subnational-labour/regional-labour-market-statistics/july-2015/stb.html (accessed 28.09.15.).

Office of Communications, 2015. Ofcom Communications Market Report: Northern Ireland. Available from: http://stakeholders.ofcom.org.uk/market-data-research/market-data/communications-market-reports/cmr15/northern-ireland/ (accessed 28.09.15.).

Office of the First Minister and Deputy First Minister, 2006. Lifetime Opportunities: Government's Anti-poverty and Social Inclusion Strategy for Northern Ireland. Available from: http://www.ofmdfmni.gov.uk/antipovertyandsocialinclusion.pdf (accessed 12.02.14.).

Oldenburg, R., 1998. The Great Good Place: Cafes, Coffee Shops, Bookstores, Bars, Hair Salons, and Other Hangouts at the Heart of a Community. Marlowe and Company, New York.

Organisation for Economic Cooperation and Development, 2013. OECD Skills Outlook First Results from the Survey of Adult Skills, 2013. Available from: http://skills.oecd.org/OECD_Skills_Outlook_2013.pdf (accessed 13.08.14.).

Osborn, H., 2008. An overview of public library research activity and developments in Northern Ireland. Library and Information Research 32 (102).

Parker, E.B., 1970. Information utilities and mass communication. In: Sackman, H., Nie, N. (Eds.), Information Utility and Social Choice: Papers Prepared for a Conference Sponsored Jointly by the University of Chicago, Encyclopedia Britannica and the American Federation of Information Processing Societies. AFIPS Press, Montvale, pp. 51–70.

Pateman, J., Vincent, J., 2010. Public Libraries and Social Justice. Ashgate, Surrey.

Pateman, J., Williment, K., 2013. Developing Community Led Public Libraries: Evidence from the UK and Canada. Ashgate, Surrey.

Pendleton, V., Chatman, E., 1998. Small worlds: implications for the public library. Library Trends 46 (4), 732–752.

Pettigrew, K.E., 1998. The role of community health nurses in providing information and referral to the elderly: A study based on social network theory. Unpublished doctoral dissertation. The University of Western Ontario, London, Ontario.

Pettigrew, K.E., 1999. Waiting for chiropody: Contextual results from an ethnographic study of the information behavior among attendees at community clinics. Information Processing & Management 35 (6), 801–817.

Pettigrew, K.E., 2000. Lay information provision in community settings: How community health nurses disseminate human services information to the elderly. Library Quarterly 70 (1), 47–85.

Pickard, A.J., 2013. Research Methods in Information, second ed. Facet, London.

Pla, I.L., 2011. Information Poverty and the Right to Access to Public Information. A Capabilities Related Issue, 40–60. Transperencia y Privacidad, Revista Mexicana.

Platt, C., December 2012. Surviving...and Thriving in New York City, CILIP Update. (hard copy).

Pollock, N., 2002. Conceptualising the Information Poor: An Assessment of the Contribution of Elfreda Chatman towards an Understanding of Behaviour within the Context of Information Poverty, Information Science. Available from: http://npollock.id.au/info_science/chatman.html (accessed 01.11.11.).

Potter, A., 2006. Zones of silence: a framework beyond the digital divide. First Monday 11. Available from: http://firstmonday.org/ojs/index.php/fm/article/view/1327/1247 (accessed 28.04.12.).

Power, A., Willmot, H., 2007. Social Capital Within the Neighbourhood, Case Report 38. Centre for Analysis of Social Exclusion, London.

Price Waterhouse Coopers, 2008. Social and Economic Value of Public Libraries, Arts and Sport in Northern Ireland Phase 1: Designing a Model. Available from: http://www.dcalni.gov.uk/valcal_-_final_report_dec_2007-2.pdf (accessed 08.11.15.).

Ptolomey, J., 2011. Government information and services: accessibility and the digital divide. In: Garvin, P. (Ed.), Government Information Management in the 21st Century: International Perspectives. Ashgate, Surrey, pp. 95–111.

Putkey, T., October 26, 2009. Information Literacy and Information Poverty, Compared, MLIS Work Theories. Available from: http://www.keypointe.ca/information-literacy-and-information-poverty-compared/ (accessed 06.09.13.).

Reilly, N., 2012. Increasing Public Library Use by Teenagers and Young Adults. MSc Library and Information Management, Available at the Ulster University Library, Jordanstown.

Roach, J.L., Gursslin, O.R., 1967. An evaluation of the concept "culture of poverty". Social Forces 45, 383–392.

Rodgers, H.R., 2006. American Poverty in a New Era of Reform, second ed. ME Sharpe, Armonk.

Rowntree, J., 2014. Monitoring Poverty and Social Exclusion in Northern Ireland. Available from: http://www.jrf.org.uk/sites/files/jrf/northern-ireland-poverty-summary.pdf (accessed 11.08.14.).

Secker, J., Price, G., 2008. Libraries as social space: enhancing the experience of distant learners using social software. In: Brophy, P., Craven, J., Markland, M. (Eds.), Libraries Without Walls: Exploring 'anywhere, Anytime' Delivery of Library Services. Facet, Cornwall, pp. 59–70.

Selwyn, N., 2003. Apart from technology: understanding people's non-use of technology in everyday life. Technology in Society 25 (1), 99–116.

Shen, L., 2013. Out of information poverty: library services for urban marginalised immigrants. Urban Library Journal 19 (1), 1–12.

Shrem, J., 2012. Public Libraries Information Brief: Impact of Public Libraries on Students and Lifelong Learners. Comprehensive Center, New York. Available from: http://www.nysl.nysed.gov/libdev/nyla/nycc_public_library_brief.pdf.

Sinclair, S., Bramley, B., 2011. Beyond virtual inclusion: communications, inclusion and digital divisions. Social Policy and Society 10 (1), 1–11.

Sinnamon, J., 2009. The Experience of Poverty in a Deprived Neighbourhood (Unpublished Ph.D. thesis). Available at the Ulster University Library, Jordanstown.

Sligo, F., Williams, J., 2002. Beyond the Digital Divide: Re-assessing Knowledge Gaps., pp. 1–8 Available from: http://unitec.researchbank.ac.nz/bitstream/handle/10652/1934/W illiams%20-%20digital%20divide.pdf?sequence=1&isAllowed=y (accessed 25.02.12.).

Spink, A., Cole, C., 2001. Information and poverty: information-seeking channels used by African American low-income households. Library and Information Science Research 23 (1), 45–65.

Spink, A., 2010. Information Behaviour: An Evolutionary Instinct. Springer, Berlin.

Sung, H.-Y., Hepworth, M., Ragsdell, G., 2012. Investigating essential elements of community engagement in public libraries: an exploratory qualitative study. Journal of Librarianship and Information Science 45 (3), 1–13.

Sweetland, J.H., 1993. Information poverty – let me count the ways. Database 16 (4), 8–10.

Thompson, K.M., 2007. Furthering understanding of information literacy through the social study of information poverty. The Canadian Journal of Information and Library Science 31 (1), 87–115.

Thompson, K.M., 2006. Multidisciplinary Approaches to Information Poverty and Their Implications for Information Access (Unpublished Ph.D. thesis). Morgan State University.

Thompson, K.M., 2011. Providing services for the underserved in public libraries through an understanding of information poverty and access. In: Bertot, J.C., Jaeger, P.T., McClure, C.R. (Eds.), Public Libraries and the Internet: Roles, Perspectives, and Implications. Libraries Unlimited, Westport, CT, pp. 131–144.

Thompson, K.M., Afzal, W., 2011. A look at information access through physical, intellectual, and socio-cultural lenses. OMNES: The Journal of Multicultural Society 2 (2), 22–42.

Thompson, K., Jaeger, P.T., Taylor, N.G., Subramanium, M., Bertot, J.C., 2014. Digital Literacy and Digital Inclusion: Information Policy and the Public Library. Rowman and Littlefield, London.

Town, S., 2011. The value of libraries: the relationship between change, evaluation and role. In: Baker, D., Evans, W. (Eds.), Libraries and Society: Role, Responsibility and Future in an Age of Change. Chandos, Oxford, pp. 303–322.

United Nations, 1948. The Universal Declaration of Human Rights. Available from: http://www.un.org/en/documents/udhr/ (accessed 01.02.14.).

United Nations Educational, Scientific and Cultural Organisation, 1998. Statement of Commitment for Action to Eradicate Poverty Adopted by Administrative Committee on Coordination, May 20, 1998. Available from: http://www.unesco.org/most/acc4pov.htm (accessed 02.08.14.).

Van Dijk, J., Hacker, K., 2003. The digital divide as a complex and dynamic phenomenon. Information Society 19, 315–326.

Van Dijk, J., 2006. Digital divide research, achievements and shortcomings. Poetics 34, 221–235.

Vinson, T., 2009. Social Inclusion: The Origins, Meaning, Definitions and Economic Implications of the Concept of Inclusion/exclusion. Australian Department of Education, Employment and Workplace Relations (DEEWR), Canberra. Available from: http://www.socialinclusion.gov.au/sites/www.socialinclusion.gov.au/files/publications/pdf/economic-implications.pdf (accessed 14.08.12.).

Weller, T., 2008. Information History an Introduction: Exploring an Emergent Field. Chandos, Oxford.

Wikipedia, 2014a. Derry. Available from: http://en.wikipedia.org/wiki/Derry (accessed 08.10.14.).

Wikipedia, 2014b. Derry/Londonderry Name Dispute. Available from: http://en.wikipedia.org/wiki/Derry/Londonderry_name_dispute (accessed 08.10.14.).

Wilson, M., 2003. Understanding the international ICT and development discourse: assumptions and implications. The South African Journal of Information and Communication 3. Available from: http://link.wits.ac.za/journal/j0301-merridy-fin.pdf (accessed 01.07.12.).

Yu, L., 2006. Understanding information inequality: making sense of the literature of the information and digital divides. Journal of Librarianship and Information Science 38 (4), 229–252.

Yu, L., 2010. How Poor Informationally are the Information Poor? Evidence from an Empirical Study of Daily and Regular Information Practices of Individuals. Journal of Documentation 66 (6), 906–933.

Yu, L., 2011. The divided views of the information and digital divides: a call for integrative theories of information inequality. Journal of Information Science 37 (6), 660–679.

INDEX

'Note: Page numbers followed by "f" indicate figures and "t" indicate tables.'